VIRGINIA MIGRATIONS
HANOVER COUNTY

Volume I (1723–1850)
Wills, Deeds, Depositions, Invoices, Letters,
and Other Documents of
Historical and Genealogical Interest

Volume II (1743–1871)
Wills, Deeds, Depositions, Letters, Marriages,
Obituaries, Estates for Sale, Absentee Land Owners,
and Other Documents of
Historical and Genealogical Interest

Compiled by
Eugenia G. Glazebrook
and
Preston G. Glazebrook

Southern Historical Press, Inc.
Greenville, South Carolina

Please direct all correspondence and orders to:

www.southernhistoricalpress.com
or
SOUTHERN HISTORICAL PRESS, Inc.
PO BOX 1267
375 West Broad Street
Greenville, SC   29601
southernhistoricalpress@gmail.com

Originally published: Richmond, VA   1943 & 1949
ISBN #0-89308-086-1
All rights Reserved.
Printed in the United States of America

VIRGINIA MIGRATIONS

HANOVER COUNTY

Volume I

-o-

1723 - 1850

WILLS, DEEDS, DEPOSITIONS, INVOICES, LETTERS
and
OTHER DOCUMENTS OF HISTORICAL AND GENEALOGICAL INTEREST

Compiled by

EUGENIA G. GLAZEBROOK
and
PRESTON G. GLAZEBROOK

Richmond - Virginia

INTRODUCTION

The County of Hanover was formed by the Act of November 26, 1720 entitled "An Act for dividing New Kent County". The Act appears in 4 Hening's Statutes by title only. When the late Morgan P. Robinson was working on his Virginia Counties a copy of this Act was procured from the British Public Rec. Of C.O. 5, 1387 and published in Mr. Robinson's book pp. 200-201. The Act was reprinted in the Vestry Book of St. Peter's Parish (1), and again in the Vestry Book of St. Paul's Parish. (2)

As originally formed Hanover County embraced all of its present area, all of the present county of Louisa, and a large part of the present County of Albemarle.

In 1742 the County of Louisa was formed from that part of Hanover County "lying above a straight course to be run from the mouth of Little Rocky Creek on the river Northanna, south, twenty degrees, west until it intersects the line of Goochland County." (3) In 1761 the western part of Louisa County was added to the County of Albemarle. (4)

Hanover is designated by law as one of the tidewater counties of Virginia. (5) From the low lands of the Pamunkey Valley and the Matadequin Creek Hanover extends westward approximately forty-five miles to the semi-mountainous hills of the southwestern part of the County.

On the North it is bounded by the North Anna of the Pamunkey and the Pamunkey River. The Little River and the Newfound River run between the North and South Annas until they merge with them shortly before they combine to form the Pamunkey. With few exceptions, all of the streams of any consequence in Hanover are tributary to the Pamunkey and the North and South Annas of the Pamunkey.

The Chickahominy which forms the larger part of the Southern boundary of the county has a very small watershed and is fed by comparatively few and insignificant tributaries in the County of Hanover.

The land is for the most part well adapted to agriculture. The lower end of the County has a light sandy soil excellent for truck crops and produces a large part of the vegetables sold on the Richmond market. In the middle and upper parts of the County heavier crops are grown, there are numerous dairies and cattle, hogs and fowls are raised.

So much for the genealogical and physical aspects of the County. It is with its history and its people that this book is concerned.

Hanover and its people have played a great role in American history. The first independent company of soldiers raised in Virginia after Braddock's defeat in July, 1755, was enlisted in Hanover County and commanded by Samuel Overton. On the Court Green at Hanover on August 17, 1755, Samuel Davies preached his famous sermon to this company in which

---

(1) Appendix 4, pp. 672-3
(2) Appendix II, pp. 595-6
(3) 5 Hening's Statutes, pp. 208-9

(4) 7 Hening's Statutes, pp. 419-20
(5) Code, Section 3156

George Washington was first publicly appraised as a man intended by his Creator as a leader of his people.

In Hanover Court House on December 1, 1763, in the famous Parson's Cause the first seed of the American Revolution was sown by the then almost unknown young Patrick Henry. From this beginning followed the Resolutions against the Stamp Act, the march on Williamsburg and the whole chain of events that finally culminated at Yorktown in October, 1781, almost seventeen years from the time of the Parson's Cause.

Patrick Henry was the real leader of the people of Hanover, but he was not the only one from Hanover who contributed to the Cause of American Liberty. The people of the County, assembled at the Court House on July 20, 1774, to instruct John Syme and Patrick Henry, their representatives, adopted one of the most remarkable documents to be found in American history.

"We are free men; we have a right to be so; and to enjoy all the priviledges and immunities of our fellow subjects in England; and while we retain a just sense of that freedom and those rights and privileges necessary for its safety and security, we shall never give up the right of taxation. Let it suffice to say, once for all, we will never be taxed but by our representatives; this is the great badge of freedom xxx", they asserted.

They called for a general Congress of deputies from all the colonies and then declared:

"The African trade for slaves we consider as most dangerous to the virtue and welfare of this country; we, therefore, most earnestly wish to see it totally discouraged."

Concluding their instructions to their representatives, the people further declared:

"While prudence and moderation shall guide your councils, we trust, gentlemen, that firmness, resolution and zeal will animate you in the glorious struggle. The arm of power, which is now stretched forth against us, is indeed formidable, but we do not despair. Our cause is good; and if it be served with constancy and fidelity, it cannot fail of success. We promise you our best support, and we will heartily join in such measures as a majority of our countrymen shall adopt for securing the public liberty."

That the general public should know the views of the people of Hanover, the meeting directed that the resolutions be published in the Gazettes. (6)

No credit is to be taken from Patrick Henry for his part in the gun powder expedition when it is said that his actions in this particular met with the whole-hearted approbation of the Hanover Committee of Safety

---

(6) William Wirt Henry's Patrick Henry, Vol. I, p. 191

which met at New Castle prior to the starting out of the expedition and again at the Court House on May 9, 1775 at which time they returned their thanks to their county volunteers. (7)

The Hanover Committee of Safety in May 1775 consisted of John Syme, William Craghead, Richard Morris, John Pendleton, Nelson Berkeley, Samuel Overton, Meriwether Skelton, Benjamin Anderson, John Robinson, George Dabney and Bartelot Anderson who acted as Clerk. (8)

Unfortunately, no list of the men who marched with Patrick Henry on the Gunpowder Expedition can be located. It is known that Patrick Henry was Captain, Samuel Meredith was First Lieutenant, Richard Morris was Second Lieutenant and Parke Goodall was Ensign. (9) It is also known that Colonel Charles Dabney and Captain Thomas Price were also members of that expedition. (10) It is probable that the majority of the young men from Hanover who later fought in the Revolution were also members of the Expedition. This Act was declared by Thomas Jefferson to have given "the first impulse to the ball of revolution". It was not Henry alone, but the great mass of the people of the County who made the expedition possible.

These were the same people who subscribed £ 100 sterling for the people of Boston, suffering from the effects of the Boston Port Bill (11); the same people who signed the fiery petition to the General Assembly of June 5, 1783 and the same people, who after their freedom had been established, could remonstrate so forcefully with the General Assembly as the County Militia did in its protest of May 24, 1782.

Hanover has always been primarily an agricultural community. It must be recalled, however, that in Colonial times, and for some years thereafter, it contained two of the most famous towns and trading centers of the Colony. Newcastle was established sometime prior to September 1744 (12). Hanovertown, long known as Page's, had grown into a town by November 1762 when it was so established by the Act of the General Assembly. (13)

Located in these towns were most of the merchants of the county who traded with the people of Hanover and the adjoining Counties, and with the British merchants. Ships from Britain called at their docks for the tobacco that grew in all parts of the colony and which was stored in Page's, Crutchfield's or Meriwether's Warehouses. The planters secured from the merchants the things they needed and when the tobacco was harvested and cured and brought to the warehouses in the fall and winter the account was balanced by tobacco certificates and a new account started. This system of trade is well illustrated by the Account and Letter Books of the Hanover Store conducted by Francis Jerdone beginning in 1736, the originals of which are in the William and Mary College Library.

(7) Burk's History of Virginia, Vol. 4, pp. 12, 14 and 15
(8) 5 William & Mary College Quarterly, 1st Series, p. 103
(9) Burk's op. cit., Vol. 4, p. 13
(10) John Blair Dabney Ms. and The Price Family of Coolwater Chart

In 1747 after the Capitol burned, a powerful combination in the House of Burgesses under the leadership of John Robinson sought to move the Capital from Williamsburg to one of the Pamunkey River towns.(14) On November 11, 1748, the House of Burgesses having resolved itself into a Committee resolved that the capital be changed from Williamsburg to a place convenient to the inhabitants and commodious for trade and navigation and then resolved that "it is the Opinion of this Committee, that it will be commodious for Trade and Navigation, and convenient for the People, that the said Town be Established, and the said Building erected on the lands of Thomas and William Meriwether adjoining the Town of Newcastle; and that Five Hundred Acres be laid off for that purpose." An amendment being offered to strike out the Meriwether land and substitute therefor the land of Richard Littlepage on Pamunkey the amendment was adopted by the close vote of 37 to 34. Due to the opposition of the Council, the resolution was defeated.

The importance of Hanovertown in 1780 may be judged from the fact that the post road from Richmond to the North ran by this place. (15)

Hanover furnished a place of refuge during the Revolution for many of the great families that lived further east. The Amblers at the Cottage, Wilson Miles Cary at Scotchtown, Robert Carter Nicholas at Mount Brilliant, which he named the Retreat, Governor Nelson's family at Offley and many others. Jacqueline Ambler, the Treasurer, sent his family to Newcastle. There his wife, Rebecca Burwell Ambler, Jefferson's fair Belinda, gave birth to their daughter Lucy Nelson Ambler on 4th August, 1776. (16)

It is one of the glories of Hanover that its people never engaged in any religious persecution.

The order books of the County have been destroyed, but, before their destruction, Foote and Semple both had the opportunity to examine them and most likely did so. Neither was able to bring any charge of persecution against the people of Hanover. It is true that some of the Presbyterian dissenters were fined by the County Court for failing to attend the Established Church on Sunday.(17) It was the law of the land that day that a man must attend the Established Church on Sunday, and a failure to do so was punishable by a fine. (18) None of the dissenters were imprisoned in Hanover, as they were in the adjoining Counties of Caroline and Spotsylvania and in Chesterfield and Middlesex. Indeed, the Rev. Patrick Henry, the minister of St. Paul's Parish, allowed a Presbyterian clergyman to preach in his church and in addition attended the service. (19)

(11) The Writings of Samuel Adams, Vol. III, pp. 223-24
(12) 5 Hening's Statutes, p. 257
(13) 7 Ibid., p. 601
(14) Journal of the House of Burgesses, April 6, 1747
(15) Official Letters of the Governors, Vol. II, p. 127
(16) Ms Letters of Betsy Ambler Carrington, 1809
(17) Foote's Sketches of Virginia, p. 124
(18) 3 Hening's Statutes, pp. 170,171 and 360, and 5 Ibid., p. 226
(19) William and Mary College Quarterly, 2nd Series, p. 266.

It should also be remembered that Hanover contained a large colony of Quakers many of whom owned large tracts of land and possessed much wealth, and learning.

The origin of the religious freedom declaration in the Virginia Declaration of Rights is attributed to Hanover's Representative in the Convention, Patrick Henry, although Madison perfected Henry's idea. (20)

Unfortunately very little work has been done to collect and preserve the source history of Hanover County. With a few exceptions all of the Deed and Will Books, the Plat Books and Order Books, and Marriage Registers and Bond Books of the County prior to 1865 were destroyed in the fire of April, 1865, that consumed the greater part of the City of Richmond. Some few deeds that had been preserved were re-admitted to record after the War and some that were lost were reestablished by Court proceedings. None of the papers and records in the Clerk's Office at Hanover, however, go back to the Colonial era.

In 1940 William Ronald Cocke published his Hanover County Chancery Wills and Notes which is a most painstaking and scholarly work. There are a good number of old suit files at Hanover. Mr. Cocke went through the papers of the early suits and abstracted their contents, except the wills which for the most part he copied in full. The book is well indexed and cannot be too highly praised. Unfortunately due to the limitations of the materials he had to work with, Mr. Cocke's book does not cover the Colonial period although it does cover another very important period in the history of the County.

Mrs. Larkin W. Glazebrook has now offered the public another contribution to the source history of Hanover County which is just as important as Mr. Cocke's book and which covers an entirely different period of its history.

The records of the United States Courts were stored in the Post Office building, which was one of the few Main Street buildings that were not destroyed by the fire of April, 1865. In these records are to be found a great many deeds, wills, accounts, letters, depositions, etc., which relate to the County of Hanover and its citizens of the Colonial and early Federal periods. Many of these suits relate to transactions that occurred before the French and Indian War and come down to the time of the late Eighteenth and early Nineteenth Centuries.

Mrs. Glazebrook has gone through these papers with diligence and care and extracted from them practically everything relating to the County of Hanover that is of interest to the historian and the genealogist. This is the first volume of what gives promise of being the foremost contribution to the source history of Hanover County of the period covered by this volume and those to follow.

In this volume, Mrs. Glazebrook has collected the essential historical and genealogical facts and documents from nineteen suits. The first, Backhouse's Adm. v. Johnson et al establishes the fact that Col. Richard Johnson and John Boswell were partners in a mercantile business conducted at New Castle. The deposition of Boswell Johnson shows that

(20) William Wirt Henry's Patrick Henry, Vol. 1, p. 430 et seq.

they were brothers-in-law. (p.10)

Colonel Richard Johnson and John Boswell were members of the County Court of Hanover in 1764.(21) They were still members of the County Court in 1767. (22) In the list for 1770 evidently amended after that date Col. Johnson is listed as dead and John Boswell as removed. (23)

Col. Richard Johnson died at New Castle on September 29, 1771. He was buried at a place now called "Solitude", which is on the road from Old Church to the New Kent line opposite the Presbyterian Church. His tomb which was a very fine one, has been badly broken by some vandal who felled a tree across it. The inscription on the tomb is as follows:

"Here lieth the remains of Collo. Richard Johnson, who was born the 7th of July in the year of Our Lord one Thousand seven hundred and fifteen and departed this life the 29th of September one thousand seven hundred and seventy-one.

"He was son to Mr. Thomas Johnson of King William County, and grand-son to Richard Johnson, Esq. of King William County who was a member of His Majesty's Council in Virginia."

This tomb-stone is mentioned in the deposition of Samuel Grantland. (p. 11)

On John Henry's Map of Virginia, printed in London, 1770, the location of Col. Boswell's place is shown as being in the southwestern part of Hanover County near the South Anna and very close to the Louisa line. The prominence of Boswell and the importance of his place may be judged by the fact that Boswell's, Dandridge's, and "Mount Brilliant" are the only places in St. Martin's Parish on the south Side of the South Anna mentioned on Henry's map. On the north side of the South Anna, Allen's Creek Church and Col. Hugh Nelson's "Chilton" are the only places referred to.

In 1783 the tract of land known as Boswells' was owned by Richard Anderson. In a mortgage from Richard Anderson and Caty, his wife, to William Anderson this tract is described as containing 480 acres. In this deed, Anderson states that he had acquired this property from Charles Thomson. (24) Richard Anderson and wife conveyed another tract of 360 acres on Turkey Creek to William Lawrence which may have been a part of the Boswell tract. (25) David Anderson acquired the 480 acre tract through foreclosure and conveyed the same to William Lawrence. (26) Lawrence conveyed this tract to Adam Toler who conveyed the same to Nathaniel West Dandridge, II. (27)

The will of John Boswell (p. 1) and the various answers and depositions disclose a wealth of information about the Johnson, Boswell and allied families; about New Castle, the methods of trade between the Virginia and British Merchants and an excellent picture of life in Colonial Hanover.

---

(21) The Justices of the Peace of Colonial Virginia 1757-1775, p. 52. Bulletin of the Virginia State Library. (22) Id. p. 73. (23) Id. p. 103. (24) Deed Book 1783-1792 - St. Martin's Parish, p. 5. (25) Id. p. 343. (26) Id. p. 412. (27) Id. p. 517 and pp. 67-68 this book.

The companion suit of <u>Donald Scott & Co</u>. v. <u>Johnson, et al</u>.
(p. 14-17) contains further information about John Boswell's estate. At
the end of this suit will be found a number of letters written by Johnson
and Boswell to John Backhouse, Merchant in Liverpool. These letters were
written at New Castle, Virginia, and bear dates 1769 and 1771.

The case of <u>Donald Scott & Co</u>. v. <u>William Clarke's Reprs</u>.
(pp. 20-26) is interesting in many respects. William Clarke was a free-
holder in St. Paul's Parish, Hanover County. (28) He was Inspector of
Tobacco at Crutchfield's Warehouse in 1776-77. (29) John Clarke, his
administrator, later moved to Kentucky and was in Bourbon County, Kentucky,
when his answer was sworn to in March, 1804. (pp. 20-21)

The inventory of William Clarke's Estate (pp. 21-22) gives an
excellent picture of the equipment and stock of a Hanover farm in 1783,
and the house furnishings on such a farm. This account would indicate
that Hanover farms were much better equipped and stocked for farming in
1783 than they are today.

The inventory also shows that his house was well furnished. The
account of the settlement also shows some interesting facts. The rum and
sugar provided for the burial cost L 1 s 9 d 4, and the rum for the sale
cost 12 s. Doctors apparently were better paid than lawyers were in those
days. The account shows that Dr. Jno. Roberts was paid L 13 s 11 d 4;
Dr. Riddock was paid L 14 s 10; Dr. Locklin McLear was paid L 2 s 10 d 2,
and Dr. John Shore was paid s 18, while John Marshall, Esq., was paid
L2 s 10 "for making defence in the General Court at the suit of Watkins",
(p. 23) and Bushrod Washington was paid L 5 for his "fee at the suit of
Rootes in the High Ct. of Chancery". (p. 25) The case also gives considerable information about the Clarke and Crutchfield families.

The fourth suit, <u>Donald, Scott & Co.v. Clay's Reprs</u>. (pp. 27-31)
relates to the estate of John Clay, the father of Henry Clay. It contains
a copy of his will, dated Novemver 4th, 1780, probated 7th February, 1782
(pp. 27-28).

John Clay, or Sir John Clay, as he is styled in a number of
deeds recorded in Chesterfield County, and as he is referred to in the
deed conveying Clay Springs in Hanover County, is claimed by the Baptists
as their chief Apostle in Hanover County. It is said that he was the
organizer of Winn's Church which was established in 1776. It will probably shock many of that denomination of this period to learn from his inventory (p. 29) that he was the owner of a thirty gallon still.

All persons interested in Henry Clay will find this a most interesting and informative suit.

The fifth suit, Gordon v. Smith (pp. 32-34) relates to the Cunninghams of New Castle and Scotland.

The next five suits, <u>Cochran Donald & Co</u>. v. <u>Underwood; Murdock
& Co</u>. v. <u>Dandridge</u>, etc.; Murdock & Co. v. N. W. <u>Dandridge's Reps</u>., <u>Under-
wood et al; Jones, Surviving Partner</u> v. <u>Dandridge's Exors</u>., and <u>John</u>

---

(28) <u>St. Paul's Vestry Book</u>, pp. 134, 200, 291, 301, 311, 312, 323, 339,
354, 355, 391, 427, 446, 455, 456, 486, 524, 544, and 555.
(29) <u>Journal of the Council of the State of Virginia 1776-77</u>, p. 285

Tyndall Ware, Exor. of Wm. Jones, decd. v. William Dandridge et al and
Cochran Donald & Co. v Underwood relate to the Dandridge and Underwood
families of the Southwestern end of Hanover.

Colonial Nathaniel West Dandridge (September 7, 1729-January
16, 1786) was the son of Col. William Dandridge of Elsing Green, King
William County and his wife Unity West Dandridge. Through his mother he
was descended from Sir Thomas West, 3econd Lord De la Warr (1555-1603).
He married 18th June, 1747, Dorothea Spotswood (1733-1773) daughter of
Alexander Spotswood. He married second, Jane Pollard, daughter of Jos-
eph Pollard, Clerk of Goochland County, who survived him and later married
Thomas Underwood.

By his mother's will he acquired most of the land in the south-
western corner of Hanover which had been granted to his grand-father,
Captain Nathaniel West, one of the original members of the Hanover County
Court and a member of the House of Burgesses from New Kent 1705-06.

Colonel Dandridge was a member of the County Court of Hanover
and represented the County in the House of Burgesses for the Sessions
1756-58, 1758-61, 1761-64.

In 1764, he vacated his seat in the House by accepting the
the Office of Coroner for Hanover. Becoming a candidate for the House
at the succeeding election, he was defeated by Col. James Littlepage,
the owner of South Wales on the South Anna. This was followed by the
celebrated, but unsuccessful election contest before the House of Burgesses in which Col. Dandridge was represented by Patrick Henry.

By his first marriage, Col. Dandridge had five sons, William,
Robert, John, Alexander Spotswood and Nathaniel West all of whom were
officers in the Revolution; William in the Hanover Militia and the others
in the Continental Service. They also had five daughters, Dorothea who
married Patrick Henry, Elizabeth who married Philip Payne, Anne Catherine
who married John Spotswood Moore, Mary C. who married Woodson Payne and
Martha Dandridge who married Archer Payne.

Col. Dandridge appointed his wife Jane Dandridge and his son
William the executrix and executor of his will. (p. 37-38).

Colonel Nathaniel West Dandridge appears to have been a poor
manager and always in debt. This may be seen from a number of Acts to be
found in Hening's Statutes and additional proof of this fact is to be
found in the pages of this book. On October 6, 1768, he executed a deed
of trust to William Dabney, William Macon, John Johnson and Robert Anderson of the County of Hanover and John Wayles of the County of Charles
City as Trustees. This deed covered the tract on which Col. Dandridge
lived, lying on Allen's Creek containing by estimation four thousand
acres and another tract on Turkey Creek containing fourteen hundred and
sixty-six acres, more or less; one hundred and sixty-one slaves and large
quantities of personal property. (pp. 54-57) Prior to this deed he had
mortgaged the Turkey Creek property to John Murdock & Co., of Glasgow,
Merchants, by deed of 3rd September, 1767, and to Andrew Cochran & Robert
Donald & Co., Glasgow, Merchants, by deed of 5th September, 1767.
(pp. 51-52)

After Col. Dandridge's death, his creditors brought numerous suits in the United States Court to collect their Claims.

The suits above enumerated and found in this volume (pp.35-68) contain a history of the debts and the litigation that followed, but what is more important they disclose many facts, heretofore unknown about the Dandridge and Underwood families, a number of deeds and statements of facts of the greatest value to anyone , interested in the history of Hanover County.

The suits of Donald Scott & Co. v. Foster's Adm. and William Morris v. Peter Foster Adm. of Thomas Foster, decd., while interesting are of slight historical importance. (pp. 69-70)

The suits of William Lawrence, Surviving Exor. of John Lawrence, deceased v. Edmund Taylor, and Smith's Exors. v. Lawrence, Exor. and Lawrence's Exors. v. Littlepage (pp. 71-76) are of very great interest.

Captain John Lawrence lived in St. Martin's Parish, Hanover County in the vicinity of the Hanover Academy. He was a captain in Heath's Independent Company in the Revolution and was a member of the County Court as early as 1770, (30) and in 1784 and 1785 he was the Sheriff of Hanover County (31).

This suit contains a copy of the will of Captain John Lawrence which, among other facts of interest, gives the names of all of his children. So far as is known this is the only source where this information is obtainable.

His daughter, Nancy Lawrence, was the wife of the celebrated teacher, Peter Nelson. A number of their descendants live in Hanover County.

The suit of Lawrence's Exors. v. Littlepage adds another chapter to the unfortunate story of Richard Littlepage, another part of which is to be found in 13 Hening's Statutes, p. 623-24.

The suit of Overton v. Honeyman & DuVal (p.77) contains considerable information about a number of people connected with Hanover County, Doctor Robert Honeyman, William DuVal, and numerous members of the Overton family. Clough Overton who was killed at the battle of Blue Licks, 19th August, 1782, was the son of John Overton and his wife Anne Booker Clough. John Overton was the son of Captain James Overton and Elizabeth Garland Overton and, therefore, a grandson of William Overton I and Elizabeth Waters Overton. (32)

The suits of Hanbury's Exor. v. Page and Lloyd, Exor. of Hanbury v. Page's Admr., etc., contains a copy of the will of Robert Carter Page and much interesting information about the Pages of Hanover and

---

(30) The Justices of the Peace of Colonial Virginia, 1757-75, p. 103
(31) Hanover Deed Book, 1783-92, pp. 66 and 100
(32) The Overton Family by W. E. Dickinson; R'd. Times-Dispatch, Sept. 5, 1915.

Spotsylvania and their property. (pp. 78-80)

The suits of John Murdock & Company v. Parke Goodall and Thomas Tinsley, and Murdock & Company v. Pearson's Heirs (pp. 81-84), contain a copy of Samuel Pearson's will, the inventory of his estate, and the deposition of one William Mann in which he located Pearson's land as being on the Pamunkey River.

Samuel Pearson was a merchant at New Castle, and a member of the Committee of merchants organized at Williamsburg in 1770. (33)

Colonel Parke Goodall had been a Revolutionary soldier. He was a member of the County Court. With John Carter Littlepage he represented Hanover in the Virginia Convention of 1788, and he was one of her representatives in the General Assembly, Sessions of 1780-81, 1782, 1785-86, 1786-87 and 1787-88. In 1790 he was sheriff of Hanover County. Samuel Pearson was one of his sureties. (34)

Thomas Tinsley was a member of the County Court. (35) He was the owner of the tavern at Hanover Town (36), and he represented Hanover in the General Assembly, Sessions of 1789-90, 1791, 1792, 1793, 1794, 1795 and 1796.

Next follows Underwood et al v. Underwood's Exor. &c. This suit arose out of a controversy about the estate of Jane Underwood, and contains a wealth of information about the family of Thomas Underwood.

Thomas Underwood (circa 1740-January 29, 1815) was a resident of St. Martin's Parish, Hanover County in 1763, and testified as a witness in the Dandridge-Littlepage Election Contest before the Committee of Privileges and Elections of the House of Burgesses. (37) He testified at that time that he lived "in the upper part of the said County of Hanover, about 25 miles above the sitting member" (Mr. Littlepage). It is believed that his home was the brick house on the Pin Hook Road leading from Vontary to Goochland lately owned by V. T. Bowles and now owned by Miss Mary Elizabeth Cochran. Later he moved to Goochland and represented that County in the House of Delegates in the Sessions of 1777, 1778, 1780, 1781, 1783, , 1784-85, 1785-86, 1786-87, 1787-88, 1789 and 1790.

The papers in this case fail to disclose the name of his first wife, although giving the names of his children.

After the death of Colonel Nathaniel West Dandridge, he married his widow, Jane Pollard Dandridge. They had no issue.

After his marriage to Mrs. Dandridge, he moved to the Dandridge

---

(33) Virginia Historical Register, Vol. III, p. 79.
(34) Hanover Deed Book, 1783-1792, pp. 430-31
(35) Hanover Deed Book, 1783-1792, p. 468
(36) Ibid, p. 543
(37) Journal of the House of Burgesses, 26 Nov., 1764

place on Allen's Creek adjoining the present Rockville High School property, which was a part of this place, and there he died the 29th of January, 1815. Mrs. Jane Underwood survived him and died the 13th of April, 1821.

His son, James Underwood, acquired the Dandridge place from Mrs. Jane Underwood about 1816, when it was transferred to him on the land book. About 1820 he acquired from John G. Childress 27 acres and the following year, 560 acres were transferred to him from Walter Boyd Gilliam. This last tract was transferred from him in 1824 and 1831 and the 27 acre tract in 1833. The Dandridge place was transferred to Joseph Nuckols in 1839.

James Underwood was a soldier in the Revolution and was captain of a troop of Cavalry of the 4th Regiment, Virginia Militia in the War of 1812. (38) He was a member of the County Court of Hanover, 1811-1836, (39) and Sheriff of the county in 1829. (40) He died prior to the 22nd March, 1847. (41) He married Frances George, daughter of James George, on June 2, 1797, his neighbor, the Reverend Charles Hopkins, performing the ceremony. (42)

Jane Pollard Dandridge Underwood was the daughter of Joseph Pollard, Clerk of Goochland County, and a sister of William Pollard of Buckeye, Clerk of Hanover County.

She was born the 25th of May, 1744, and died the 13th of April, 1821, "much known, respected and regretted". (43)

Joseph Rogers Underwood was born in Goochland County the 24th of October, 1791, and died in Kentucky the 23rd of August, 1876. He was the son of John Underwood and Frances Rogers Underwood, and, therefore, a grand-son of Thomas Underwood. He moved to Kentucky in 1803 to live with his maternal uncle, Edward Rogers, and was educated in various schools, graduating at Transylvania College in 1811. Later he studied law in Lexington, Kentucky. He was an officer in the War of 1812, was wounded and captured. He was a member of the Kentucky Legislature, 1816-19 and 1825-26 and a judge of the Kentucky Court of Appeals 1828-1835. He was a member of Congress from Kentucky 1835-1843, and United States Senator from Kentucky 1847-1853. He was the ancestor of Oscar W. Underwood, the great United States Senator from Alabama.

Warner L. Underwood, born in Goochland County, Virginia the 7th of August, 1808, was also the son of John Underwood and Frances Rogers Underwood. He was educated at the University of Virginia, graduating there in 1830. He was a member of the Kentucky Legislature in 1848-49, and a member of Congress 1853-1859. (44)

---

(38) Muster Rolls of the Virginia Militia, War of 1812, p. 795
(39) Cocke, p. 179
(40) E. F. 48, Hanover Clerk's Office, Underwood v. Starke
(41) Cocke, p. 108
(42) Goochland Marriage Register, pp. 63 and 341
(43) Richmond Enquirer, April 27, 1821, p. 3, col. 3, and an article by
    John Pollard, Sr., of King and Queen County written in 1870 and
    published in the Argus.
(44) Appleton's Enc. of American Biography, pp. 210-211

John Underwood, the husband of Frances Rogers and father of Joseph Rogers Underwood and Warner L. Underwood, lived in Goochland and represented that county in the House of Delegates in the Sessions 1807-08, 1808-09, 1812-13, 1813-14, and 1814-15. Judging from the contents of Mrs. Jane Underwood's letter to him of the 14th of September, 1817, he was rather neglectful of his family. In the article on his son, Joseph Rogers Underwood, in Appleton's Cyclopaedia of American Biography, it is said that he was adopted by his uncle, Edward Rogers, because his family was in adverse circumstances. It appears from this suit that Thomas and Jane Underwood took into their home John Underwood's children, Malvina, Elizabeth, Jane and Warner and apparently Mrs. Underwood continued to support them in her home after Thomas Underwood's death. From this fact and the contents of the above mentioned letter, it is reasonable to believe that he was not only in adverse circumstances but extremely neglectful of his family as well.

The last item in Mrs. Glazebrook's book is the will of William Winston, Sr., who died the 3rd of February, 1781. The Winston family of Hanover is one of the leading families of the county to the present day. It was a remarkably numerous family, and due to the loss of the county records and many of the personal family records, it has been a source of unending confusion to genealogists. Anything that that throws light on any member of this family is, therefore, of interest.

In a letter to John Adams, Thomas Jefferson said, "A morsel of genuine history is a thing so rare as to be always valuable. (45) This book is packed with one hundred pages of genuine source history of Hanover County and its people which is to be found in no other published work.

Every person who loves the County of Hanover and who is interested in its history and its people should read this book. By so doing he will find himself indebted to Mrs. Glazebrook whose industry and painstaking care have made this possible.

LEON M. BAZILE

November 17, 1943

(45) The Writings of Thomas Jefferson (Washington), Vo. VII, p. 82

PREFACE

Book I, for Hanover County, is the first of a series of volumes, - others of which will follow in the near future, - composed of documents relating to Virginia families of the latter half of the eighteenth and early part of the nineteenth centuries. Numbers of these files concern counties whose original records are no longer extant, many of them having been destroyed by fire, a fate which has befallen all too much of our Virginia material. From these papers the movement of the people from County to County, State to State, and in some instances from the Mother Country to the Colony, is clearly shown, thus enabling the researcher to establish the connection between these early Virginians and their scattered descendants. Depositions included in the chancery suits often prove conclusively relationships hitherto in doubt, or in many cases quite unknown.

The compilers are deeply indebted to Judge Leon Bazile, of the Fifteenth Judicial Circuit, without whose interest and encouragement this volume would not have been possible. Judge Bazile, whose circuit includes the Counties of Hanover, Caroline, Spotsylvania, Stafford and King George, as well as the City of Fredericksburg, has long been a student of Virginia history, and his thorough knowledge of Hanover and its people is shown in his very fine introduction to these records.

To Mrs. Nell Nugent and Mr. Beverley Fleet for their unfailing confidence and advice; to Mr. Carroll K. Moran, Deputy Clerk of the United States District Court for the Eastern District of Virginia, and to Miss Sally Carlton, Mr. Glover N. Buck, and other members of the staff of that Court, for their kind and courteous assistance while this material was being gathered, the compilers wish to express their very sincere appreciation.

Eugenia G. Glazebrook
Preston G. Glazebrook

Richmond, Virginia
December 8, 1943

MAP
of
RICHMOND HANOVER COUNTY

NEW KENT COUNTY

NEW CASTLE

KING WILLIAM COUNTY

HANOVER TOWN C.

CRUMPS C.

PIMUNKEY R.

TETOTOTOMOY R.

CHICKAHOMINY C.

CHICKAHOMINY R.

N. WALES

S. WALES

C.H.

LITTLE PAGES

LITTLE BRIDGE

WINSTONS B

N

Henrico County

JAMES RIVER

STONEY R.

STRG C.

STONEMORE C.

GOLDMINE C.

SHOP C.

ALLENS C.

TURKEY C.

Goochland County

CAROLINE COUNTY

N. ANNA RIVER

LITTLE RIVER

NEWFOUND RIVER

TAYLORS C.

S. ANNA RIVER

LOUISA COUNTY

Backhouse's admr.) 1349 (157)   1
     vs   ) U. 3. Cir. Ct.
Johnson & als   ) 5th Cir. Va. Dist.
(1806)

         John and Jane Backhouse admr. & admx. de bonis non of
John Backhouse decd Pltf
                         against
         Richard C Johnson exor of Thomas Johnson Senr who was
exor of John Boswell - Richard C Johnson - John B Johnson - Thomas
M Johnson - Chapman Johnson - William Johnson - Patrick Michie
and Dorothy his wife - Jane Johnson - Ludlow Branham - James Watson - John Daniel - John White - James Barbour Junr - Charles
Quarles - Thomas Lipscomb and Agnes Ragland admor & admx of William Ragland .decd. who was security for Thomas Johnson, minor, exor
of John Boswell decd - Rhodes Ragland another security of the said
Thomas Johnson minor - Elizabeth Johnson exx of Thomas Johnson
Sheriff another security of the said Thomas Johnson minor   Defds

                        In Chancery

Richmond - December 1806 -

         In the course of the month of October all the defendants
now living were notified of the appointed day (10 day November)
except John B Johnson who is said to be no inhabitant of this State -
Richard C and William Johnson are said to be dead -

                    WILL OF JOHN BOSWELL
                    d. 14 April, 1738
                    p. June 9, 1738

         In the name of God amen I John Boswell of the parish of
Fredericksville in the county of Louisa being sick and weak but of
sound mind and memory, (god be thanked for the same) and considering the frailty of human nature, and that it is appointed for all
men once to die I do make and constitute this my last will and testament in form and manner following and desire it may be received as
such first and principally I commit and commend my soul unto god
that gave it in hopes of his gracious acceptance of the same only
in and through the merits and mediation of Jesus Christ his only
son and my own blessed Saviour as for my body I commit it to the
earth from whence it came to be buried in such a decent manner as
my executors hereafter named shall think proper and as for such

worldly goods as it hath pleased god to bless me with after all
my lawful and just   are paid I will and depose of the remainder
in the following manner that is to say - I give to Boswell Thornton
the land I bought of Burr Harrison in Orange County known by the
name of the brick chimney, and the following negroes viz - James,
Suck & hir three children and Usley & hir three children & their
increase and mountain Tom, Nancy, Speed, Bill & hir child nan and
two children & all their increase and one fourth of my stock to be
delivered to him when he comes of age if the said Boswell Thornton
should die without lawful heir and I likewise lend him Isaak on the
same terms and if the said Boswell die without heir lawfully begotten then the whole and all to Thomas Boswell & Thomas Johnson
minr. Lucye captain & hir child Maney, I do sett free a yellow boy
James & his mother Luce I do sett free I give to the said James
the tract of land bought of John Goodman & desire my exors to give
the said James a horse saddle worth nine pounds & cow & calf and
a tolarable education and William Captain I do give the land purchased of Thomas Gibbens if he does not redeem it if he does the
money to him and to my beloved wife Ann Boswell twelve choyes negroes & the plantation whereon I now live and all my stock and
furniture I do lend for hir life and at her death to be equally
divided between Thomas Boswell & Thomas Johnson minr. to the sd
Thomas Johnson minr. I give the land lent to my wife but if the
british debts should be paid that is to be sold for that purpose.
I give to the Thomas Johnson minr. the land in Orange bought of
Charles Smith and the mill land bought of Matthew More and Paines
tract bought of the sheriff & likewise the land that was Raglands
bought of the sheft and my brother Thomas Boswell the tract of
land bought of William and the tract bought of Elkanah Ray and
to Mitchum Boswell I give the negroes Bass and Francey and to
Fanney Boswell I give Rose and hir child Winney and to Jane Boswell I give Moll and hir child Jacob and to Nancy Boswell I give
the   Matt   I likewise give to Boswell Thornton Dick & John
Scott on the same terms and to go to the same in the same case
as the above and to John Bourn, Jim boy and all my estate not
mentioned to be divided between my brother Thomas Boswell & my
niffue Thomas Johnson, minr. I ordain and make this to be my last
will & testament and disannull all other wills heretofore made
and do appoint my friends Thomas Boswell Thomas Johnson minr.
John Bourn & Boswell Thornton my exors Signed sealed &c this
14th of April 1788

Test   John Boswell   (Seal)
Butler Bradburn
Thomas Guthry
John (X) Self

At a court held for Louisa county June 9th 1788

     This will was this day exhibited in Court & proved by
the oaths of Butler Bradburn Thos. Guthry & John Self & by the
Court ordered to be recorded and at a Court held for the sd
County Oct - 13th 1788 Thomas Johnson (minr.) one of the executors therein named came into Court & took the oath of an exor.
& entered into & acknowledged his bond with approved security
whereupon (on the motion of the sd exor) a certificate is granted
him for obtaining a probat thereof in due form -

                            Teste   Jno. Nelson Clk

           A Copy

                            Teste John Poindexter CC

12 Jan 1789

Anthony Thornton - Gdn for Boswell Thornton, acknowledges receipt from Capt. Thomas Johnson exor of Colo. John Boswell of
slaves & stock Devised to sd Boswell Thornton -

                            Anthony Thornton

ANSWER OF PATRICK MICHIE AND DOROTHY HIS WIFE

   ... Dorothy is the daughter of Thomas Johnson (nr) who
was the exor and one of the Devisees of John Boswell ...

Albemarle County Sct -

   Sworn to before Charles B Hunton Justice of the Peace for
said County 21 April 1806

ANSWER OF CHAPMAN JOHNSON
Filed 30 April, 1805

... It is true that John Boswell of Louisa died in the year 1788 possessed of a very large real and personal estate

That Thomas Johnson (minor) one of the exors named in the will died in 1795 possessed also of a considerable estate -

That Richard Chapman Johnson was his only acting exor. who died intestate in December 1802, and that this respondent is a son and devisee of Thomas Johnson (minr.) and a brother and one of the heirs of Richd. C. Johnson -

This respondent was not more than 16 yrs. old at the death of his father (1795) It is believed that Richard Johnson one of the partners of Boswell & Johnson died in September, 1771 ... Anthony Thornton, father of Boswell Thornton (a man of large property, it is believed) ... Boswell Thornton is dead, without children - Mrs. Lucy Thornton of Fredericksburg it is believed, is his sole legatee and devisee, and Thomas Rootes of the same place his exor. or administrator -

Major Thomas Boswell is also dead - His children were, Martha Boswell, Nancy Boswell, Frances Boswell (married, not known to whom) Jane Boswell married to Major   who is dead), another daughter married to Churchill Armistead, and another, it is said is married to one Churchill - Martha is dead - It is believed that Benjamin Dabney of King & Queen is guardian to his orphan children & exor to his estate -

The representatives of Richard Johnson the other partner to the firm are supposed to be the following -- William Johnson of Hanover, the exor. John B. Johnson of Hanover, Nicholas Johnson, Nicholas Syme who married Elizabeth Johnson & Elizabeth Johnson, William Cunningham, John Cunningham, John Syme & Nancy his wife formerly Nancy Cunningham, Isaac Butler who married Dorothy Cunningham now dead (these Cunninghams being heirs of Nancy Cunningham formerly Nancy Johnson) and the reprs. of Doctr. William Marshall who married Jane Johnson and whose exor. is a Mr Fox of Gloucester - Thomas Johnson (minor) the father of this respondent was also one of the sons of Richard Johnson -

Colo. Reuben Lindsay, a man of respectibility and a monied man purchased the land containing 633 acres devised by Boswell to Thomas Johnson (minor) which land adjoins a tract of land which had been devised by Thomas Johnson (minor) to his four sons,

Backhouse's Admr. vs Johnson, cont.:
Answer of Chapman Johnson, cont.

5

John B., Richard C., Thomas L. Chapman & William Johnson.

While this respondent was at college in Williamsburg 430 acres of this land were sold to Ludlow Bramham. Robert Michie also purchased a part of same.

One of the Slaves of Col. Boswell, Cob, a blacksmith, was sold to a company of Gentlemen, consisting of Colo. Richard Morris, Majr. James Watson, Captain Turner Anderson and others, who it is believed have liberated him.

Chapman Johnson

ANSWER OF JOHN B. JOHNSON
Filed Nov. 30, 1803

This respondent, being duly sworn, etc. ... states that he is one of the sons and Legatees of Richard Johnson late of the Town of New Castle in the County of Hanover deceased, whose Testament and last will among the records of the County court of said County of Hanover he will be ready to produce at the hearing if required - He had a daughter named Dorothy to whom he advanced in his lifetime, and who having intermarried with Anthony Thornton of the County of Caroline departed this life in the lifetime of the said Richard leaving the said Anthony Thornton & an only child by him named Boswell, to which Boswell the said Richard gave a Legacy in and by his said Testament, wherein he the said Richard also provided for his wife Dorothea, afterwards his widow, & for his five sons, to wit Richard, Thomas, William, this Defdt., John Boswell and Nicholas Meriwether, and three daughters to wit, Anne, Jane and Elizabeth, all of whom survived him. His son Richard departed this life possessed of a considerable estate as did also his son Thomas & his sons, William, this Defdt & Nicholas Meriwether are still alive - His daughter Anne intermarried with John Cunningham & died under coverture, leaving the said John Cunningham and four children to wit Dorothe who intermarried with Isaac Butler, and died under coverture leaving the said Isaac and an only child named Lucy Anne, both of whom are still alive - William who is made a party to the sd Bill, John who is since dead and Anne Johnson who intermarried with John Syme both of whom are still alive, and for all these her children she provided by an Instrument in the nature of a last Will - Jane another daughter of the said Richard intermarried with Doctor William Marshall, and both of them are dead, without ever having had issue, and Elizabeth another of his daughters intermarried with

Nicholas Syme, and is now deceased leaving the sd Nicholas and
four children by him, to wit John M., Nicholas, Elisa, and Clar-
issa -

The said first named Richard Johnson departed this
Life on the 29th Day of Sept. 1771, and in & by his Testament
afsd. constituted his wife Dorothea, & his sons Thomas & William to be his Exorx. & Exors thereof all of whom took upon
themselves the burthen of that office before the County Court
of Hanover aforesaid and possessed themselves of the whole estate of their sd Testator, both real & personal, and the sd
William who is the only survivor among them & the Representatives of the said Dorothea & Thomas can best account for their
administration thereof -

Dorothea died intestate & her son Williamafsd had
the administration of her Estate committed to him by the sd
County Court of Hanover -

Thomas died testate and his Representatives are supposed to be before this Court as Defdts.

After the decease of the sd Dorothea in the month of
March 1781 the estate of the first named Richard was divided
by his Exors (both of whom survived her)...

In the year 1770 this Defdt became an assistant in a
Store kept under the firm of Boswell & Johnson, the Partners
concerned in which were the sd John Boswell, this Defdts uncle,
and Thomas Johnson afsd this Defdts Brother whose Partnership
(as he believes) commenced in the year 1768 or 1769

John B. Johnson

Sworn to in Court November 30, 1803

William Marshall Clk.

ANSWER OF ELIZABETH ARMISTEAD, LATE ELIZABETH BOSWELL

Elizabeth Armistead, late Elizabeth Boswell, one of the daughters of Thomas Boswell, decd., says that no part of the estate of the said John Boswell in the Bill mentioned was devised to her. That her father Thomas Boswell did devise to her for life a Slave named Polly aged about 48 or 9 years. to the best of her belief & of about forty Pounds value which slave this defendant believes was of the estate of the said John Boswell, devised to her Father -

Eliza Armistead

Gloucester County towit -

Sworn to before Frans. Whiting a Magistrate for the said county 14th day of Octr. 1807

ANSWER OF JOHN HART AND JANE, HIS WIFE

... Jane Hart, late Jane Major was formerly Jane Boswell daughter of Thomas Boswell and sister of Machon Boswell ...

Matthews County to wit -

Sworn to before Fdr. Hudgins, Justice of the Peace for the said county 23rd day of September 1807

SUPPLEMENTARY BILL OF BACKHOUSE'S ADMRS.

Dated April 1807 - Mentions Machin Boswell deceased, Frances Boswell widow of sd Machin Boswell, and the sisters of the sd. Machin Boswell, towit: Jane who hath intermarried with John Hart, Elizabeth who hath intermarried with Churchill Armistead, Dorothy who hath intermarried with Benjamin Churchill, Frances who hath intermarried with Thomas Mullings and Anne who hath intermarried with --- and are descendants of Thomas Boswell -

SUBPCENA DATED 23 September 1806 SHOWS:

... Ann (Boswell) wife of Robert N. Hongess (?), Frances Boswell widow of Machin Boswell, deceased, Jane Major late Jane Boswell ...

ANSWER OF WILLIAM CUNNINGHAM

This Deponent saith ... that he is a grandson of Richard
Johnson in the Bill named, who was formerly of the Town of New Castle
in the Co. of Hanover - That gentleman had five sons, and three
daughters at the time of his death besides --- who was the wife of
Anthony Thornton, Junior of the County of Caroline - The five sons
were Richard, William, Thomas, John Boswell, and Nicholas Meriwether,
and the three Daughters of whom this Deft can say anything correctly,
from information or otherwise, were Anne, this Defdts. mother, who
intermarried with his father John Cunningham, if he can judge from
a marriage settlement between them some time soon after the 15th Day
of April 1774, and departed this life on the 26th day of May 1788,
having first made her will which was probated in Hanover county
Court, in the lifetime of the said John Cunningham, leaving issue
by him, Dorothea Fairley, who after the death of her father intermarried with one Isaac Butler and is since Dead - leaving him and
issue by him Lucy Ann now an Infant, this Defendant, John who is
since Dead, and Anne Johnson now the wife of one John Syme, now of
the County of Nelson. The Testament and last will of this Defdts
grand father Richard Johnson, bearing date, on the 25th day of
September 1771, was admitted to proof before the worshipful Court
of the County of Hanover in Virginia on the 25th Day of March 1772 ...
All the transactions mentioned in the Bill happened long before the
birth of this Defdt.

                                                    William Cunningham
Henrico County towit

            Sworn to before David L Hylton 26 day of November 1808

ANSWER OF JOHN DANIEL

This Deponent saith that he bought of Lucy Thornton the
widow executrix and devisee of Boswell Thornton deceased about 420
acres in the County of Orange which he understood and believed to
have been part of a Tract of land devised by John Boswell in the Bill
named to said Boswell Thornton by the name and Description of the
Land which he had bought of Benjamin Harrison called the Brick
Chimnies -

                                                    John Daniel

Richmond

            23 November 1805

ANSWER OF WILLIAM JOHNSON

This respondent was not fourteen years old at the death of his father - He cannot therefore have any personal knowledge of his fathers administration of Boswell's estate.

This respondent recollects the sale made by Richard C. Johnson of the land charged by Boswell, with the payment of his British debts - He was present at the sale ... Thomas M. Johnson was the purchaser. He understood the land was purchased for the five sons of Thomas Johnson (mr) - This respondent has received his fifth part of the two tracts of land divided between the five brothers - In his division there was contained none of the land purchased of Boswell's estate ... No part of the personal estate of Thomas Johnson (minor) has ever been received by this respondent - Some money is supposed to have been paid to Parson Nelson, of Hanover, for about a quarter of a year's board and tuition of this respondent - A few dollars, at this time, were furnished this respondent and a bed was furnished him, when going to Tennessee, and $95 on his return from that Country ...

Louisa Co   Sc -

Sworn to before Peter Crutchfield a justice of the peace for the said County 25 April 1805

ANSWER OF MRS. LUCY THORNTON

This deponent states that she intermarried with Boswell Thornton some time in the year 1790 and the said Boswell departed this life some time in the year 1799. He devised his whole Estate to this Defendant subject to the payment of his debts which were numerous & some of them large, making this defendant executrix. This defendant sold off the estate of her husband and paid the debts & had expended a considerable part of the proceeds of the estate for her own comfort and maintenance long before any supn. of this cause was executed upon her.

Fredericksburg, Va. -

Sworn to before Tho. Goodwin a Magistrate 11th day of may 1808

DEPOSITION OF JOHN BOSWELL JOHNSON

By Virtue of a Commission hereto annexed we have proceeded
to Take the Deposition of John Boswell Johnson a witness on behalf of
the Defendant at the House of Francis Taylor in the Town of New Castle
& County of Hanover, now Occupied by John Tinsley, this 8th day of
February 1796 ...

John Boswell Johnson, being first sworn on the Holy Evange-
lists of Almighty God. deposeth & saith that he is the son of Colo.
Richard Johnson late of the Town of New Castle in the State of Virginia, and Nephew to the late Colo. John Boswell of the County of
Louisa in the State aforesaid, - that between the Year 1769 and 1774
he was some Times at his Fathers in New Castle and most of his Time
at his Uncle Boswells in the upper end of Hanover where he then resided - that he never heard nor understood nor does he believe that
Colo. William Johnson the present Defendt. was ever concerned or connected in Trade with Colo. Boswell - that his Father Colo. Richd.
Johnson and his Uncle Colo. John Boswell formerly carried on the Trade
of Merchandize in importing and vending Goods under the Firm of Johnson & Boswell - that long before the correspondence commenced between
the sd. Johnson & Boswell & John Backhouse there Trade in goods &
Merchandize were at an end, and that he this Deponent has heard both
from his Father and Uncle that the nature of there correspondence with
Mr. Backhouse was to ship him there Crops of Tobacco, import Family
goods & draw Bills of Exchange for the supposed Value of there Tobacco -
that on the Death of this Deponent's Father who had given discretion-
ary powers by his Will to his Executors Col. John Boswell & this Deponents Brother William Johnson and his Mother, to conduct his Estate
to the best ---* for the Interest of his Wife & Family, the said Executors on a Consultation of the Affairs of the Estate of the sd. Richd.
Johnson, came to a resolution to continue the Correspondence with Mr.
Backhouse and shipd. him the Estates and Colo. Boswell's Tobacco, Import Family Goods and draw Bills of Exchange on the Tobacco - that
this was done by the Executors after this Deponents Fathers Death, to
his knowledge and further this Deponent saith not

John B Johnson

State of Virginia
Hanover County, to wit
Sworn to before Bartt. Anderson and Merir. Jones, Magistrates for the
sd. County of Hanover ...

Notation on back of deposition: "We of the Jury find for the Plaintif
Twenty seven thousand five hundred and twenty nine dollars and Six
Cents, damages -

David Lambert

*mutilated

DEPOSITION OF SAMUEL GRANTLAND

        taken at the Tavern of Harrison Ball in New Castle
the 9th day of November 1811

        Saith that he lived in the Town of New Castle in the
County of Hanover from the fall of the year 1767 until the death
of old Colo. Richard Johnson of New Castle which happened from
the inscription on his Tomb stone the 29th of September 1771 -

DEPOSITION OF ABRAHAM KENT

        taken at the same place on the same day

        He deposeth and sayeth that for three or four years
before the death of old Colo. Richard Johnson of New Castle he
was in the habit of working almost every day in the said years
at the Tobacco Warehouses in New Castle which was within fifty
yards of old Colo. Richard Johnsons dwelling-house and well
knows that during the time of his working at the Warehouses that
Colo. Richard Johnson had no Store in New Castle, he further
saith that during his working at the Warehouse David Cockran,
Colo. John Syme, Samuel Pearson, Joseph Thropp and William Johnson and Charles Tinsley had Stores in New Castle -

        Question by William Johnson: How many House-keepers
were there in New Castle during the time you worked at the Tobacco Ware Houses?

        Ans.: I don't think there were more than twelve -

        Sworn to on the 9th day of November 1810 before John
Kilby and Benjn. Brand

DEPOSITION OF JOHN BROWN

        taken at Fredericksburg, Thursday 4th day of May, 1809,
Banjn Parke Master Commissioner -

        Sayeth that he was well acquainted with the firm of
Johnson & Boswell of Hanover ... that he this affiant lived with
the said John Boswell from the year 1761 to 1736 excepting two
years & he believes the partnership was dissolved in the summer
of the year 1762 ... Mentions contract to ship 100,000 pounds of
Tobacco annually to Backhouse & to receive one thousand Pounds in
Specie ... but had not received the Specie ...

DEPOSITION OF FRANCIS IRWIN

Deposition of Francis Irwin of lawful age, taken at the Commissioner's office in the Town of Fredericksburg on Monday the 1st day of May 1809 -

This Deponent sayeth that he was well acquainted with the firm of Johnson & Boswell who formerly carried on business in the town of New Castle & County of Hanover; that the firm was composed of old Colo. Richard Johnson & John Boswell; that said Richard Johnson lived at New Castle and that John Boswell lived in the upper end of Hanover County near the line of Goochland County, and that the said John Boswell was in the habit of coming to the store at New Castle & stayed a week at a time and when they received Goods from Liverpool, London and elsewhere, the said Boswell took an active part ... That there was a store kept at the place where John Boswell resided in which store he believes the said Richard Johnson & John Boswell were equally concerned as in the store in New Castle -At one time the said Johnson & Boswell shipped about 150 Hogsheads of Tobacco to the address of Walker & Co of Liverpool -

The deponent refers to letters dated August 9 1770 and 26 May 1771 - New Castle - written by the late Charles Tinsley of New Castle formerly a partner of William Johnson now living near New Castle, afterward under the firm of Johnson & Tinsley -

DEPOSITION OF MARY COCKBURN

The deposition of Mary Cockburn, of lawful age, taken at the Tavern of Harrison Ball in New Castle in the County of Hanover this 9th day of November 1811 - who sayeth that she came to live in New Castle in the County of Hanover about five and forty years ago, and lived there until the death of old Colo. Richard Johnson of New Castle and that she well knows that Colo. Johnson had no store in New Castle - During the time between her coming to New Castle and the death of Colo. Richard Johnson she was in the habit of intimacy with his family - She believes Francis Irwin to be an Englishman & came to live at New Castle some time after she did ...

ANSWER OF JAMES BARBOUR

... Thinks it unjust and oppressive that he should be disturbed in the possession of property which he purchased & paid for, which has passed through so many hands & when the present claim has lain dormant for so many years and was never heard of by this respondent until he had bought and paid for the land - John Boswell by his last will gave Thomas Johnson a tract of land lying in the County of Orange which he sold to William Alcock, which said Alcock sold to Richard Bruce who sold it to this Respondent, containing 700 acres upon which were valuable improvements

Albemarle County

Sworn to before G. Carr a Justice of the Peace for the said County 3rd day of November 1806

ANSWER OF JOHN WHITE

This Respondent saith that he is in possession of 600 acres of land part of the tract given by Col. Boswell to Boswell Thornton and sold by his widow, devisee and executrix before he heard of this claim and he fully paid for the same and obtained his deed before the emanation of the ---- of this cause -

City of Richmond -

Sworn to before Anderson Barret 23 May 1307

DEPOSITION OF JOHN BROWN

taken at Ludlow Branham's in Louisa County on the 12th day of May 1810

... Saith that Backhouse was to return £1000 specie for every 100,000 lbs. of Tobacco upon its receipt to Boswell according to contract ...

Donald Scott & Co.) 1820 (90)
    vs   ) U. S. Cir. Ct.
Johnson & al:) 5th Cirt. Va. Dist.
(1805)

ANSWER OF CHARLES QUARLES

    This Defendant saith that he knows not anything of the
Justice of the Complainants claims but hath been informed that it
hath been a custom to Strike of_ eight years Interest from British
debts.

    That he is in possession of the Land designated in John
Boswells Will as bought of William estimated at 885 acres & devised
to Thomas Boswell the Brother of sd John; under a fair purchase
for a full and valuable consideration of the sd Thomas, that sd
Thomas is dead; but he is informed & verily believes he should be
able to prove that in the life time of sd John who lived in Louisa
County he promised the sd Thomas who lived in Gloucester County
that If he the sd Thomas would remove from sd County of Gloucester
to sd County of Louisa & be his neighbor that he the sd John would
give him the sd Thomas the Land foresaid, and that the sd Thomas
did so remove & he the sd John Did so give & put in possession the
sd Thomas of the sd Land in his the sd John's life time, for the
Term of   years or thereabouts all that Time continuing to be the
neighbor of sd John. That sd John was a Wealthy Man & the sd
Thomas, perhaps, being & (sic) only Brother & having further expectations from the Bounty of said John did not urge or did not
obtain the legal title of sd Land from sd John during his life.
That said Devise is only in affemence & fulfillment of the promises
of sd John in order to vest the legal Title in sd Thomas, that sd
promis of sd John was about the   Day of   1785 & the removal
of sd Thomas was on the   Day of   1786 ...

    This defendant further states that at the time of making
the Will of sd John there was a well grounded Doubt pervading all
Men's minds as to British debts being ever paid a Doubt the Testator had as appears from his Will. That add to this he directed
certain Lands, Sufficient perhaps to pay all his own proper debts
as this defendant has been informed, to be sold for the payment of
British debts, the debt of the complainant & others of like description ...   That Thomas Johnson (Minor) proved the Will of sd John
and qualified as Executor thereto & acted from the 13th day of
October 1788 ... til the   day of   1795 or Thereabouts, when he
dyed leaving a large Estate in Lands, negroes & other personal
property, during all which Time this defendant is Informed & ex-
pects to be able to prove that the complainants did not use due
diligence for the recovery of their debt ...

City of Richmond to wit

    Sworn to before Wm Richardson a Justice of the Peace
for sd City 22 Novr 1805

DEPOSITION OF WILLIAM WASH

This Deponent saith that some time in the fall of the year one thousand seven hundred & eighty five this deponent was at the house of Colo. John Boswell, when the said John introduced this deponent to a gentleman saying, Sir, this is my only brother Thomas Boswell. He is going to become one one of your nearest neighbors - He now lives low down in Gloucester county where he and his family are frequently sick - I have prevailed with him to leave the place although he is well fixed - I have given him the tract of land which I purchased from Capt. William Harris provided he will come & spend the balance of our days together - Thomas then said brother John I meet a difficulty in thinking how I shall get up - John replied do not let that distress your mind I will send down my waggon & help you up & will also furnish you with what corn you may need next year - In the course of the year one thousand seven hundred and eighty six the said Thomas did move with his family to the said tract of land where he resided until the death of his said brother John & for some time afterwards & then sold the said land to Charles Quarles one of the defendants to the bill aforesaid, & further this deponent saith not -

Louisa County Sct -

Sworn to before John Downing a magistrate for the said county -

Notation:

I admit this affidavit as if the same had been legally taken -

Thomas Wilson
for
Donald Scot & Co
22 November 1805

ANSWER OF JOHN RHOADES RAGLAND AND THOMAS LIPSCOMB

Surviving administrator of Wm Ragland decd (Agness Ragland the admr being dead)

Uninformed on the subject of the claim etc.

Louisa County towit

Sworn to before John Downing Justice of the Peace for Louisa County 7 November 1808

ANSWER OF LUDLOW BRANHAM.

This Defendant saith that he is a stranger to the affairs
of the said Colo John Boswell, Thomas Johnson (minor) & Richard C.
Johnson as also of any of the other Defendants any further than
from report - That Colo. John Boswell by his last Will & Testament
devised that in case British debts should be paid that then a certain Tract of Land containing as this Defendant is informed about
600 acres should be sold for that purpose - that he this Defendant is in possession of about 296 acres part of the said Tract
under a fair purchase for a full consideration of Richard C. Johnson who was the only executor of Thomas Johnson (minor) who qualified to his will, who the said Thomas Johnson (minor) was the
only acting executor of the said Colo. John Boswell decd. That
this Defendant purchased the same at the price of £1000 payable
at three annual instalments the first principal to become due at
Christmas 1800 & the two last to carry Interest from that date till
paid ... That in pursuance of such purchase this Defendant paid
in part of the purchase Money & Interest £792.2.4½ whereupon
the said Richard as executor aforesaid executed a deed in fee
simple to this Defendant for said Land which hath been duly recorded in Louisa County - That the balance of this purchase
money this Defendant holds subject to the order & decree of the
honorable court ... That since this Defendant purchased the
said Land he has gone on to make considerable repairs & improvements, all of a useful nature, to the value in the opinion of
this Defendant of two hundred pounds or upwards - That this
Defendant hopes said purchase will be confirmed to him ...

Richmond City Sct -

Sworn to before Snml Pleasants jr 28 November 1805

ANSWER OF JAMES WATSON

This Deponent knows nothing of the affairs of John
Boswells estate of his own knowledge ... He believes that
said John Boswell decd did devise the plantation on which he
lived at the time of making his will, to be sold (on certain
conditions) for the payment of his British debts ... As to
that part of the complainant's bill which states that this
defendant is in possession of part of the land devised by John
Boswell for the payment of his British debts it is not true
but is totally erroneous, nor is this defendant in possession
of nor did he ever claim or hold any land that was ever the

property of or claimed by said Boswell, or by any person holding
or claiming under or thro' the said Boswell. This defendant supposes this mistake in plaintiff's bill proceeded fra the fact
that Thomas Johnson (minor) above named, was at the time of his
death as well as at the death of the said John Boswell, in possession of a certain tract of land which sd Johnson (minor) had
possessed and lived on for many years before the death of said
John Boswell which said land the said Johnson (minor) claimed
in fee simple, and had acquired not fram sd Boswell, or any person claiming under or through him but from others, no way connected, as this defendant has always heard and believes with
John Boswell or his affairs - At the death of said Johnson
(minor) he the said Johnson (minor) devised this land and others
to be divided among sundry of his children, who in a division
allotted the land now held by this defendant to John Boswell
Johnson, son of said Johnson (minor). This defendant so long
ago as the   day of October 1799 at a fair sale and for a full
and valuable consideration, purchased this lot containing ---
acres of the said John Boswell Johnson and others, paid for it
and received a fee simple deed therefor, which has been recorded
according to law in Louisa County This lot of land does not
lie adjoining to any part of the tract of land on which said
Boswell lived at the time of his death and which is said to have
been devised by him for payment of British Debts -

Louisa County -

          Sworn to before Ludm. Branham, J. P. for the County of
Louisa 11 November 1805

Backhouse's Admrs. vs Boswell (1799-1800 - #18):

          LETTER - JOHNSON & BOSWELL TO BACKHOUSE

                              New Castle Virginia Augt 16th 1769
Sir
    As our friend & Correspondent, Mr. John Walker Late Mercht of
Liverpool is deceased, it puts us under the necessity of Looking out
for some other, and as your Charactor has recommended you to us, we
have thought proper to make you the following proposals, in the first
place we want you to advance us one Thousand pounds Sterlg. and that
we may have the Liberty to draw for it, in our next April General
Court, which money we desire to have the use of, for two years allow-
ing you 5 pct. Interest, without being obliged by Law, or honor to repay till the aforesaid Time is Expired, in the next place we desire
to have Leave to draw for Ten pounds Sterling on each Hhd we Ship you;

Letter, Johnson & Boswell to Backhouse, cont.:

we make in mean years about Sixty Five hhdg, & in good years Seventy
odd, & that of the best Sort of York River Tobacco, the sum of money
we propose borrowing together with drawing on our Tobacco, pays all
our debts both here and in England, & Leaves a Balance of out standing
debts to the amount of Seven or Eight hundred pounds, but they are
chiefly such as will take us a Year or two to Collect, if you Should
come into our Terms, we shall not draw on you for any more money,
untill the money borrowed is paid, and shall only Send for as many
Goods as we think our Familys may have occasion for, which we Suppose
will amount to upwards of two hundred pounds Annually, and the over-
plus to go to the Credit of the money borrowed; if we make Tolerable
good Crops, & the prices of Tobacco keeps up, we shall pay it up in
two years, but Supposing the Tobacco sent you shou'd prove short, we
Expect we Shall be able to remit you some Money from our Debts -
There are two young men Messrs. Johnson & Tinsley in Trade the one
the Son to our Richard Johnson that is next to be considered. We have
given them Letters of Credit, and they have Corresponded with the Late
Mr. Walker, they will want goods twice a year to the amount of Eight
or Nine hundred pounds each Cargo, which goods we will undertake to
see you paid for, tho we don't make the Least doubt but they will
punctually comply with their payments, you'll receive their Letters
covering a Scheme for Goods, & their proposals by Capt. Clarke who
brings you this ...
Col. Humphrey Hill has been Long acquainted with us, & make no
doubt but that he has a Tollerable Idea of our circumstances, therefore we have made him acquainted with this, & hope it will meet with
your approbation, we are

                              Sir
                    your mo. obedt. & Honble Servts.
N.B.   Johnson & Boswell
    if you think proper to come
    into our terms you'll be pleased
    to let us know it by the first Ship -
                    J & B

To
    Mr. John Backhouse
              Mercht. in
                    Liverpool

P Capt. Clarke

LETTER - JOHNSON & BOSWELL TO BACKHOUSE

Virginia New Castle 14 Oct - 1771

Mr John Backhouse

SIR -

Its with the greatest concern we acquaint you of the
death of our late worthy friend & relation Colo. Richard Johnson
on the 29th of Septemr. Last, after a Short illness, whom we most
Sincerely regret - he has willed his whole Estate to his Widow during her Life, or Widowhood, and appointed her Executrix & ourselves
Executors thereto, with full power to Act as we shall think necessary. We have maturely considered all Matters thereto relating, &
Judge it most Expedient to cultivate that correspondence our departed
friend had the pleasure of Establishing with you, and in consequence
of which we shall send you in the Spring, between Eighty & Ninety
Hhds of Tobacco, by whichever of your Ships you may think proper
to direct ...
        The Correspondence of our Johnson & Mr. Chas. Tinsley
with you, our John Boswell desires may be continued, with himself as
Security, for all further Cargos you may send them ...
        Bills payable in your port are Ginerally ½ pct. Lower
than those upon London, therefore we must beg the favor of you, to
permit us to make ours on you payable in that port, provided it would
not be attend_ with any inconvenience of consequence to you ...
        We are Sir
                        Yr. Mo. obedt. Servts.
                        John Boswell & W Johnson

LETTER - JOHNSON & BOSWELL

Sir   Virginia, New Castle July 30th 1771
        Inclosed you have a Bill of Lading for seventy Hhds. To-
bacco Shipt you by the Tom, and wish them safe to hand, the other Ten
was ready but Capt. Clarke could not take them in ...
        There is 22 Hhds. Shipt you that we Bought of a nephew of
ours, that lives at the Mountains, which we expect is equal to our own:
the Reason we bought them was, our R. J. could not get down all his
Mountain Crop by 20 Hhds. from the repeated Rains that distressed his
Plantations ... The extraordinary wett weather and the repeated Freshes
we believe will render the ensuing Crop very Short, as well as Mean...
        We have in repeated letters mentioned our indorsement of
a Bill of Exchange drown on our relation Mr Richd. Chapman ...
        We are Sir with great respect
To Mr. John Backhouse   Yr. Most Honble. Srt.,
   Mercht in Liverpool   Johnson & Boswell
P the Tom Capt. Clarke

Donald Scott & Co.,   ) 1805 (#30)
    vs   ) U. S. Cir. Ct.
William Clarke's Reprs.) 5th Circt. Va. Dist.
    (1803)

Donald Scott & Co., british subjects sheweth That a certain William Clark of Hanover County on the 1st Septr. 1775 gave his bond to Donald Scott & Co. for the sum of £385.13.5 of the value of $1286.40. That William Clark departed this life intestate in or about the -day of - . A certain John Clerk took out letters of adm on his estate and gave bond according to Law with Thomas Tinsley his security.-

THE ANSWER OF JOHN CLARKE

This Defendant saith ... that not having the bond of William Clarke stated in the bill, he requires the sum due thereon to be proved in the course of law.... That this Defdt. admits the bond stated to have been given by himself, Thomas Tinsley, Thomas Clerke, and Zachariah Clerke for this Defdt's due administration of said William Clarke's estate. That the Inventory and appraisement of the estate of William Clarke and the administration account settled and returned to the Court of Hanover County show assets not disposed of in the payment of debts was divided on the 7th day of January, 1793 and on the 11th of May, 1795 without this defendant having any notice of the debt now claimed by complainants, in the following manner(To wit) To this defendant a Negro woman named Lucy and her two youngest children named Edmund and Sarah, and two boys named Billy and John. To Samuel Crutchfield in right of his wife Mildred a Daughter of the said William Clarke, a negro woman named Mary and her child named Charles, Alexander a boy and Betty a girl with £3.6.0 from this defendant to compensate a deficiency of value. To Elender alias Alice the wife of Peter Crutchfield the slaves, Fanny, Sampson and Peter with 16/8 from the defendant to compensate the deficiency of value and the balance of £06.10.6 aforesaid was divided equally among the distributees. That the said Peter Crutchfield and Elender alias Alice his wife are living in the County of Hanover. That the said Samuel Crutchfield is dead leaving three daughters Caroline, Cynthia and Eliza and that the aforesaid Mildred is now married to Samuel Whitlock. That this defendant's father left a small tract of land which this defendant has long since sold fairly and bona fide without having any notice of the debt now claimed by the complainant. This defendant claims as credit against the bond now sued on various sums of Money from the transactions of the agents of the Complainants, Thomas Sympson and Thomas Steel and Richard Anderson, according to the annexed account found stated in the said William Clarke's books and a note of Thomas Sympson with the endorsement of Richard Anderson thereon, and a note or receipt of Thomas Steel herewith exhibited as part of this answer: from all which this defendant believes it will appear that the said bond is overpaid and this Defendant prays that the balance due to him, if any, may be decreed to himself ...

                              John Clarke

State of Kentucky Bourbon Co Sct

John Clarke personally came before me the subscriber a Justice of the Peace for the said County and made oath to the truth of the above ... 18th day of March in the year 1804

Thomas Hughes

RECEIPT OF THOS. STEEL

Hanr. Court 2d. November 1775

Recd. of Capt. Wm. Clarke Twenty five Pounds curr. which I promise to pay on demand

Thos. Steel

INVENTORY OF ESTATE OF WILLIAM CLARKE, DECD.

15 Slaves	£752.10.	8 Chairs £	2.
1 Bay mare	30.	3 Walnut frames	. 6.
1 Sorrel horse	30.	4 ditto corner chairs	4.
1 Bay Colt	13.10.	1 large lookg. glass	1.
1 Bay horse	7.	1 small ditto	6.
1 white horse	7.	1 Bed & furniture	8. 6. 8
1 yoke steers	10.	1 ditto & ditto	8. 6. 8
1 ditto	8.	1 ditto & ditto	8. 6. 8
1 cow & calf	3.10.	1 ditto & ditto	7.
1 ditto ditto	3.	1 ditto & bolster	4.
1 ditto & ditto	3.	1 ditto & ditto	5.
1 ditto & ditto	3.	1 Clothes press	1.
1 ditto & ditto	3.	2 Chists	.15.
1 Cow with calf	2.15.	1 Trunk	1. 3
1 Cow	2.15.	2 Cases	3. 6.
1 ditto	2.10.	1 Tea board)	1. 4.
4 Yearlings	6.	2 Waiters & 1 slider)	
1 Steer	2.	Parcel of window	
1 Desk	3.	glass	1. 1. 6
2 Sqr. foldg. tables	5.	2 Rum hhds.	10.
2 Round ditto	3.15.	3 Casks	6.
1 Side board	1.15	Parcel Pewter	1.10.
1 tea table	15.	4 Candlesticks	1. 4.
½ doz. walnut chairs	3.12.	Parcel Knives & forks	5.
½ doz. ditto	3.	Parcel lumber	9.

Inventory of Estate of William Clarke, cont.:

2 fruit dishes &	£	.10.	4 hoes	£	.5.
pickle do.			3 Axes		7. 6.
Parcel China		.5.	Parcel old iron		4. 6
1 Soup spoon	)		1 plow coller & haimes		10.
3 Table do.	)		Pair and irons		16. 8
11 Tea ditto	)	4.10.	2 Pair ditto		5.
1 pair sugar tongs	)		7 Butter potts		15.
1 Carte		4.	Quantity of Bacon		6. 5.
Parcel Leather in tan		1. 5.	Parcel Cotton		6.
1 Grind stone		5.	1 Plow, coller & hames		5.
Parcel lumber		5.	1 Grubbing hoe &		
3 Potts		1. 5.	Trowel do.		5.
1 Jug 1 sugar box		5. 6	Quantity Corn	30.	
1 Dutch oven		6.	1 Hand saw		2. 6
1 Spice morter		10.	2 Window Curtins		12.
Pair flat irons		2. 6	28 Sheep	14.	
1 Salamander		6.	1 Saddle & bridle	3.	
Parcel lumber		6.	2 Table cloths		5.
3 Pot racks		1.10.	Cash in hand		6. 8
1 Spit		5.	1 Grissell sow		1.10.
1 Scythe		5.	1 White ditto		1.
1 Brass kittle		10.	7 Shoats		2. 2.
1 Tea kittle		10.	1 White sow & 4 pigs		15.
Skillet & Coffee pot		6.	1 Sow & 5 pigs		1.10.
1 Loom Slay & harness		1.	1 Spotted sow & 7 pigs		1.10.
1 Pail		1. 3	Gun		1. 5.
1 Pewter Bason		3.	Saddle (old)		10.
Quantity of wool		2.	Corn @ 12/ p. 11.		3.12.
Parcel leather		6.	60 feet tops		3.15.
Wheat fan		1.	2500 bundles fodder 2/6		3. 2. 6

John Clarke a.

Agreeable to an order of Hanover court made on the 1st day of May
1783 & hereto annexed, we the subscribers proceeded to appraise the
estate of William Clarke deceased as will appear by the foregoing
inventory. Given under our hands this 28th day of May 1783

John Parker
Thos. Green
Wm. Gardner

Recorded at a Court held for Hanover County at the courthouse on Thursday the 2d. of July 1795

Teste   William Pollard C H C

November 1802 Copy   teste   Tho. Pollard D C H C

EXTRACTS FROM THE SETTLEMENT & DIVISION OF

THE ESTATE OF WILLIAM CLARKE, DECEASED

Dr the Estate of William Clarke decd. In Account with John Clarke
Administrator of the said Estate

1783

April 28	To Cash paid for Rum and suger) for burial)	₺ 1. 9. 4
	To ditto paid for butter & flower for Do.)	11. 4
	To William McClary for coffin	2.10.
	To cash paid for mourning for) the Girls)	1. 6.
May 7	To ditto paid the sheriff for) taxes of 1782)	9. 6. 2
June	To do. paid for Rum for the sale	12.
Aug. 14	To paid Sheriff of Hanover for) Co. & Parish leve. & 785 hs. Tob. @ 25/.)	9.16. 3
Septr. 5	To do. paid Docr. Jno. Roberts pr. acct.	13.11. 4
12	To acct. paid Charles Lewis for Cotton for the negrs.	7. 6
Novemr. 5	To Bacon & Corn consumed in the family	36. 5.

1784

Jany. 1	To a quantity of wool, Cotton & leather) made use of in the family)	3.17.
	To 17 Barrels new Corn) consumed in the family)	10. 4.
2	To cash paid Docr. Riddock p acct. & rect.	14.10.
April 15	To George Hollins for schooling J.B.Clarke	17.
24	To the sheriff of Hanover for Certif. tax	8.14.
May 20	To do. for specie tax of 1783	14.14.
June 13	To Docr. Locklin McLear as pr. Voucher	2.10.2
Aug. 12	To Docr. John Shore pr. do.	18.
Oct. 2	To John Marshall esqr. Atty. for making) defence in the Genl. Court at the) suit of Watkins)	2.10.

1783 Cr

May 11	By 1 Hhd tobacco nett 1176 11. @ 25/.	14.14.
June 4	By 1 lamb sold for 15/. before the sale	15.
July 19	By cash received of James Turner) for the hire of Joe)	2.10.
Septr 15	By Samuel Pearson for hire of Nat	6.

Settlement of Estate of William Clarke, decd., cont.:

1784			£	...
Feby. 9	By Ralph Crutchfield for the hire of Julius - 700 t. Gross pork settled @ 22/6			7.17. 6
June 13	By Docr. L. McLean for the hire of Joe from) the 3rd. Augt. to 24th Decemr. 1785) at 40/ p mo.)			9. 8.
15	By Matthias Abbott for a provicion Certif.) amg. to 13.8			8.14.
Sept 11	By Richard Littlepage for hire of Jack			9. 5.

£ 643. 9.10½

Dr Brought forward   £ 214. 7. 4½

1785		£	...
June 10	To Claudius Vial for 20,000 ll. Tobo.) settled at £264)		264.
July 20	To Ann Durham p Voucher		.11. 3
10	To Charles Hundley Adm. of Geo. Hundley		42.10.
Apr. 29	To cash pd. an express sent to Prince) Edward on business of the estates		1.10.
Mar. 31	To Elizabeth Hooper as p Voucher		1. 4.
1789			
Jany. 17	To the Orphans of Benjamin Clarke decd.		12. 2. 4¼
Feby. 15	To John Watkins's exor for a Judgt.) obtained in Hanr. Court)		222. 5. 7
1792			
Octr. 5	To paid Charles Hundley Admr. &c of) Zachary Hundley decd. as P Vouch.)		2. 2.10½

£1185.11.11½

Cr Brought forward		£ 648. 9.10½
1785		
Jany. 1	By hire of Peter £10, Ditto) of Nat £11.16, Isaac £7 &) Gloucester £2 for last year)	30.16.
	By Thomas Foster for the hire of Joe last year	20.
1786		
Jany. 1	By Geddes Winston for the hire of Peter & Isaac last year	24.
	By Thomas Talley, hire of Delilah last yr	4.
	By Thomas Foster, hire of Joe last year	22.

Settlement of Estate of William Clarke, decd., cont.:

1786 (cont.)   ...
Octo. 1 By Violet & her Child Charles sold Feby
             1st 1785 for   ℔ 110.
1787
Jany. 1 By the James River Co. for the hire of
             Peter & Nat last year   42.
          By Ro. Fleming for the hire of Isaac last yr   10.
Sept. 10 By Edward Voss for hire of Nat for yr 1785   16.10.
Feby. 15 By the sale of Joe, Nat, Isaac & Delilah)
             by the Sheriff   )   206.18.
                                                          ────────
                                                          ℔ 324. 5. 8¼

                                                     ℔ 1459. 2. 5½

Dr   Brought forward   ℔ 1186.11.11½
1793
Feby. 19 To Paid Samuel Earnest as p acct. &c   5.12.6
1794   To Z. Clarke as p ocnd &c   191.15.0¾
1795
Feby. 28 To cash paid Bushrod Washington)
             his fee at the suit of Rootes)
             in the High Ct. of Chancery   )   5.
Apl. 14 To paid Peter Foster admor of   )
             David Clarke decd. the bal-   )
             ance due from my estestate   )
             (sic) who was admor of the   )
             said David Clarke decd. (in   )
             the first instance) as re-   )
             ported by the Commissioners   )   90. 0.2
Apl. 18 To paid Thomas Bowles per Voucher   2.10.
          To paid Peter Foster admor of   )
             David Clarke decd. the said   )
             David Clarke's proportion of)
             his fathers Estate   )   22. 2.11¾
          To paid Do. as exor of Zacha-   )
             riah Clarke his the said   )
             Zachariah Clarke's propor-   )
             tion of his father's estate   )   22. 2.11¾
                                                          ...
                                                      ────────
                                                  ℔ 1591.11. 5¾
                               To balance   86.10. 6
                                                      ────────
                                                  ℔ 1678. 1.11¾

Settlement of Estate of William Clarke, decd., cont.:

Cr.	Brought forward		£ 1459. 2. 5¼
1793			
Feby. 20	By 90 Gallons brandy recd. of)		
	Colo. Temple in the year 1789)		9.
1794			
	By Zach. Clarke for interest on)		
	his purchases at the sale of)		35. 0. 0
	the estate of Wm. Clarke, dec.)		
			£ 1642. 1. 5²
	By Interest &c		36. 0. 6
			£ 1678. 1. 11¾
	By Balance P Debit due Estate		86. 10. 6

In Obedience to an Order of the County Court of Hanover, we have
stated and examined the Vouchers, of the within Account of the Administration of John Clarke of the estate of William Clarke decd.
and have found the within balance due the estate, we have also (some
time previous to this settlement) divided the negroes belonging to
the said Estate between John Clarke, Samuel Crutchfield, in right
of his wife Mildred, formerly Mildred Clarke, & Ellender Clarke
(being the only persons entitled to distribution) in the following
manner ... The whole amount of the negroes, we estimate at £422.10
which divided into three parts is £140.16. 8 apiece. Certified
under our hands this 11th day of May 1795

                            Thos. Tinsley
                            William Gardner
                            Nathl. Talley

At a Court held for Hanover County, at the Courthouse, on Thursday
the 2d. of July 1795 This Account & report of the Administration
& division of the estate of William Clarke deceased were returned
& are ordered to be recorded

                Test   William Pollard C. H. C.

July 1807   A Copy
                    teste
                            Tho. Pollard D C H C

Donald, Scott & Co.) 1803 (90)
vs   ) U. S. Cir. Ct.
Clay's reprs.   ) 5th Circt. Va. Dist.

        Donald, Scott & Compy., subjects of the King of Great
Britain and Ireland, against Henry Watkins, exor. of the last
Will & Testament of John Clay, and Wm. O. Winston his security,
George Clay, Sally Clay, John Clay, Molly Clay, Henry Clay and
Porter Clay, children and devisees of John Clay, deced. -

                    WILL OF JOHN CLAY
                    d. 4 Novr. 1730
                    p. 7 Febr. 1732

        In the Name of God Amen, I John Clay of Hanover County,
being very sick & weak but of a disposing mind and sound memory,
doe make and Ordain this to be my last Will and testament in manner & form following IMPRIMIS First of all I recommend my soul to
God that gave it, hoping that through the Mediation & sufferings
of my Lord and Saviour to receive free pardon of all my sins, and
my body to be decently buried at the discretion of my Execurs.
hereafter mentioned Item I desire my stock of horses & Cattle
may be sold and all my just debts be paid. Item my will and desire is that all my estate real & personal be kept together untill
my eldest son George Clay shall arrive to the age of twenty years
old except my loving wife should intermarry betwixt this & then -
If she should marry then in that case, I desire all my estate real
and personal may be delivered up to my execrs. except such part
as I shall hereafter mention for her use. Item I lend to my loving Wife Elizabeth Clay, after my son arrives to the age above
mentioned or the time she does intermarry If before the use of
my plantation at Euphraim in Henrico County together with seven
negroes Charles, Judea, Ceasar left her by her father's will, Sam,
Paul, Cheeter, Bob and Fanney during her natural life, and also
two foather beds & furniture, also a Child's part of Stock, that
may be at the time she marries, or my son comes to the age above
mentioned. and after her decease all the above lent to be sold
and equally divided among all my children as shall be alive at
that day, and to their heirs forever. Item I give & bequeath to
my son George Clay too negroes (to wit) Hanover Bob & Ben to him
and to his heirs forever - Item I give & bequeath to my daughter
Salley Clay two negroes (to wit) Sus & Frank to her & to her heirs
forever - Item I give & bequeath to my Daughter Molley Clay two
negroes (to wit) Annaca and Little Judea to her & her heirs forever - Item I give & bequeath to my son John Clay two negroes
(to wit) Daniel & Arthur to him and his heirs forever Item I
give & bequeath to my son Henry Clay two negroes (to wit) James
& Little Sam to him and his heirs forever - Item I give & bequeath to my son Porter Clay two negroes (to wit) Dick & harry

Will of John Clay, cont.:

to him and his heirs forever. Item I give & bequeath to the
Child my wife is now Pregnant with If it should live equal with
my other Children out of my other negroes not mentioned above,
to its heirs and assigns forever. Item my will and desire is
that all the rest of my estate except land, should be equally
divided amongst all my Children, and if any should die before
they arrive, to the males to the age of twenty years, & the
females if not married to the age of eighteen years, that then
their part should be equally divided amongst ye surviving Children and if any of my Children should loose any of their negroes
above mentioned in their Lotts that then such loss is to be made
good out of my estate to them and their heirs forever- Item my
will and desire is that the land I now live on or any part thereof
may not be sold untill my son George Clay arrives to the age herein mentioned, or until my wife intermarries that then it may be
sold, by my Exors. and the money arising by the sale be equally
disposed of among my sons, or to be laid out in land at their
Discretion and be equally divided amongst my sons as they come
to the age of twenty years to them and their heirs forever -
Item I Desire my estate may not be appraised, and I doe appoint
my loving wife Elizabeth Clay my Executrix and Colo. Nathaniel
Wilkerson and Mr. Richard Chapman Execrs of this my last will and
testament revoking all other wills heretofore made

             IN WITNESS Whereof I have hereunto set my hand and seal
this 4th day of November 1780

Signed sealed & delivered)   John Clay (Seal)
In the presence of   )
John Starke Senr.
Charles Wingfield
Isaac Perrin
Charles Bridgewater

At a Court held for Hanover County on thursday the 7th day of
February 1782

             This last will & testament of John Clay decd. was of-
fered to proof by Richard Chapman an executor therein named and
was proved by the oath of John Starke Gentn. and Isaac Perrin
witnesses thereto and also by the oath of the said executor and
is ordered to be recorded
                          Test   William Pollard Junr CHC
November 1802   A Copy
                          Test   Tho. Pollard D C H C

INVENTORY OF THE ESTATE OF
JOHN CLAY
Dated January 15th, 1784

An Trew Inventory of the estate of the deceased John
Clay taken January 15th 1794 - 24 negroes 4 feather beads
4 beadsteads 3 Cords 4 sheets 2 Coverlids 1 rug 7 Leather
Chairs 4 flag bottom Chears 1 Deask & Bookcase 1 eight day
Clock 2 Black walnut Tables 1 pine table 1 corner Cupboard
3 pine Chests 1 walnut box 1 Case & bottles 1 Dozen of Queens
Chaney plates 1 Chaney tea pot one earthen Dish 1 dozen pewter
plates 3 dishes & 3 basons 1 duch oven 2 pots 1 tea Cittle
1 Coffee pot 1 paire of pot hooks 1 gug 1 Loome 6 Stays e paire
old Harnisses 3 Axes 3 hilling hoes 2 grubing hoes 2 Trowel
hoes 1 paire of iron wedges 1 thirty Gallon Still 1 paire of
Sissers 3 butter Pots 1 Jar 1 Crosscut saw 1 han saw 1 paire
of pinchers 1 shew Hammer 4 nifes & 4 forkes 2 Candle moles
28 bookes 1 Gun 2 old gun barrels 1 old pistol 1 wayter
2 Brass Candle Sticks 1 mans saddle 1 womans Do. 5 horses
16 head of Cattle 1 ink stand 1 sand Glass one hone and strop
1 rasor 1 sett of iron streaks for a pair of Cart wheals with
a parcell of old lumber

The property in the County of Henrico

To 1 riding Chair 1 flacks wheal 2 large bottles
55 ls. of seed Cotten 1 loome 1 paire of old Cart Wheals 6
head of Cattle one horse Colt 1 pot 24 Bushels & 3 pecks of
wheat 66 Bushels of Oats parcel of straw 1 thousand bundles
of fodder 1 stack of tops parcel of trash Corn

Henry Watkins Admr.

At a Court held for Hanover County on Thursday the 1st day of
April 1790

This inventory of the estate of John Clay deceased
being returned is ordered to be recorded

Test

William Pollard jr C H C

INVOICE OF JOHN CLAY

Mr John Clay

                To Donald Scott & Co   Dr

1775
Septr 8   To your bond of this date   £ 74.14.5½
          Sundry Goods not included in   )
          bond.as under viz.   )
          Augst. 30th   500 Pins 8d. 15 ^{a})
          Bro. Sugar   9/4½   )   10.0½
Septr 5th   1 Gilt bible   4.6
         1 lb Pepper   2.6
         1½ yds. of. bro. Cloth   2.10.3
         1 yd Shalloon   3.6
         1 hank thread   .5
         ½ yd Buckram   1.
         2 Quarts rum   2.6
         24 Small & 3 large Buttons   1.3
         2 yds blue duffle   6.3
October 3   To 3 Quarts Rum   3.9
        " Sundries pd John Crutchfield   3.
Decr 14   To 1 Almanack   .8
1776   "   1½ yards Shalloon   4.6
Feby 27   "   1 Snaffle Bridle   4.6
March 23 "   2 Bunches Lace   2.6   £83.8.-

Morrison-Doe Lessee &c vs Thos. Cocke, 1824 (#110):

DEED TO ESTATE CALLED "EPHRAIM" - CLAY'S EXOR. & ADMOR. TO COCKE

       This Indenture made this 3rd day of January 1791 Be-
tween Nathaniel Wilkinson of Henrico county exor and Henry Wadkins
of Hanover admor of John Clay decd of Hanover and Elizabeth Wadkins
wife of the said Henry Wadkins and late wife of the said John Clay decd
of the one part; and Richard Cocke of the sd county of Henrico of the
- part; wit., that the said Nathaniel Wilkinson exor and Henry Wadkins admr. of the sd John Clay decd for and in consideration of £30
our money of Virginia in conformity to the last will & Testament of
the sd John Clay decd directing a sale of the lands which he died
seized of, doth sell &c unto Richard Cocke his heirs &c that parcel
of land lying in the county of Henrico containing 227 acres more or
less, bounded by Thomas Ellis, William Tinsley and Porterfield Trent,
Harwood Ford, Nathaniel Holloway, Samuel Jones, Benjamin Jones, Peter
Cottrell, John Lacy, Jesse Smith ...

Witnesses: William Williamson   Nathl. Wilkinson Exor (Seal)
Harod Ford Jno Williamson Junr   Henry Watkins Admor   (Seal)

Deed to "Ephraim" - Clay's Exors & Admrs. to Cocke, cont.:

Recorded in Henrico County Court on monday the 3rd of January 1791 -

                         Test   Adam Craig CC
        A Copy
                         Teste   J B Whitlock C H C

Memo on back of deed: "This Land lies on the Richmond turn-Pike
Road about eight miles from town & three from Burton's Coal Pitts -
is still own'd & occupied by R. Cocke is worth from $15 to $20
per acre - Lands on the same turn-Pike (one mile nearer town)
have sold for $40 -   The information of Ben: Sheppard" - no date

Memo: "Richard Cocke has departed this life (Thos. M. Shoemaker
is his repr.) agd. Jno. James D M. 1821."

Hanover county Court, Feb. 7th 1782 - Elizabeth Clay widow & relict
of John Clay decd. came into Court and declared that she would not
accept legacies to her given in the will of her decd. husband, and
renounced all benefit which she might claim ...

        A Copy

                         Teste   Tho. Pollard D C H C

              DEPOSITION OF HENRY WATKINS

        Deposition of Henry Watkins taken in Franklin Co., Ky.,
aged abt 65 years, saith that he married the widow of John Clay,
decd., formerly of the county of Hanover in the state of Virginia;
that George Hudson Clay was the eldest son of the said John Clay &
died in the City of Richmond the latter end of 1796 or Spring of
1797 without ever having been married & without issue & intestate -
... That the surviving children of the said John Clay are John Clay,
Henry Clay & Porter Clay -

        Sworn to before Thomas Todd an Associate Justice of the
Supreme Court of the United States, the 17th day of October, 1823

        Papers show that James Morrison was admr. of the estate of
George Hudson Clay, decd., and was a citizen & inhabitant of the
State of Kentucky on the 1st day of April, 1820.

        Estate called "Ephraim" was occupied by Thomas M. Shoe-
maker, as tenant, on November 22, 1821.

Gordon   ) 1801 (23)
  vs   ) U. S. Cir. Ct.
Smith   ) 5th Circt. Va. Dist.

(John Gordon of Springfield, Northumberland County, Va.,
against Thorowgood Smith of Baltimore, regarding protested Bill of
Exchange of John Cuningham of New Castle, Hanover County, Va.,
1783, drawn on his brother, Sir William Cuningham, of Robertland,
Scotland.)

Extract of Bond of Provision
SIR WM CUNINGHAM BART
To
HIS YOUNGER CHILDREN
(1781)

AT AYR the thirtieth day of October Seventeen hundred and Eighty
one Years In Presence of William Wallace Esqr Advocate, Sheriff
Depute of Ayrshire Compeared James Neill Writer in Ayr as provt
for Sir William Cuninghame Bart. after designed and gave in the
Provision after copied (being wrote on Stamped Paper) desiring it
to be registred in the Sheriff Court Books of Ayr Conform to the
Clause of Registration therein mentioned which desire the said
Judge found reasonable and ordained it to be done accordingly
whereof the tenor follows - "KNOW ALL MEN BY THESE PRESENTS I
Sir William Cuninghame of Robertland Barronet Whereas in the event
of my death Lieut. Wm. Cuninghame my eldest son will by Law succeed
to my whole lands and Heretable Subjects and that Alexr. John
Charles and Fairlie Cuningham's my younger Children are hitherto
unprovided by me in any Share of my means & Effects except what
Sums I have thought proper to advance and pay to them in my own
lifetime and it being Just and reasonable that such rational &
competent provisions should be made in their favours as are suitable to my fortune and circumstances THEREFORE and for the love
and affection I have and bear to my said Younger Children after-
mentioned Have become bound and obliged likeas I by these Presents
with and under the reservation and Declarations afterwritten Bind
and oblige me my heirs Executors and Successors whomsoever thank-
fully to content and pay to each of the said Alexr. John Charles
& Fairlie Cuninghame's my Younger Children the respective Provisions
and Sums following Vizt - to the said Alexr Cuninghame the sum of
Three Hundred Pounds Sterling To the said John Cuninghame the sum
of Three Hundred Pounds Sterling To the said Charles Cuninghame
the sum of Four Hundred Pounds Sterling and in the event that the
said Charles shall have lost his three negroes by the present
Capture of Granada the sum of One Hundred and Fifty Pounds Sterling more and to the said Fairlie Cuninghame the sum of Six Hundred
Pounds Sterling and in case any one or more of them should die

Bond of Provision of
Sir Wm Cuninghame Bart, cont.

before Majority or disposing of the Sums Provided to them as
aforesaid then and in that event the sum or sums so provided to
them shall fall and accrease to and be equally divided amongst the
Survivors of them and which Provisions before written I Bind and
oblige me & my foresaids to pay to each of the said Alexr. John
Charles and Fairlie Cuninghames my said Younger Children their heirs
or assigneys at the first term of Martinass or Whitsunday next &
immediately following my decease with five pounds Sterling of Liquidate penalty for each One Hundred Pounds Sterl. of prinl. in
case of Failure and the lawful Interest of the said respective
Sums from and after the foresaid term of Payment and Yearly thereafter during the not Payment of the same Declaring always that my
heirs Executors & Successors foresaid shall be bound and obliged
to pay to the said Fairlie Cuninghame, my Youngest Daughter over
and above the provision in her favours before specified An Yearly
Annuity of twenty five pounds Sterling & that ay & untill she shall
remain unmarried & untill the first term of Martinass or Whitsunday
after that event shall happen and no longer with a fifth part more
of the said annuity of Liquidate Penalty in case of not Punctual
Payment of the said Yearly annuity after the said terms of payment
and beginning the first terms of payment thereof at the term of
Marts. or Whits. which shall first happen immediately after my decease with the legal Interest of the same after the said respective terms of Payment and untill payt. of the same during the time
foresaid WHICH PROVISIONS before written in favour of my said
Younger Children shall be aughted of by them in full of all Portion
natural Bairns Part of gear Legittim exeoütry Legacy former Provisions or any other thing whatever which they or either of them can
ask claim or demand by or through my death when the same may happen
Reserving always full power and Liberty to me at any time of my life
and even on Deathbed to revoke or alter and make void these presents
in whole or in part as I shall Judge proper Declaring nevertheless
that if these Presents if not alter'd or revok'd by me shall be valid
& Effectual evident in favour of my said Younger Children to all In-
tents and purposes although the same shall be found in my own custody
or in the keeping of any Person undelivered --- the time of my decease any law or Custom to the Contrary notwithstanding And in
respect that some of my said Children are as yet under age I hereby
nominate and appoint Dame Margaret Fairlie my wife the said Lieut.
Wm. Cuninghame my eldest son Alexr. Fairlie of Fairlie Esqr. and
John McAdam of Craigengillan Esqr. or any two of them the said Dame
Margt. Fairlie my wife being sine qua non to the tutors and Curators
to such of my said Children till they attain the age of Twenty one
Years complete with power to them to do everything necessary in the
Management and administration of their affairs Declaring that they
shall only be liable for their actual Intromissions but not for
omissions or in Solidum Consenting to the registration hereof in the

Gordon vs Smith, cont.:

Bond of Provision of
Sir Wm. Cuninghame, Bart., cont.:

Books of Councill & Session or any other Judges Books competent
for preservation and if needfull that all legal Dilligence on a
Charge of Six days may Pass and be derected hereon in form as
effeirs and thereto Constitute James Neill Writer in Ayr Provst
In Witness Whereof I have subscribed these Presents consisting
of this and the two Preceeding pages (written on Stamped Paper
by John Boswell Writer in Ayr At Ayr the twenty ninth day of
October One thousand Seven Hundred and Seventy nine Years before
these Witnesses John Cameron my servant and the said John Boswell
Writer hereof and of the two Marginal Notes on the first Page
signed before the said Witnesses

      (Signed) Will. Cuningham

John Boswell Witness John Cameron Witness

Extracted upon this and the three preseeding pages By

        Will Crooks Cl. Sub

    Papers show that before the 3rd Day of November 1783
Charles Cuningham, brother of John Cuningham of New Castle had
died and that John Cuningham considered himself entitled to a
share of Charles's inheritance "set apart and secured to him
by the foregoing bond of provision of their father, William
Cuningham"?

     AFFIDAVIT OF ROBERT CAMPBELL

    Robert Campbell of the City of Richmond maketh oath
that he was long and intimately acquainted with John Cunningham late of the Town of Newcastle, and County of Hanover, having for many years lived in the same Town, only a small village,
with him, and Part of the Time in the House and family of the
said John Cunningham. That in the years one thousand seven
hundred and eighty four and five this Affiant well knows, that
the said John Cunningham was possessed of a Considerable number
of Slaves, as he thinks over Twenty, in Right of his, the said
John Cunningham's wife, and that he the said John Cunningham
was possessed in these years, in his own Right, of personal
Estate, in the opinion of this Affiant much more than sufficient to raise two hundred and fifty Pounds Sterling Money -
And further this Affiant saith not -
City of Richmond - Sworn to 28th Day of Novr., 1798, before
Wm. DuVal, an Alderman of the said City -

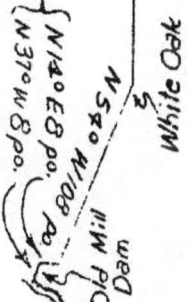

N 15° on Hawses line
W 46 po. Reed

N 96° W 412 poles on line Wm. Dandridge decd.

Begin at a poplar on Underwoods line

2 Underwoods line

N 40° E. 294 poles on Underwoods line to the beginning.

Ditch Mosby's & Underwood's corner

S 85° E 140 poles on Mosby's line

Red Oak on Wm. Dandridge decd.

Wm. Dandridge decd.

2 Spanish Oaks

S 132 poles on Robt. Dandg. decd. line.

Great Allens Creek

This tract of 1132 Acres of Land belonging to Nathaniel West Dandridge, Esqr. lying in the county of Hanover on Allen's Creek, the courses, distances &c expressed in this Plot. Surveyed May 13th 1803 at the request of Mr. Dandridge.

White Oak

N 14° E 8 po. N 37° W 8 po. on Wm. Dandridge Decd.

S 54° W 108 po.

Old Mill Dam

Reuben Ford of Gr. Allens Cr.

Spanish Oak on Middle Branch of Gr. Allens Creek

S 83° E 244 poles on Robt. Dandg. decd. line.

S 2° W 72 po. on Robt. Dandg. decd. line

MATCH LINE

From Sd Mill Dam (formerly Boswell's) up the Sd creek as it meanders 528 poles to the head

1132 ACRES

Stake near the Middle Branch of Robt. Dandg. decd.

S 68° E 404 po. on line of Robt. Dandg. decd.

MATCH LINE

Saplin in a slash on Dandg. decd. line

To the Judges &c ...

        Humbly complaining anew &c, Your Orators Andrew Cochran,
Robert Donald & Company, subjects of the King of Great Britain &
Ireland ... That a certain Nathaniel West Dandridge in his life
time on the 5th of Sept. 1767 in consideration of the sum of
L1062.1.7½ of the value of $5540.27 then justly due and owing from
the said N. W. Dandridge to the said Andrew Cochran, Robert Donald & Co. for securing the payment thereof ... conveyed unto the
said Andrew Cochran, Robert Donald & Compy. all that tract of land
lying on Turkey Creek in the County of Hanover containing 1465½
acres, more particularly described in the deed of Indenture of
same date as above & recorded in Hanover Court on the 7th day of
April 1768. Provided always that the said Nathl. W. Dandridge
his heirs &c. paid and satisfied to your Orators the said A. Cochran R. Donald & Co. or to their attorneys the said sum of L1062.1.7½
with lawful interest on or before the 1st day of April next ensuing, from date of Deed of Mortgage hereto annexed. Further ...
that the said N. W. Dandridge departed this life on or about the
year 1786, having made his last Will and Testament, and having
appointed his executors, of whom William Dandridge qualified as
executor and took upon himself the burthen and execution thereof
and gave bond, with Patrick Henry and Philip Payne his securities.
The said N. W. Dandridge died seized of considerable estate which
he devised to his wife Jane Dandridge, since intermarried with and
now the wife of Thomas Underwood, William Dandridge, his daughter
Dorothea Henry, Elizabeth Dandridge, Anna C. Dandridge & Mary Claiborne Dandridge, his sons Alexander Spotswood, John, Robert and
Nathaniel.

        The land contained in the said deed of Mortgage was
given to his sons & the use of a part thereof containing 700 acres
given to his wife Jane Dandridge during her natural life on which
the said Jane & her husband Thomas Underwood now reside & after
her death the said land was given to his son William and his heirs -

        Your Orators are informed that Jane Dandridge and Nathl.
Dandridge are still surviving, that William, Alexander Spotswood
& Robert have departed this life and that Ann Dandridge is the
executrix of the said William (who) was executor of the said N.
W. Dandridge but your Orators are uninformed who are the repre-
sentatives of the said Alexander Spotswood & the said Robert -
Your Orators have been inform'd that a certain Samuel Mosby also
lives upon a part of the said land ...

AMENDED BILL (1807 ?)

... With the leave of the Court your Orators beg to shew
further ... that Nathaniel W. Dandridge in the said bill mentioned,
by his said Will devised and directed that after the death of his
wife certain personal property given to her during her natural life
should be sold & the money equally divided between his four daughters
Dorothea Henry, Elizabeth Dandridge, Anna Catharine Dandridge & Mary
Claiborne. He also gives to his Daughter Dorothea Henry one negroe
slave nam'd Mary then in her possession as her absolute property
to his daughter Elizabeth a negroe Girl nam'd Sucky and a sorrel mare
as her absolute property, to his Daughter Catharine a negroe Girl
nam'd Sally & a sorrel mare as her absolute property. He also "devises" all the residue of his slaves after his wife if she survives
him shall have chosen hers according to their marriage agreement &
those at her death he gives to be equally divided between his said
daughters & their respective heirs ... He further devises all the
residue to his Exors. or the survivors of them in trust to sell the
same & the money to be equally divided between his said four daughters & their respective exors. or creditors. Your Orators would
further shew that the said Dorothea intermarried with Patrick Henry
who has departed this life and that his widow has administered on
his estate and has since intermarried with Judge Winston and that
Elizabeth intermarried with Philip Payne, Anna Catharine intermarried with John Spotswood Moore and Mary Claiborne intermarried with
George Woodson Payne - Your Orators have been informed that Samuel
Mosby has in his possession 1200 acres of land given by Nathaniel
W. Dandridge to his sons Spotswood and John - that Nathl. W. Dandridge has about 1500 acres of land given to him by his Father. That
the widow of William Dandridge and her son William Dandridge have in
their possession about 600 acres of land formerly belonging to the
estate of said Nathl. W. Dandridge and that the widow of Robert Dandridge has also in her possession 8 or 900 acres formerly the property
of Nathl. W. Dandridge & given by him to his son Robert -

Your Orators would further shew that the said Deed of Mortgage had a covenant of the following tenor and effect, that he the said
Nathl. W. Dandridge for himself his heirs exors. & admrs. covenanted
& promised to & with the Plaintiffs their exors., etc., that he, his
exors., etc. would pay or cause to be paid unto the Complts. the said
full sum of ₤1062.1.7 with interest, etc. From this deed of Mortgage
& covenant in which his exors., heirs, &c are bound not only the
mortgaged property in the deed mentioned but all the property real &
personal of which the said Nathl. W. Dandridge died seized & possessed
is liable for the payment of said sum of Principal & interest.

Amended Bill, cont.:

     To the end therefore that the Bill above mentioned already
filed may be amended this be received and considered as a part thereof
and that the said Judge Edm. Winston and Dorothea his wife, Philip
Payne and Elizabeth his wife, John Spotswood Moore and Anna Catharina
his wife, George Woodson Payne & Mary Claiborne his wife, Anna Hunter,
widow of Moses Hunter formerly Anna Dandridge the widow and relict of
Alexr Spotswood Dandridge son of the sd N. W. Dandridge, Dolly, John,
Susanna, Alexander, Elizabeth & William children of John Dandridge and
Basil Brown and Fanny his wife who was a daughter of the said John
Dandridge who was a son of Nathl. W. Dandridge, and Mildred Dandridge
the widow of Robert Dandridge & his children Richard, Alexr. Spotswood, Robert, Elizabeth and Mildred, and Nathaniel W. Dandridge, Archibald B. Dandridge, William, John, Jane B., Robert Bolling and Washington children of William Dandridge & Frederick, James & Nancy his
wife also a daughter of William Dandridge dec'd who was a son devisee
& Exor of Nathl. W. Dandridge decd. all citizens of Virginia & within
the Jurisdiction of this Court may be made Defendants hereto ...

     WILL OF NATHANIEL WEST DANDRIDGE, of HANOVER CO.
     d. 24 September, 1782;   p. 2 February, 1786
     (Murdock & Co. vs Dandridge &c. #109)

     In the name of God Amen   I Nathaniel West Dandridge of
the County of Hanover being infirm, but of sound & disposing memory, do make this my last will and testament for setling my tempo-
oral concerns

     Imprimis I give my beloved wife Jane Dandridge the use
of the tract of land I live on containing about seventeen hundred
acres, being what I reserved for myself when I laid off the several
tracts for my sons; also my Chariot & Harness & four Chariot horses;
a fourth part of my household and kitchen furniture, and of my stocks
of Cattle sheep & hogs, during her natural life and after her death
I give the said land to my son William Dandridge and his heirs, and
the personals to be sold and the money equally divided between my
four daughters Dorothea Henry, Elizabeth Dandridge, Anna Catharina
Dandridge & Mary Claiborne Dandridge.   I also give my wife a black
mare called hers, as her absolute property -

     Item I give to each of my sons William, Alexr. Spots-
wood, John, Robert & Nathaniel & to his heirs the lands laid off
& allotted to them respectively, together with the slaves & other
things I have delivered to them; for which I intend to make them
Deeds in my life time, which if I do, will fulfill this part of
my will -

Will of Nathaniel West Dandridge, cont.:

     Item. I give to my daughter Dorothea Henry One negroe slave named Mary now in her possession as her absolute property; to my daughter Elizabeth a negroe girl named Sucky daughter of sary, and a sorrel mare called hers, as her absolute property; to my daughter Anna Catharina a negroe girl named Salley, daughter of Sary & a Sorrel mare called hers, as her absolute property; and to my Daughter Mary C. Dandridge a negroe girl named Sucky, daughter of Doll, and a Bay mare called hers as her absolute property: Nevertheless each of my said daughters shall account for the negroes herein given to them, as so much received of their share upon the general division of slaves hereinafter directed, so as to make the part of each of my said daughters in Slaves equal, & my daughter Henry to account also for Patty, wch. I gave her & is since dead.

     Item. All the residue of my slaves, (after my wife if she survives me shall have chosen hers according to our marriage agreement, and those at her death) I give to be equally divided between my sd daughters Dorothea, Elizabeth, Anna Catharina & Mary Claiborne & their respective heirs they collating into the stock the negroes herein before given them, so as to make an equal division as before directed.

     Item. All the rest of my estate I give to my Executors or the survivor of them in trust to sell the same and the money to be equally divided between my said four daughters Dorothea, Elizabeth, Anna Catharina & Mary Claiborne and their respective Executors or Admrs

     Lastly I constitute my said wife Jane Dandridge & my son William Dandridge Executrix & Executor of this my last Will & testament, sealed & published by me this twenty fourth day of September One thousand seven hundred & eighty two

Seald. & Published before us   N W Dandridge
who subscribed the same in presence
of the testator & at his request

John Taylor
Edmd. Pendleton jr
Jno. Rogers

                        I give my still to my wife for
                        life & at her death to my son
                        Wm., in every thing else I con-
                        firm the above Will Octr 8th 1782
                              N W Dandridge
              Teste Edmd Pendleton

Probate of Will of N. W. Dandridge

At a Court held for Hanover County on Thursday the 2d day of February 1786 This last will and testament of Nathaniel West Dandridge
decd was offered to proof by William Dandridge the Executor therein
named and was proved by the oath of Edmund Pendleton jr and John
Taylor Esqrs. two of the witnesses thereto and also by the oath of
the said Executor and is ordered to be recorded

                         Test   William Pollard junr C H C

At a Court continued and held for Hanover County on Friday the 6th
day of May 1791

        The Codicil to this will of Nathaniel West Dandridge deceased,
was proved by the oath of the Honble Edmund Pendleton esquire a
witness thereto, and is ordered to be recorded

                         Test   William Pollard jr C H C
        November 1802 A Copy Teste Tho. Pollard D. C. H. C.

        William Dandridge as Executor gave bond dated 2d. day
of February 1786 with Patrick Henry and Philip Payne as security -
William O Winston, Ambrose Lipscombe, Elisha White, Thos. Tre-
vilian, John Garland & Chapman Austin Gentn. Justices of the County
Court then sitting; bond for £20,000.

        Recorded at a Court held for Hanover County on thursday the
2d day of February 1786

        November 1802 A Copy Teste Tho. Pollard D. C. H. C.
        Memo: "Wm Dandridge is dead & his widow Ann Dandridge has
qualified as his executrix

                         INVENTORY & APPRAISEMENT
                              of the Estate of
                         NATHANIEL WEST DANDRIDGE

Negroes Viz -   £   S   D

    Rachel & her children)
       Alexander   )
       John   4   )   130 . .
       Milly   )

Inventory & Appraisement
Estate of N. W. Dandridge, decd., cont.:

Negroes, cont.:		£	S	D
Patience & her children)				
Billy)				
Isaac 5)		180	.	.
John)				
Nathaniel)				
Nancy & her children)				
Rose)				
Billy 5)		120	.	.
Nancy)				
Dinah)				
Hannah & her child)				
Molly 2)		85	.	.
Mary Ann & her children)				
Mary)				
Sally 4)		145	.	.
Queen)				
Dosia 1		35	.	.
Pompey & his family)				
Sarah)				
Sally 3)		70	.	.
James Carpr. & his family)				
James)				
Chandler)				
Janey 7)		300	.	.
Patt)				
Betsy)				
Cambridge)				
Nelly & her children)				
Milly 3)		100	.	.
Pat)				
Lucy & her children)				
Betsy 3)		100	.	.
Patience)				
Mary & her children)				
Tom 3)		100	.	.
Sally)				

Inventory & Appraisement
Estate of N. W. Dandridge, decd., cont.:

Negroes, cont.:		L	S	D
Will, the Doctor	1	50	.	.
Dolley's Betty & family)				
Lucy)				
Billy)				
John)	7	220	.	.
Isaac)				
Cato)				
Dolly)				
Milly & her family)				
Dinah)				
Lucy)	5	180	.	.
Sam)				
Creety)				
Little Molly & her family)				
Andrew)				
Dolly)	4	220	.	.
Charity)				
Delphia	1	40	.	.
Bull Robin	1	100	.	.
Gib	1	75	.	.
Weaver Sam	1	90	.	.
Molly's Sam	1	75	.	.
Coachman Jack	1	30	.	.
Manuel	1	40	.	.
Carter Jincy	1	25	.	.
Peter	1	75	.	.
Charles	1	40	.	.
Judith	1	75	.	.
Dolly	1	75	.	.
Patt	1	75	.	.
Frances	1	.75	.	.
Mary an	1	70	.	.
Little Dolly	1	50	.	.
Sukey	1	70	.	.
Little Nelly	1	70	.	.
Phillis) from Mr Robt Dandridges	2	50	.	.
Nelly)				
Vaul	1	50		
	78	L 3285	.	.

Inventory & Appraisement
Estate of N. W. Dandridge, decd., cont.:

Horses, Viz.:	L	S	D
1 Old sorrel horse	10	.	.
2 black horses	27	.	.
1 Bay Mare	22	. 10.	
1 Small bay horse	8	.	.
1 Dark bay horse	15	.	.
1 Sorrel mare	30	.	.
4 Colts	48	.	.
4 Chariot horses	160	.	.
43 hogs	21	. 10.	
1 Sow & 5 pigs	1	. 10.	
8 Work Oxen	40	.	.
14 Cattle (yearlings)	14	.	.
21 Cattle	40	.	.
1 Calf		10.	
5 Cows	15	.	.
32 Sheep	16	.	.
1 Ox cart & chain	5	.	.
1 Waggon & geer	25	.	.
1 Small horse cart	2	. 10.	
1 Pr Cart wheels (old)		12.	
1 Chariot & harness	50	.	.
1 Single Chair	15	.	.
Corn Judged 105 barls.	94	. 10.	
Oats Judged 50 bushls.	7	. 10.	
Hay, fodder, tops & straw &c	59	. 26.	
50 Geese	3	. 15.	
7 Axes	1	. 15.	
1 large plow	1	. 10	
17 plow hoes & some coulters	1	. 18.	
18 broad hoes	1	. 16	
13 Grubbing hoes	1	. 13.	6
1 X Cut saw	1	. 5.	
1 Pitt-saw	1	. 15.	
1 Pitt-saw foil		1.	3
6 Scythes & cradles	2	.	.
2 Cuting boxes		. 10.	
1 pr. old Steelyards		. 5.	
9 old barrels		. 15.	
2 flax hatchets	1	. 10.	
1 Copper kittle	6	.	.
4 Stocks of timber	1	.	.
150 Hhd. staves		. 7.	6
2 Looms, warping Carrs & boxes	1	. 10.	
5 old spinning wheels	1	.	.

Inventory & Appraisement
Estate of N. W. Dandridge, decd., cont.:

Furniture & Household Goods: L   S   D

	L	S	D
16 pr. Sheets	16	.	.
21 pillow cases	2	2	.
8 Counterpaines	6	.	.
7 Bed quilts	9	.	.
13 Table cloths	5	4	.
3 Duffle blankets	1	7	.
1 Bed blanket bedstead cord &c	8	6	.
9 towels	.	9	.
1 pine table	.	5	.
1 Walnut Do.	.	10	.
1 Dressing glass	1	5	.
1 Do.	.	10	.
1 Bed & 3 bed steads	6	.	.
3 Doz. Queens china plates	.	9	.
8 Do. dishes	1	4	.
1 Do. tureen	.	2	6
A parcel of Queens china	.	7	6
9 China plates	.	6	.
1 Doz. do. tea cups bowl &c	.	15	.
1 China bowl	1	.	.
7 Wine glasses 1 tumbler)			
1 vinegar crewet 2 Salts)	.	6	.
17 old pewter plates	.	8	.
8 do. dishes	.	12	.
4 Old candle stands and)			
6 paddy pans)	.	2	.
4 brass candlestands	.	12	.
1 Cullender 2 sauce pans 1 pint tin)			
4 old spoons, 1 quart pot, 1 funnel,)			
1 pr steelyards, 2 pr snuffers)	.	12	.
1 Silver soop spoon 7 table)			
3 tea spoons)	7	.	.
1 Marble morter & pestle	.	15	.
4 sad irons 1 tea kittle)			
1 tribit 1 pr scales)			
1 Iron skillett)	.	15	.
17 knives & folks	.	8	.
2 Copper stew pans	.	15	.
1 Cherry table	2	5	.
2 Walnut do.	2	10	.
1 Walnut do.	1	15	.
1 tea table	.	10	.
1 marble slab	2	.	.
11 Cherry chairs	5	10	.
13 Walnut do.	5	4	.

Inventory & Appraisement
Estate of N. W. Dandridge, decd., cont.:

Furniture & Household Goods, cont.:	L	S	D
1 Bible 2 Vol with cuts	3 .	.	
6 Mahogany chairs	6 .	.	
2 beds bedsteads & cords	11 .	.	
1 Cherry desk & book case	8 .	.	
1 parcel old lumber	5 .		
2 tea boards		. 6 .	
1 Warming pan		. 6 .	
6 pr broken and irons	1 . 10 .		
2 pr iron wedges		. 8 .	
5 flax wheels	1 . 10 .		
1 Cotton gin & reel		. 6 .	
5 Iron pots 2 dutch ovens	2 . 10 .		
2 Iron pot racks 1 do. spit)			
1 ladle 1 skimmer 1 flesh fork)			
2 Iron spoons 2 fyg. pans)		. 13 . 6	
8 wash buckets		. 8 .	
A parcel of pails & tube		. 10 .	
3 Candle moulds		. 5 .	
1 meal sifter		. 2 . 6	
2 Small pine tables		. 5 .	
1350 ll. bacon @ 6d	33 . 15 .		
2 tubs & some Salt		. 15 .	
375 ll. iron @ 4d	6 . 5 .		
5 Casks & barrels		. 10 .	
5 Casks & a few tubs		. 12 . 6	
13 ll. steel		. 16 . 3	
2 Casks		. 8 .	
1 Jar with hogs lard		. 10 .	
180 ll. beef @ 4d	3 . .		
1 Cooler		. 6 .	
24 ll. tallow		. 12 .	
1 Currying knife & a parcel of old tools		. 15 .	
3 Cow Hides	1 . 5 .		
2 Grass scythes		. 8 .	
1 pr. tongues		. 2 .	
1 Ink stand		. . 26	
2 Chamber pots		. 2 .	
1 old bed 2 bed steds	1 . .		
Certificates £90. 0 . 0	45 . .		
	L 4265 . 16 . 8		

Murdock & Co. vs Dandridge &c.,

Inventory & Appraisement
Estate of N. W. Dandridge, decd., cont.:

Agreeable to an order of Hanover court we the subscribers being
duly sworn have appraised the estate of Nathaniel West Dandridge
to four thousand, two hundred & sixty five pounds sixteen shillings
& eight pence A p Inventory

John Richardson
Jas. Vaughan
John Hughes

February 8th 1786

At a court continued and held for Hanover county, on Friday the
6th day of June 1788

        This inventory & appraisement of the estate of Nathaniel West Dandridge decd. was returned & is ordered to be recorded

        Test

                                William Pollard jr C H C

    November 1802

        A Copy

            Toste

                                Tho: Pollard D C H C

Murdock & Co   ) 1323 (#109)
     vs   ) U. S. Cir. Ct.
N W Dandridges reprs) 5th Circt. Va. Div.
Underwood & al   ) (May 1816)

MARRIAGE CONTRACT
Nathl. West Dandridge, Esqr., of Hanover County
and
Miss Jane Pollard, of Goochland County

This Indenture made the 2d day of August one thousand
Seven hundred & Seventy nine between Nathl. West Dandridge. of the
County of Hanover Esqr. of the first part, Miss Jane Pollard of
Goochland County of the second part & her father Joseph Pollard
of the third part, WHEREAS a Marriage is intended by God's grace
to be solemnized between the sd. Nathaniel West Dandridge & the
sd. Jane Pollard between whom it hath been agreed that the latter
shall retain the sole power over her own fortune & future acqui-
sitions, & shall moreover be entitled to certain lands & slaves
herein after described whereof the sd Nathl. West is seized &
Possessed in case she shall be the Survivor to hold for her Life
in lieu of her Dower & other claim in his Estate. THIS INDENTURE
therefore Witnesseth that pursuant to the sd. agreement & for the
sum of five shillings to the sd. Nathl. West Dandridge in hand
paid by the sd. Joseph Pollard the receipt whereof is hereby acknowledged he the sd. Nathl. West Dandridge hath granted bargained
& Sold & by these presents doth grant bargain and sell unto the
sd. Joseph Pollard his heirs & assigns the Mansion House whereon
the sd. Nathl. West now resides together with four hundred Acres
of Land to be laid of_ in a reasonable manner so as to include
the sd. House, the plantation whereon it is, and the Garden, out
Houses & other appurtenances thereto. To have & to hold the sd.
House Land & premises hereby conveyed unto the sd. Joseph Pollard
his heirs & assigns IN TRUST to & for the following uses, that is
to say, to the use of the sd. Nathl. West Dandridge as of his former Interest therein until the said Marriage shall take effect &
from thence forth to his use during the Coverture & if he shall
survive the sd. Jane then to the use of the sd. Nath. West & of
his heirs or assigns forever. But if the said intended Marriage
shall take Effect & the said Jane shall be the survivor then from
& after the death of the sd. Nathaniel West to the use of the sd.
Jane for her natural life for her Jointure & in lieu, bar & full
satisfaction of Her claim of Dower in or to the real estate whereof
the sd. Nathaniel West Dandridge may be seized at any time during
the coverture; and from the time of her Death then to the use of
such person or persons as shall become entitled thereto by the gift
or devise of, or legal descent from the sd. Nathl. West Dandridge.
And the sd. Nathl. West Dandridge for himself his heirs Executors
& Administrators doth covenant & grant & to and with the sd. Joseph
Pollard his heirs & assigns in manner & form following, that is to
say that in case the sd. Marriage shall happen & the sd. Jane shall

Marriage Contract, cont.:

be the Survivor, she shall in that case enjoy during her Natural life,
any three of his household Slaves which she shall chuse, also Six
good labouring slaves half males & half females not to be under Sixteen nor above thirty years of age which several slaves with their
after increase shall at her Death go to the Donee, Devisee or heir
of the sd. Nathl. West Dandridge, as above express'd for the lands
And further that the sd. Nathl. West Dandridge his heirs Exrs or
Admr̄s. shall not and will not claim any estate, right, title or
Interest in or to the Slaves or personal Estate to which the said
Jane is now entitled in possession reversion or Remainder: or to
which she may become intitled at any time hereafter, by donation
devise, or descent (for the slaves herein before settled on her for
life only excepted) But that the sd. Jane Pollard if she survives,
or such person or persons to whom she shall dispose of the same by
any Deed or Will or writing purporting her Deed or Will notwithstanding her coverture or if she dies before the sd. Nathaniel &
makes no disposition or appointment thereof then her child. or children equally if she hath any, or if she hath none her Brothers &
Sisters equally or their representatives according to the law of
distribution shall respectively be intitled to hold or enjoy all &
every such Slaves & Personal Estate in like manner as if such Marriage had not happened. And the sd. Jane Pollard for herself her
heirs Extrs. or Admrs. doth covenant & grant to & with the sd.
Joseph Pollard, his heirs Extrs & Admrs. that in case the said
Marriage shall take Effect & she shall overlive the said Nathl. West
Dandridge, she will take & accept of the Jointer & Provision herein
& hereby made for her in lieu & full Barr, of all claim of Dower or
Distribution in or of the lands, slaves, or Personel Estate of the
sd. Nathl. West Dandridge whereof he shall be seized or possessed,
or entitled to at any time during the coverture. And the sd. Jane
Pollard for the consideration aforesd. & for the sum of five shillings to her paid by the said Joseph Pollard Hath & doth hereby bargain,
sell, assign & transfer unto the sd. Joseph Pollard his heirs & assigns
the several negroe Slaves, money goods & Chattels mentioned in a
Schedule hereunto annexed; to hold to him the sd. Joseph Pollard his
heirs & assigns In trust, to and for the uses herein before mentioned
concerning the same IN WITNESS Whereof, the parties have hereunto
set their hands & Seals the day & year first within mentioned

Sealed & Mutually deliver'd)   N. W. Dandridge (Seal)
In Presence of us   )   Jane Pollard   (Seal)
Robin Poor (?)
Jno. Curd, Senr.
Jas. Meriwether
Signd. 3d. Augt. 1779

Murdock & Co. vs N. W. Dandridge, cont.:

Marriage Contract, cont.:

A Schedule to wch the annex'd Deed refers -

      Margarett, Sylva, Daphney, Lucy, 2 feather beds, 2
boulsters, 4 pillows, 4 pr. sheets, 4 pr. pillowbers, 2 Blanketts,
11 Bed Quilts, 2 Counterpains, 2 table Cloths, 6 Towels, 2 chests
Drawers, 5 Trunks, Loan Office Certificate for two hundred &
Seventy pounds - Sixty pounds eighteen Shillings paper bills, a
riding Horse & Womans Saddle

                          N W Dandridge
                          Jane Pollard

At a Court held for Goochland County Septr. 20, 1779

      This Instrument of writing was presented in Court and
admitted to Record
      A Copy from the Records Teste G: Payne Cl Ct.

ACT OF ASSEMBLY
N. W. Dandridge

      An Act to vest certain Lands in Nathaniel West Dandridge,
Esqr. in fee Simple, and for setling Slaves in lieu thereof -

      1 - Whereas Unity Dandridge, widow, formally of King
William deceased, was in her Life time Seized in fee Simple of
and in a large Tract of Land, Containing four Thousand Eight hundred and thirty two acres, situate in the parish of St. Martin, in
the County of Hanover; and being so seized, in and by her last
will and testament in writing bearing Date the ninth Day of July
one thousand Seven hundred and fifty three She the said Unity,
did devise Twelve Hundred Acres, part of the said Tract of Land
which had been Granted to her Father, Nathaniel West Gentleman
deceased by Patent bearing date the thirteenth day of October
one thousand Seven hundred and twenty three, unto her son Nathaniel West Dandridge, Esqr. and Dorothy his wife During their natural
lives and after their Deceases to their Daughter Martha Dandridge
and the Heirs of her body for ever; and in Default of such Heirs
to Elizabeth Claiborne the wife of Philip Whitehead Claiborne
Gentleman, and her heirs for Ever, and the said Unity, by her
said Will did devise all the Residue of the said Tract of Land
unto her son Nathaniel West Dandridge and Heirs male of his Body
lawfully begotten with several Remainders over as in and by the

Act of Assembly, cont.:

said Will duly proved and recorded in the said County Court of
King William may more fully appear; and soon after making the
said Will the said Unity died So Seized of the said Land and the --
Nathaniel West Dandridge her Son entered into the said Land and was
and is seized thereof for such Estate and interest as is devised
him by the said Will aforesaid, and whereas by an Act of Assembly
passed in the twenty eighth year of the Reign of His late Magesty
King George the Second intitled an Act to dock the Entail of certain Land whereof Nathaniel West Dandridge Gentleman is seized,
and for Setling other Lands and Slaves of Greater value to the
same use, four hundred and ten acres of Land, adjoining the tract
aforesaid and fifty negroe Slaves therein named, with their future increase where among other things, vested in the said Nathaniel West Dandridge and the Heirs of his body with Several
Remainders; in default of such Issue as the said Act is more
particularly mentioned, and whereas the said Nathaniel West
Dandridge is possessed of Sundry other Slaves as his absolute
property and Being indebted in Large Sums of Money must sell
those Slaves or they will be Taken in Execution and sold for
payment of His Debts, whereby Burthen to him as the entailed
Slaves are mostly females - or young ones unfit for Labour
unless He can be allowed to Sell part of the said Land to enable
him to pay his Debts upon setting Slaves to the same uses from
the Profits whereof he may Support himself and Family and make
Provision for his younger children, and whereas it is most convenient to sell part of the said Land to be laid off at one end
of the Tract which cannot be done without including the Houses
and plantation where the said Dandridge lives at one end or the
other twelve Hundred acres of Land so devised by the Will of the
said Unity Dandridge to her Grand Daughter Martha Dandridge after
the Death of the said Nathaniel West Dandridge and Dorothy his
wife and the beforenamed Philip Whitehead Claiborne and Elizabeth
his wife the next in Remainder, under the Will of the said Unity
on the Death of the said Martha without Issue are consenting to
the sale of that part of the said Land upon settling Slaves in
lieu thereof in manner herein after mentioned; But whether the
two hundred Sixty-six and a Half acres Residue of the fourteen
hundred Sixty Six and a Half acres herein after vested in the
said Nathaniel West Dandridge in fee simple including any part
of the four hundred and Ten Acres in said Act mentioned is not
certainly known and whereas notice hath been published three
sundays successively in the several Churches of the said parish
of St. Martin that application would be made to this Present
General Assembly, to Dock the entail of fourteen hundred and sixty
six and a half acres of Land Part of the Tract aforesaid and to
Settle Slaves in Lieu thereof pursuant to your Magestys Instructions; may it therefore please your Most Excellent Magesty, at the
humble suit of the said Nathaniel West Dandridge that it may be
Enacted by the Lieutenant Governor Council and Burgesses

of this Present General Assembly and it is hereby enacted by the
Authority of the same that fourteen Hundred and Sixty Six and an
half acres of Land part of the Tract aforesaid to be laid off and
Bounded as follows, that is to say Beginning at William Atkinsons
Corner White Oak and poplar at Turkey Creek; thence north thirty-
three and a half degrees east three hundred and forty-four poles
to a poplar in Walker's branch; thence north forty-nine degrees
east one hundred and forty poles to a white-oak corner to Boswell
and Richards; thence north fifty degrees east twenty poles; thence
south four and an half degrees east one hundred and thirty poles
to a corner pine at the head of the Cat-tail branch; thence down
the water course of the said branch to a hickory now marked as a corner for dividing this land from the residue of the tract; thence
across the tract, along several lines now marked, to a hickory in
Atkinson's line another dividing corner; thence south sixty-six
degrees west one hundred and sixty-two poles to two persimmon trees
corner to Atkinson; thence north seventy-six degrees west one hundred and ninety-two poles to a corner ash on Turkey creek aforesaid,
and down the said creek to the beginning, be, and the same hereby is
vested in the said Nathaniel West Dandridge, his heirs and assigns,
forever; to his and their own proper use and behoof: And that the
following negro slaves whereof the said Nathaniel West Dandridge is
now possessed, as his absolute property, that is to say, a woman,
named Mary, and her children, named Sarah, Judy, Dinah, Daniel, and
Peter; a woman, named Betty (daughter of Nell) and her children,
named Lucy, George, and Frank; a woman named Molly, and her children
Jack, Sam, and Charity; a woman named Tamar, and her child Anthony;
and seven men, named Booth's Sam, Peter, Yellow Peter, George, Jack,
Robin, and Pompey, with the future increase of the females, be, and
the same are hereby vested in the said Nathaniel West Dandridge, his
heirs, executors or administrators IN TRUST, to and for the following
uses, that is to say, to the use of the said Nathaniel West Dandridge,
and Dorothea his wife, and to the survivor of them, for his or her
life; and from and after the death of such survivor, to the use of
the said Martha Dandridge, the daughter and the heirs of her body,
forever, & in default of such issue, the said slaves and their increase, or such of them, as shall be then living, shall pass and go
to such person or persons, and for such estate and interest therein,
as the above mentioned twelve hundred acres of land would have remained, descended and gone by virtue of the limitations in the will
of the said Unity Dandridge if this Act had never been made.

DANDRIDGE TO MURDOCK
Deed of Trust
d. 3 September, 1767

Nathaniel West Dandridge of the County of Hanover Gent
of the one part & John Murdock & Co. of Glasgow Merchants of the
other part - Whereas Nathaniel West Dandridge is justly indebted
to sd John Murdock & Co. in the sum of £963.3.2 Virginia Current
money advanced by & goods purchased of John Johnston & Hugh McMickin
Merchants & factors for the said John Murdock & Co. in this colony
& the said John Johnston & Hugh McMickin are willing to continue
to supply the said Nathaniel West Dandridge with goods for the
use of his family from time to time as there shall be occasion,
on having secy for the payment thereof, which the said Nathaniel
West Dandridge is willing to give, Now therefore this Indenture
witnesseth that the said Nathaniel West Dandridge for & in consideration of the sum of £963.3.2 like money from him to the said
John Murdock & Co. & for securing to them the payment of such
further & other sums as he may hereafter owe them and also for &
in consideration of the sum of five shillings by sd John Murdock &
Co. to sd Nathaniel West Dandridge pd., etc., grants all that tract
of Land on Turkey Creek in the parish of Saint Martin County of Hanover
containing 1466½ acres more or less which was lately vested in sd
N. W. Dandridge in fee simple by an Act of the General Assembly of
this Colony of Virginia made in the 7th year of the reign of his
present Magesty King George the third, intitled "An Act to vest
certain intailed Lands in Nathaniel West Dandridge esq in fee simple
& for settling slaves in lieu thereof" in which act the bounds of
said land are particularly described ... also the following slaves
Bartlett, Moses, Great Robin, Nathl., Elias, Sam, Roger, Dover,
Scipio, Thyphas, Great Sam, Harry, Abraham, Warwick, Cuffy, Will,
finnie, fellows & boys, Bett, Patience, Rose, Isbell, women & girls,
wth. all their future increase & the reversions &c... In Trust ...
Provided always that if sd Nathaniel West Dandridge his heirs &c
shall truly pay to sd John Murdock & Co. or their proper agents
£963.3.2 like money with lawful interest thereon from the 1st day
of May next on or before the 3rd day of the same month
and such further sums of money as may hereafter be due & owing
sд td John Murdock & Co for goods sold & money advanced him or for
any other debt to be contracted by sd Nathaniel West Dandridge or
any other account or dealings with sd Murdock or their agents ...

Sealed & delivered)   N W Dandridge   (Seal)
in presence of   )
James Thompson
Richd Anderson Junr
Alexr Henderson

Dandridge to Murdock, cont.:

    Received of John Murdock & Co. the sum of five shillings being the consideration money herein mentioned to be paid by them to me

James Thompson   N. W. Dandridge
Richd. Anderson Junr
Alexr. Henderson

At a Court held for Hanover County on Thursday the 7th day of April 1768

This mortgage indented & receipt thereon endorsed were proved by the oath of James Thomson Richard Anderson Junr & Alexander Henderson the witnesses thereto & ordered to be recorded -

           Test   William Pollard C H C

November 1802 A Copy Teste   Tho: Pollard D C H C

        A Copy Teste   Wm Marshall Clk

DANDRIDGE TO COCHRAN
Deed of Trust
d. 5 September, 1767

    Nathaniel West Dandridge of the County of Hanover Gent. of the one part & Messrs. Andrew Cochran Robert Donald & Co. of Glasgow Merchants of the other - Whereas Nathaniel West Dandridge is justly indebted to the said Messrs. Andrew Cochran Robert Donald & Co. in the sum of £1062.1.7.½ ... Now therefore this Indenture witnesseth that the said Nathaniel West Dandridge for securing the payment thereof, as for & in consideration of 5 shillings by the sd Cochran & Co. to the sd Nathl. West Dandridge pd., grants unto the sd Cochran & Co. all that tract of Land on Turkey Creek in the Parish of Saint Martin in the County of Hanover containing 1465½ acres more or less, and is the same tract of land lately vested in the sd Nathaniel West Dandridge in Fee Simple by an Act of the General Assembly of Virginia made in the seventh year of the Reign of his present Magesty King George the third intitled "an Act to vest certain intailed lands in Nathaniel West Dandridge Esqr in Fee Simple and for settling slaves in lieu thereof" in which act the bounds of the said land are particularly mentioned ... To have & to hold the said Tract of Land ... Provided always that if the sd Nathaniel West Dandridge his heirs &c shall truly pay to sd Andrew Cochrane Robert Donald & Company or to their agents & attorneys in this Colony the sd sum of £1062.1.7.½ with interest thereon from date on or before the 1st day of April next

Dandridge to Cochran, cont.:

ensuing the date of these presents that this present Indenture
&c shall cease ...

Sealed & delivered in)   N W Dandridge   (Seal)
presence of   )

Thilman
John Richardson
Edmund Taylor

Received of Messrs. Andrew Cochran Robert Donald & Company the
sum of five shillings it being the consideration money within
mentioned to be by them paid to me this fifth day of September
1767

Edmund Taylor   N. W. Dandridge
Thilman
John Richardson

At a Court held for Hanover County on Thursday, the 7th day of
April 1768

        This Mortgage Indented & receipt thereon endorsed were
proved by the oath of Paul Thillman and Edmund Taylor two of the
witnesses thereto. And at a Court held for the said County on
Thursday the 5th day of May next following the said Mortgage &
receipt were further proved by the Oath of John Richardson the
other witness to the same & ordered to be recorded

              Test   William Pollard C H C

    May 1818   A Copy

                    Teste   Tho. Pollard D C H C

Jones Surv. Partner   ) 1801 (#22)
        vs   ) U. S. Cir. Ct.
Dandridge s Exors &c) 5th Circt. Va. Dist.
      (1791)

John Tyndall Ware exor.)
  of Wm. Jones decd.   )
      vs   )
William Dandridge & al)

      William Jones of the City of Bristol, in the Kingdom of
Great Britain, who is an Alien, surv. Partner of Joseph Farell &
William Jones, late Merchts. & Partners of the said City and King-
dom, acting under the firm of Farell & Jones,   against

      William Dandridge and Jane Dandridge executor and executrix
of Nathaniel West Dandridge dec'd, William Macon, John Johnson and
Robert Anderson, survising Trustees, John Dandridge, Robert Dandridge,
and Nathaniel Dandridge, Sons, Patrick Henry and Dorothea his Wife,
Philip Payne and Elizabeth his wife, John Spotswood Moore and Anna
Catharina his wife, Woodson Payne and Mary his Wife, and Archer
Payne, the said Dorothea, Elizabeth, Anna Catharina and Mary, Daugh-
ters of the said Nathaniel West Dandridge and devisees in his said
Will and --- Dandridge, --- of Alexander Spotswood Dandridge, Defts.

DANDRIDGE to DABNEY & Others - DEED OF TRUST

      THIS INDENTURE made the 6th day of October in the year of
our Lord 1768 Between Nathaniel West Dandridge of the County of Hanover esqr of the one part and William Dabney, William Macon & John
Johnson of the County of Hanover John Wayles of the County of Charles
City & Robert Anderson of the County of Hanover Gentn. of the other
part WHEREAS the said Nathaniel West Dandridge is considerably indebted to sundry persons in this Colony & in Great Britain, and is
possessed of a valuable estate in lands & slaves but greatest part
being entailed on him & the rest under Mortgage to some of his
Creditors, he cannot sell the said estate to discharge his said
debts, but is willing that his Creditors shall receive the profits
thereof, till their debts are satisfied & that all his estate shall
be vested in the said William Dabney, William Macon, John Johnson,
John Wayles, and Robert Anderson as trustees for that purpose saving to the said Nathaniel West Dandridge only a reasonable allowance
out of the said profits for the maintenance of himself & his family
during the time aforesaid NOW THEREFORE THIS INDENTURE WITNESSETH
that the said Nathaniel West Dandridge as well for providing for the
payment of the said debts as for and in consideration of the sum of
five shillings by the said William Dabney, William Macon, John
Johnson, John Wayles & Robert Anderson to him in hand paid, &c,
HATH Granted unto the said William Dabney, William Macon, John
Johnson, John Wayles & Robert Anderson ... all that tract or

Deed of Trust, cont.:

parcel of land whereon the said Nathaniel West Dandridge now lives
lying on Allen's Creek in the Parish of St. Martins in the County
of Hanover containing by estimation four thousand Acres be the
same more or less, and all that other tract & parcel of land situate on Turkey Creek in the said Parish & County containing one
thousand four hundred & sixty six acres more or less ALSO one
hundred and sixty Slaves now on & belonging to the several plantations settled on the said land which slaves are particularly named
in Schedule No. 1 hereto annexed and likewise all the household
& kitchen furniture Stock of Cattle, Hogs, horses, & Sheep, Tools,
Utensils, goods & chattels belonging to him the said Nathaniel
West Dandridge ... TO HAVE AND TO HOLD ... IN TRUST, that they
the said William Dabney, William Macon, John Johnson, John Wayles
& Robert Anderson, &c., shall and may receive & take the rents
issues & profits of all the said land, slaves, stocks, &c. aforesaid
(except the part thereof that is and shall be hereinafter reserved
for the use of the said Nathaniel West Dandridge) until all the debts
now justly due and owing from the said Nathaniel West Dandridge
shall be fully paid & satisfied out of the said rents, &c, to the
persons intitled to receive the same, and also upon the trust that
they the said William Dabney, William Macon, John Johnson, John
Wayles and Robert Anderson, &c., or some one of them under the
direction & by advice of the rest & the survivors, etc., of them,
shall manage the estate hereby conveyed to them in the best manner
they can in order to raise & receive profit from the same & will
yearly & every year sell & dispose of the tobacco, Corn, Wheat,
Pork, Beef, and everything else made & raised on the said land
and estate hereby conveyed for the best price that can be had for
the same ... and pay the money arising (after delivering & paying to the said Nathaniel West Dandridge the allowance herein
reserved for support of himself & family & deducting all costs &c)
unto and amongst all the present Creditors of the said Nathaniel
West Dandridge ... PROVIDED always & it is hereby agreed it shall
be lawful for the said Nathaniel West Dandridge & his family to
use, occupy & possess the Dwelling house on the plantation where
he now lives with the outhouses and offices thereon & thereto belonging and the garden & pasture adjoining without interruption,
in the same manner as if this deed had never been made, and that
the said Nathaniel West Dandridge shall & may retain & keep for
the use of himself & family all the servants & slaves that are
now imployed in and about his house & family provided they do not
exceed sixteen in number, but the increase of the said slaves shall
be under the direction of the said trustees to be left with the
said Nathaniel West Dandridge or removed as they shall think fit
and in case of the death of any of the said servants others may
be put in their places ... & the said trustees shall furnish &
allow the sd Nathaniel West Dandridge the following provision

Deed of Trust, cont.:

out of the grain & stock made & raised on the sd estate, that is
to say 100 Bu. of Wheat, 150 Bu. of Corn, fifty fat hogs, 3 Grass
Beeves, three stalled Beeves, six Muttons, six Lambs, twenty
Shoats, all the wool shared from the Sheep, the use of --- Horses
with a sufficient Quantity of fodder to support them & all the
milk and butter that the sd Nathaniel West Dandridge & his family
shall have occasion for, and shall also moreover pay to the said
Nathaniel West Dandridge yearly & every year out of the profits
of the sd estate the sum of ₺100 all which the said trustees covenant & agree to do ...

	N W Dandridge	(Seal)
No witnesses		(Seal)
	William Macon jr	(Seal)
	John Johnson	(Seal)
	Robert Anderson	(Seal)
		(Seal)

Memo - it is hereby agreed & the trustees are hereby directed in
case of the death of the sd N W Dandridge before the debts are
paid out of the profits, that the sd trustees shall sell all the
estate conveyed to them by this deed that the sd N W Dandridge
has the absolute property in & divide the money between the
creditors that shall sign the Letter of Licence hereto annexed in
proportion to their several Debts -

                                    N W Dandridge

At a Court held for Hanover County on thursday the 6th day of
October 1768

          Nathaniel W. Dandridge, William Macon, John Johnson &
Robert Anderson, Genm. acknowledged this deed indented, and the
sd N W Dandridge acknowledged the Receipt thereon endorsed &
schedule thereto annexed which were ordered to be recorded

                    Test
                                    William Pollard   C H C

          March 1801
              A Copy
                        teste

                              Tho. Pollard   D C H C

SCHEDULE TO WHICH ANNEXED DEED REFERS

Schedule No. 1 ists by name 161 Slaves, including 49 men, 7 boys, 44 women, 61 children part of whom were eleven or twelve years old.

Furniture &c at Home House: 14 Beds with Bolsters and Pillows, 5 pr of Blankets, twelve Ruggs, 4 Quilts, 5 Counterpins, 12 pr. of Sheets, 4 pr. of Pillow bears, ten Towels, 15 Bedsteads, 1 Desk and Book Case, one Chest of Drawers, 10 Tables, one Marble table, 4 Doz. of Chairs, 2 Arm chairs, one great Chair, 2 Glasses, 12 table Cloaths, 7 pr and Irons, 2 Spits, 4 iron potts, 1 large Copper Kettle, one small kettle, 4 doz. pewter plates, 14 Dishes, 1 Doz. tin pans, 4 Pewter Basons, 6 Candle Moulds, one Silver Bowl, one silver Coffee Pot, one dozen large Spoons, one Doz. tea Spoons, one Charrot & Harness, one Chair & Harness, one Ox Cart, one Horse Cart, one Tumbrell, two Looms & Slays with harness, one large Silver Spoon, four silver salts, 8 Brass Candlesticks, 2 pr. snuffers, one Wilton Carpet, one Japan tea board & China, a sett, six spinning wheels, 4 flax wheels, 21 stone jugs, one large stone Jarr, 8 butter Potts, 3 flax Hackels, one Waggon & Harness, John Avera, a white servant man, Ploughs, Hilling hoes, weeding hoes, grubbing hoes, Axes

N W Dandridge

Stocks &C, vizt.: At home House: two small mares, one small Horse, one Chair horse, one riding horse, one ball face bay horse.

AT GRAVES Plantation twenty four Cows, ten work Oxen, two Stears, one Calf, one Bull, five plow horses, three mares, twenty six head of hogs -

AT DAVERS PLANTATION twelve Cows, ten young Cattle, one Stear, one Bull, one Calf, eighteen hogs, sixteen Pigs

AT JAMEYS PLANTATION eight Cows three Stears seventeen young Cattle, four Colts nine hogs sixteen Pigs.

AT SIMS PLANTATION twenty three cows, six stears, nineteen young Cattle, eight Calves, four work horses one young black horse, two young mares thirty six hogs eighteen pigs

AT BAGBYS PLANTATION eleven Cows four Stears, eleven young Cattle, three Calves, one bull, two work horses four mares, two Colts, forty four hogs twenty nine Pigs.

AT ANTHONYS PLANTATION one Cow fifty Sheep

THE ANSWER OF PATRICK HENRY & DOROTHEA, HIS WIFE

... Saith That some time in the year one thousand seven hundred & sixty eight he the said Deft was present at the House of Nathl. West Dandridge, Esqr. decd., when he agreed to execute the Trust Deed in the Bill mentioned - That he was induced to do so on Account of his being only Tenant in Tail of by far the greater part of his Land & Slaves more than on account of the amount of his Debts - His Creditors urged this Consideration as well as the very infirm State of Health in which he constantly remained - This Deft. was consulted by the said Dandridge as his Counsel upon that & on many other Occasions & was privy to most of his Transactions relating to his Debts for many Years - When the aforesaid Trust Deed was executed it was understood & agreed that John Johnson therein named should be the Receiver of the Money raised by the Trust Estate & agreeably thereto several Dividends were made from Time to Time amongst the Creditors who acceded to the Terms held out by the said Deed - And after several Years the said Dandridge came to the Resolution of selling off so many of his Slaves & so much of his Lands as would make up the Deficiency of his Debts which the profits of his Estate had not paid - This Deft further says he remembers that two Sales of the said Dandridges Slaves were made for that purpose & a considerable Quantity of valuable Land, but what was the amount of these Sales this Deft cannot ascertain; but well remembers the said John Johnson being privy to & advising Sales to be made of the said Estate & his mentioning & recommending particular Persons as purchasers - This Deft verily believes that large Sums must have been received by the said Johnson from these Sales made as this Deft ever understood by the Consent of the Creditors of the said Dandridge in order to accelerate the Receipt of their Claims - and which this Deft supposed would have been solely applyed to that purpose & accounted for by the said Johnson as the Receiver for all the said Creditors .. This Deft has seen a Statement of one Sale of Negroes made by the said Johnson amounting to near or about nine hundred Pounds which Negroes this Deft saith were given up by the said Dandridge & sold by the said Johnson for the purpose of paying his Debts - The Number of Negroes this Deft cannot recollect but supposes they were nearly Twenty included in that particular Sale - This Deft saith that the said Dandridge complained of Injustice in the Credits for his Tobaco shipped to the House of Farell & Jones & a certain Mr. Alexr. Donald Merchant did examine the accounts current & he said on his looking over the several Documents there appeared to be a very capital Error in Crediting the Tobacco shipped as aforesaid - The said Dandridge upon complaining of this received a Letter from the honble Peter Lyons their Attorney or Agent for the said Farell & Co telling him that every Error in the said Farells Accounts should be rectified notwithstanding any Judgement he might suffer to pass against him, or to that Import to the best of this Defts Recollection. But whether the Error really existed or was rectified this Deft knoweth

The Answer of Patrick Henry, cont.:

not certainly but believes it was not - This Deft. saith that he
received with his Wife as her portion Negroes valued to about four
hundred Pounds as well as he remembers but that they were rated or
valued very high & above their true Value as he thinks - That one
of the most valuable is dead & that he heretofore refunded a considerable sum of Money to the Executor Wm. Dandridge to satisfy in
part a Mortgage of the said N. W. Dandridge's Estate made to Philip
W. Claiborne decd which as he is informed & verily believes was
executed by the said Dandridge before the Date of the said Trust
Deed - That a large sum is still due to the Estate of the said
Claiborne for which a suit at Law is now depending against the executors of the said N. W. Dandridge for the said Debt to secure
which the said Mortgage was given but whether the Negroes possessed
by this Deft. are named in the said Claiborne's Mortgage this Deft.
cannot say - But the said Executor took from this Deft. a Bond to
refund as is usually given by Legatees & retains the same - This
Deft. further saith that he is well satisfied that the negroes he
possessed are of the Stock from the said Dandridges Estate of entailed Negroes belonging to the said Dandridge in his Life Time,
denying that he hath any other property or Estate whatsoever to his
knowledge which ever belonged to the said N. W. Dandridge; & how
far the Alienation of the Tenant in Tail for a greater Estate than
vested in him can affect this Deft. or avail the Complainant is
submitted into the honble Court this Deft. avering that the Partys to
the Trust Deed & in particular the agent for Farell & Jones well
understood that the said N. W. Dandridge held his Estate in Tail
as to the greatest Part of it & that part of it which was not entailed was sold as aforesaid - This Deft. ever expected the Debt
really due to Farell & Jones from the said N. W. Dandridge was fully
discharged, as the profits of the Trust Estate added to the aforesaid
Sales seemed by the View which this Deft. was able to take of the
subject were sufficient for that purpose - And lastly these Defts.
denying all unjust combination &c pray to be hence dismissed with
their Costs &c

                                        P Henry

Henrico County Sc

                  Swn. to in the usual form the 30th May 1796 before

                                        Jno Pendleton

THE ANSWER OF WM. MACON

... Saith that all the profits made from the estate conveyed
by the said Deed from the yearly 1768 untill the year 1775 were applied to the discharge of the debt due from the said Nathaniel West
Dandridge according to the intent and meaning of the said Trust. After
the last mentioned period, and after the late War had broken out between the United States of America and Great Britain the said N. W.
Dandridge took into his possession the whole of the estate conveyed
by the said Deed, and used and enjoyed the same until the time of his
death ... but this defendant verily believes that during that period
the nett profits of that estate if any could be made after discharging all the expences imposed upon it in consequence of the War must
have been very trifling... That the debts due to the subjects of the
King of Great Britain having been at a very early period of the war
sequestered, the intention of the said Nathl. W. Dandridge in making
the said Deed of Trust became thereby, as well as by the consequences
attending that War entirely defeated, and therefore it was unnecessary
for the Trustees to retain possession of an estate which under their
management could produce no profits during that period of general
distress, if indeed it could have been made to defray the expences
which it incurred. After the War had ceased, the legal impediments
to the recovery of british debts still continued, and so fully was
the sd Nath. W. Dandridge convinced that they never would be paid,
that this defendant is well satisfied that if the possession of the
said estate had been demanded by the Trustees, that he would have
refused to deliver it to them ... That John Johnson one of the Trustees
kept the accounts of the profits of the said Trust Estate and made a
just and accurate distribution thereof amongst the several Creditors
untill the year 1775 ... that some time in the year 1776 he left this
Country and went to Great Britain or to some part of the Dominions of
the King of Great Britain, and is not to the knowledge of this defend-
and a resident of this Commonwealth - the rest of the Trustees are
since dead, except this defendant who hath no money or other property
in his hands due or belonging to the said Trust Estate, nor does he
believe that any other of the Trustees had in their hands any money
or property due or belonging to the estate except the profits which
were received until the year 1775 and which were honestly fairly and
accurately distributed amongst the respective Creditors as above
stated... This defendant conceives that it would be highly inequi-
table and oppressive to compel him at his advanced period of life to
Resume the laborious office of a Trustee, and to undertake singly
those burthensome duties which were originally intended to be borne
by five or six ...

Wm Macon

Hanover county towit -

    Sworn to before Elisha White a Justice of the peace for
the county afsd the 15 day of May 1794

THE ANSWER OF THOMAS UNDERWOOD AND JANE, HIS WIFE

These Defendants are not in possession of any part of
the lands mentioned in the deed which are described as situated
on the Waters of Turkey Creek whereas the lands of which these
Defendants are in possession & not mentioned in the aforesaid
Deed of Mortgage are situated on Allen's Creek. When this Defend-
and Jane intermarried with her first husband Mr. Dandridge he settled on her for life 400 acres of land including the houses and
orchards where these Defendants now live, and nine slaves, and at
his death he gave her by his last Will for life 700 acres all which
land was given to the said Jane for life & after her death to William Dandridge son of the said Nathaniel W. Dandridge & Jane afterwards purchased of the said William the Reversion of the said land
& has actually paid the purchase money for the same. Afterwards
suit was instituted in the Federal Court by Farell & Jones against
these Defendants to obtain a Decree for the sale of this land which
had been mortgaged to the said Farell & Jones by Mr. Dandridge in
his life time & before his intermarriage with the Defendant Jane.

The land was afterwards sold under a Decree of the said
Court at public auction and this Defendant Thomas Underwood became
the purchaser. The Slaves that the Defendant Jane had on the division of her dec'd husband N. W. Dandridge's estate now living and in
the possession of these Defendants are eight in number together with
four children born since the death of the said Nathl W Dandridge.
This Defendant Jane also received of said estate an old chariot now
totally destroyed, 5 horses, some Cattle, hogs and sheep, some household and kitchen furniture. The residue of Mr. Dandridge's estate was
divided among his children except those things which were sold by his
Exor amounting to about £700. These Defendants have understood and
believe that Mr. Dandridge gave to his son Spotswood 9 slaves, to
John Robert & Nathl 25 slaves and several to William ... These Defendants believe that nearly 40 slaves of the said Nathaniel W Dandridge
were divided among Patrick Henry, John S. Moore, Philip Payne and
Woodson Payne who intermarried with Mr. Dandridge's daughters, - that
Mr. Samuel Mosby is in possession of about 1200 acres of land given
by Mr. Dandridge to his sons Spotswood and John. That Nathl. W. Dandridge is possessed of about 1500 acres, that the widow of Robert Dandridge has about 900 acres in possession formerly belonging to the estate of Mr. N. W. Dandridge & that the widow of William & his son
William have in possession about 600 acres also a part of the estate
of the said N W Dandridge dec'd -

                                        Tho Underwood
(Filed 29 Sept 1804)   . Jane Underwood

Hanover County to Wit:

Personally appeared before me a Magistrate of the said
County Thomas Underwood and Jane his wife and made oath that the
above answer contains the truth so far as they know or believe

Certified under my Hand this 6th Sepr. 1804

John Woodson

THE ANSWER OF ANNE DANDRIDGE EXX OF WILLIAM DANDRIDGE, DECD.

Anne Dandridge executrix of William Dandridge dec'd eldest
son and heir in tail of the said N W Dandridge, saith that N. W.
Dandridge on the 30th day of May 1780 executed a writing under seal
confirming in fee simple to William Dandridge, a water mill and two
acres of land and one fifth part of his lands in Hanover exclusive
of the lands, slaves and personal estate of which the said N W Dandridge had given to him the possession, and for which he undertook at
any time to execute a proper conveyance in fee simple. The lands
were 618 acres on Allen's Creek in Hanover County, also 119 acres
adjoining the 618 acres ...

THE ANSWER OF NATHANIEL WEST DANDRDIGE

... Saith that he is not in possession of any part of the
tract of Land in said Deed of Mortgage mentioned - That Nathl. West
Dandridge, father to this Defdt., left to this Defdt a tract of Land
containing about 1600 acres. That the said tract of Land being conveyed by said Nathl. West Dandridge in trust to secure payment of his
Debts a suit was filed in this Court agst him & others by Farell &
Jones & decree entered for the sale of the Land devised to this Defdt
together with other Lands that were held by said Nathl. W. Dandridge
& conveyed in trust as afsd. & that a decree was entered for the sale
of sd Lands & sale taking place accordingly this Deft was obliged to
buy in the Land before held by him under his Father's will All which
will more fully appear reference being made to the said Decree & proceedings &c ...

He further saith and he hath heard and hath reason to believe that the sd Mortgage Debt was long since paid off & Discharged
whether under the sd trust Deed or not he cannot say ...

City of Richmond To Wit -

Sworn to before ? Carrington a Magistrate for the said
City 19 May 1806

THE ANSWER OF MILDRED DANDRIDGE

Mildred Dandridge widow of Robert Dandridge, saith ...
the sd Nathl. W. Dandridge dec'd did by his last Will & testament
bequeath to her dec'd husband, Robert Dandridge, 618 acres in the
county of Hanover lying on the waters of Allen's Creek which Land
sd Robert Dandridge died possessed of and after his death the reprs.
of sd Ro. Dandridge retained possession of sd Land until the --- day
of --- in the year 180- when the whole of the afsd tract of Land was
sold by Benjamin Mosby then a Deputy Marshall in Virginia under a
decree of this Honourable Court to satiafy a Debt due from the estate of Nathl. W. Dandridge deced to the reprs. of --- Jones.

Hanover Co towit

Sworn to before Walter Coles a Justice of the Peace for
the said County 16 May 1806 -

THE ANSWER OF ADAM S. DANDRIDGE

Adam S. Dandridge, son and heir of Alexr. Spotswood Dandridge, saith ... that he knows nothing of the circumstances ...

Adam Stephen Dandridge

Berkeley County Sct

Sworn to before William Riddle 31 day of Octr. 1806.

Note on Subpœna dated 17 January 1806, for Spotswood Dandridge,
Mildred Dandridge, Elizabeth Dandridge, Robert Dandridge and Ann
Hunter:

"Executed on -- day of April 1806. 180 miles and 160
extra. A Hunter lives in Martinsburg, Berkeley County."

Also: Subpoena dated 24 August, 1808: "Elleanner wife of Peter
Foster was the widow of John Shelton. - Service 12 miles."   *

Papers show: "Nathaniel West Dandridge who was a son and devisee
of Nathaniel W Dandridge the elder deced. departed this life be-
fore the 22 day of October 1810, leaving Watson N. Dandridge, Mary
Ellis, late Mary Dandridge, Martha Fontaine, late Martha Dandridge,
Unity Dandridge, heirs at law of the said Nathaniel West Dandridge,
Junr."

* The connection with the Dandridge suit is not apparent. E. G.

PASLEY TO BOSWELL

This INDENTURE made this fifth day of October in the Year
of our Lord Christ MDCCL Between William Pasley of the Parish of St.
Peters in the County of New Kent, Planter, and Frances his wife, of the
one part, and John Boswell of the Parish of Ware in the County of
Gloucester Gent. of the other part WITNESSETH that in consideration
of the sum of one hundred and fifty five pounds and fourteen shillings
current money of Virginia, etc., the said William Pasley and Frances
his wife do hereby convey, etc., unto the said John Boswell, his heirs,
etc., all those two tracts or parcells of Land and plantations containing in the whole five hundred and nineteen Acres, — one of the said
Tracts of Land contains by estimation 200 acres, situate, lying and
being on the South Side of the South Ann River, and the other contains 317 acres being on the same side of the said River, opposite
and contiguous to each other. Both of the said tracts or parcells
of land are in the County of Hanover. The tract that contains 200
acres was purchased by the said William Pasley of one Robert Clopton,
and is bounded as followeth towit, Beginning at a corner red oak by
the road side at the upper corner of the said Tract, running thence
South sixty four Degrees, East two hundred pole to a corner red oak,
thence north sixty four degrees East one hundred and twenty pole to
a corner red oak, thence north thirty one and a half degrees, West
one hundred and ninety two poles to a corner at several pointers
thence South fifty six degrees, West two hundred and twenty three
poles to the corner where it first began —   The other above mentioned tract or parcell of Land was granted by Patent bearing date
the xxviij th day of August in the year of our Lord Christ MDCCXLVI
to the said William Pasley and is bounded as followeth to wit, Beginning at a red oak corner of the said Pasley's and Joseph Morris,
thence north sixty three degrees West seventy seven poles to a corner
red oak in William Gooch's Line thence South fifty Degrees, West two
hundred and six poles to a corner pine in James Massie's line thence
South one hundred and sixteen poles to a pine, on the north side of
Cattail Branch thence down the said Cattail Branch by the meanders
to a white Oak in Mrs. Anne Aylett's line, thence on the said Aylett's
line, north sixty degrees West two hundred and eighty poles to the
said Pasley's and Meriwethers corner red oak, thence on the said
Pasley's line to the beginning place, ... and all the appurtenances
whatsoever, to the said tracts or parcells of land belonging ...

Sealed and Delivered in   Wm Pasley   (Seal)
presence of   Frances (X) Pasley   (Seal)
George Clopton
George Taylor
William Pasley junr

Pasley to Boswell, cont.:

October the fifth MDCCL, then received of the within named John Boswell one hundred and fifty five pounds and fourteen shillings current
money it being the consideration for the land and premises within
mentioned   Pr me   ₺155.14.0

Teste   Wm. Paslay
George Clopton
George Taylor.

At a Court held for Hanover County on Thursday the 2d Day of May 1751
George Taylor and William Paslay junr. made oath that they did see
the within named William Paslay and Frances his wife seal and deliver
this Deed (Indented) as their proper Act and Deed, and also that they
did see the said William sign the receipt on the sd Deed Endorsed as
his Act and Deed and the sd Deed and receipt are thereupon admitted
to record

                        Test

                                 Henry Robinson C H C

                 DANDRIDGE & ALS TO WATKINS & TO GRAVES

N W Dandridge & others)
           to   )
Tho. Watkins Jr and   )   Extract from Deeds for Land
           to   )
Wm. Graves   )

        By Deed recorded in the County Court of Hanover bearing
date on the 10th June 1773 between Nathaniel West & wife of the
first part, Andrew Cochrane, Robert Donald & Co: of the second part,
John Murdock & Co: of the third part & Thomas Watkins jr of the
fourth part, - 760 acres of Land conveyed to the said Watkins which
was sold to him for the sum of ₺760 under a deed of trust from the
said Dandridge to the said John Murdock & Co & being part of 1466½
acres vested in the said Dandridge by Act of Assembly -

        By another Deed also of record in the County Court of
Hanover bearing date on the 22nd July 1773 between the same parties
as the 1st, 2nd & 3rd parties to the above mentioned deed & William
Graves of the 4th part, 146 acres of Land was conveyed to the sd
Graves which was sold to him for the sum of ₺146 under the said deed

of trust to Murdock & Co. & being part of the said 1466½ Acres.

The first of these Deeds was acknowledged by John Johnson as
Attorney for Donald Cochran & Co. & Murdock & Co., and the second Deed
was acknowledged by Archibald Govan as Attorney for the said Donald
Cochrane & Co. & Murdock & Co. There are receipts on the Deeds for
the Consideration of money but neither the Deed nor those receipts
state whether it be in full or in Part of the Money due under the
Mortgage or deed of trust ...

Deed for 760 Acres to Thomas Watkins, junior, bounded as
follows: Beginning at a poplar in Turkey Creek running thence north
28 deg. E. 366 poles along a line of marked trees to a corner spanish
oak thence South 66 & a half degrees E 268 poles to sassafras bushed in
an old field, thence South 4 deg. E 52 poles to pointers, thence South
10 deg. West 72 poles to a corner red Oak, thence South 27 degrees
East 14 poles to Pointers, thence South 33 deg. West 82 poles to pointers, thence South 16 deg. West 15 poles to a corner hickory, thence
South 17 deg. West 54 poles to a hickory, thence South 72 deg. West 48
poles to a black Oak, thence South 6 deg. West 80 poles to Persimon
Trees, thence north 76 deg. West 197 poles to an Ash in Turkey Creek,
thence down Turkey Creek 94 poles to the beginning.

At a Court held for Hanover Co. on thursday the 5th day of
August 1773 this deed ... was proved by the oath of William Graves,
one of the witnesses thereto, and at a Court held for the said County
on thursday the 4th day of November 1773 the same was further proved...
by the oath of Josiah Tompkins another witness thereto - And at a Court
held for the said County on thursday, the 6th of January 1774 the said
Deed was acknowledged by Andrew Cochran, Robert Donald & Co. & by John
Murdock & Co., by John Johnson, their Atty. And at a Court held for the
said County on thursday the 7th day of December 1775 The said deed and
receipt were further proved by the oast of William Dandridge, another
witness... and ordered to be recorded. Test   William Pollard C.H.C.
December 1818 A Copy teste Tho. Pollard D. C. H. C.

Deed for 146 Acres to William Graves, of the County of Hanover, Planter, bounded as follows: Beginning at a corner pine at the
head of Cat-tail branch, thence South 10 degrees West 138 poles to a
corner stooping hickory thence North 66½ deg. West 123 poles to a
spanish Oak, thence North 28 degrees, E. 17 poles to the point where
a pine formerly stood, thence North 74 poles to a corner poplar on
Walker's branch, thence North 36 deg. East 50 poles to a red oak near
a Glade, thence North 52 deg. East 108 poles to a white oak where
Massie's pine formerly stood, thence South 4 deg. East 122 poles to
the beginning, being part of said 1466½ acres...

At a Court held for Hanover County on thursday the 5th day
of October 1773 this deed was proved by the oath of Alexr. Spotswood
Dandridge ... And at a Court held for the said County on thursday the

Dandridge & others to William Graves, cont.:

7th day of December 1775 the same was further proved by the oath of
Paul Thilman and Paul Woolfolk two other witnesses. And at a Court held
for the said County on thursday the 5th day of December 1776, Andrew
Cochrane, Robert Donald and Co. and John Murdock & Co. by Archibald
Govan their attorney acknowledged the said deed indented and the said
receipt, which were thereupon ordered to be recorded. Test William
Pollard, C. H. C. December 1818 A Copy teste Tho Pollard D.C.H.C.

DEED - TOLER TO DANDRIDGE
D. 23d day of March 1791

        Adam Toler and Mary his wife by deed bearing date the 23d
day of March 1791 and of record in the County Court of Hanover, conveyed unto Nathaniel West Dandridge one certain tract or parcel of land
in the County of Hanover, it being part of the tract of land the said
Toler now lives on, known by the name of Boswell's old tract, containing 150 Acres as appears from under the hand of Mr. John Street, surveyor for the said County, bounded as followeth: Beginning at a bunch
of Laurells on the ditch of dry slash, running thence North one degree,
East 174 poles along a new line of marked trees to pointers three small
pines on the main road, thence down the said road 105 poles to a corner
white oak bush thence South 2½ degrees East 41 poles along a line of
marked trees to a corner Post Oak, thence along a line of marked trees
South 72 degrees East 140 poles thence South eight degrees East four
poles to a rock stone in Allen's Creek thence up the run of the said
Creek to the mouth of the dry slash, thence up the middle of the same
to the beginning ... Teste William Pollard C. H. C. Hano.Office
May 20th. 1818.

DEED - TOLER ET UX TO DANDRIDGE
D. 15th. day of September 1796

        Adam Toler and Mary his wife, by deed bearing date the 15th
day of September 1796 and of record in the County Court of Hanover,
conveyed to Nathaniel West Dandridge one certain tract of land in the
County of Hanover and Parish of St. Martins, bounded as followeth:
Beginning at a corner bunch of Laurels on the dry slash, and running
thence North 1 degree East 174 poles along a new line of marked trees
to a corner pointers three pine bushes on the road thence up the road
one hundred and nine poles to a corner red Oak, thence North 79 degrees
West 85 poles to a corner on the Hill, thence N 1 degree West 6 poles
& 17 links to a corner large white Oak, thence South 47½ degrees West
141 poles through the field to a corner near the head of a drean,
thence 40½ degrees West 92 poles to a corner on Turkey Creek, thence
up the said Creek as it meanders to a corner beach on the Road, thence
down the road 6 poles to a corner white oak, thence along Jenning's
line South 30 degrees thence South 48 degrees West 13 poles to pointers

Toler et Ux to Dandridge, cont.:

thence South 27½ degrees East 65 poles to a white oak stump on William
Hardin's line, and on his line North 51 degrees East 42 poles to a Post
Oak, thence South 3 degrees East 136 poles, thence South 3 degrees West
105 poles to two Oaks and a Hickory on Letcher's road, thence on Claiborne Watkins line South 60 degrees East 97 poles to a heap of stones
on Robert Dandridge's line and on his line North 16 degrees East 54
poles, thence North 25 degrees East 173 poles to a corner Post Oak,
between Robert Dandridge and Richard Anderson, thence along Letcher's
road as it meanders north 15 degrees East 16 poles thence North 6 degrees West 18 poles, thence North 15 degrees West 76 poles to a branch,
thence down the said branch as it meanders to a dry slash & along the
said slash to the beginning & containing five hundred & twenty three
acres -   Teste William Pollard, C. H. C. Hano. Office May 20th 1818.

MANTLO ET UX TO DANDRIDGE
17th. day of April, 1798

        James Mantelo and Lucy his wife by deed bearing date the 17th
day of April, 1798, conveyed unto Nathaniel West Dandridge all that
tract or parcel of land whereon James Mantelo then lived in the County
of Hanover containing 140⅔ acres lying on the branches of Turkey Creek
and bounded as follows, Beginning at a corner white Oak and pine stump,
thence South 60½ East 60 chains thence So. 8 West 67 chs. to a white
Oak & red Oak, thence North 68 West 23½ chs. thence North 69 West 39½
chs. to a spanish and red oak, thence North 1½ East 44 chs. to a dead
poplar in Walker's branch, thence North 34 East 46 chs. to a blasted
pine thence North 80 east 5½ chs. to a persimmon thence 49 East 33 chs.
to the beginning. Teste William Pollard, C. H. C. Hano. Of.20 May,1818

Donald Scott & Co)
vs) Hanover
Foster's admrs & al) 1803 (43)

William Morris, Plt.)
vs) Hanover
Peter Foster, admr) 1797
of Thomas Foster, decd. Dft.) (43)

      In Hanover County Court September 4, 1794, Robert Fleming, William B. Christian, James Parker and Samuel Crutchfield, or any three of them, being first sworn before a Justice of the Peace, are appointed to appraise all the personal estate of Thomas Foster, decd.
      A Copy   Teste   Thomas Rogers D C H C-

      Admrs. Bond; dated 4 Sept., 1794. Peter Foster, admr. of Thomas Foster, Deced. Bartlett Anderson & George Nailor, securities. Thomas Tinsley, Thomas White, Wm. O. Winston & Wm. Winston, Gentn., Justices of the Court of Hanover. L200. Rec. Hanover Co., Thursday, the 4th of Septr., 1794. Peter Foster, Bartlett Anderson & George Nailor ackn. bond. Test William Pollard C H C
A Copy Nov. 1802 Teste Tho Pollard D C H C

      1794. Mr. Peter Foster to John Brown, Clerk of the General Court - To Recording the certificate of administration of Thomas Foster's estate - 18 cents   J. Brown

      In Hanover County Court April 22, 1797, William Morris, Plt., against Peter Foster, admor. of Thomas Foster deced., Deft. - Jury: Abraham Netherland, William Corley, Major Winfree, Walter Chisholm, James Hart, John Batkins, Francis Timberlake, Nathaniel Whitlock, James Byars, William Mallory, William Barker & John Gibson, "who joined upon their oaths do say that the said Peter Foster, at the time of plaintiff's suing out of the original writ had fully administered all the goods & chattels which belonged to said Thomas Foster, at the time of his death, in his hands to be administered ... dismissed
      A Copy   Teste   Tho   Pollard D C H C

      Bond - Thos. Foster to Eleasabeth Jinnings - both of Hanover Town; dated 10 December 1785; L91.2. Wit. Peter Foster, Mary Foster: Dec. 15, 1785 - By 1 Bead L10. By 1 Chest drawers L3. By Cow Earling L1.10. By 1 Tea Table L.10. By 1 Square do L3. By 1 Cubbird L2. - L18.

      Bond - Thomas Foster to John Clarke, Adm. of Wm. Clarke, late of the County of Hanover, deced. L57.4, Gold or Silver. D. 6 June, 1783. Peter Foster, Sec. Witnesse - Jono. Gardner.

      Subpoena, d. 4 Mar., 1803. Sheriff's report: "Executed upon Peter Foster May 7, 1803. I am informed that Bartlett Anderson is dead and George Nailor is not an Inhabitant." Sgd. T. D. Harris, D. M. for Jos. Scott, M. V. D.

THE DEPOSITION OF LUCY CLARKE

The deposition of Lucy Clarke taken upon oath at Her House in Hanover Town on the 2nd day of June 1809, who saith that she was living with the testator or intestate at the time of his death and remained at the place until the property belonging to his estate was sold by the admr. She also saith that she believes the estate of Thomas Foster decd was mortgaged to Robt Johnson or Robert & Christopher Johnson some time before his death. Certified under our hands the date above -   J. Starke   Wm White

THE DEPOSITION OF LUCY CLARKE

The deposition of Lucy Clarke of Lawful age taken at the Dwelling House of Capt Peter Foster, who saith that the articles entered upon the Bond given by her father Thomas Foster decd to Elizabeth Jennings were sold at the sale made by the Administrator on the 6th day of October 1794 as the estate of sd Thomas Foster ... She well recollects that the Bed was purchased by Samuel Richardson - the Chest of Drawers by Peter Crutchfield - the Cupboard by George Nailor, the Square Walnut Table by Zachariah Clarke & the Tea Table by Doctor Murchant - She further saith that it was not known that the above recited articles were entered on the Bond until it was presented for payment - She further saith that she well recollects that William D. Yeal boarded with her father Thomas Foster decd. while he was in the employment of Thomas Simpson on his Acct but the year she does not recollect - She thinks it was about the year 1774 - but how long she does not know - Hanover County to wit - Sworn to before us 18 Oct., 1809, J. W. Ellis and William White.

Sales of the estate of Thomas Foster Decd. made 5th Oct 1794; purchasers were: Nathaniel Anderson, Jr., L25.5.6; Saml. Crutchfield, L16.19.6; John Clarke, n .19.; James Parker, L2.3.6; Peter Foster, L13.17.3.; Robert Foster, L.19.6; Wm. B. Christian, L.19.6.; Zach. Clarke, L23.14.10.; Alexr. Hallam, L1.16.3.; Peter Crutchfield, L21.4.6; George Nailor, L7.12.3.; Saml. Bird, L.17.0.; Wm. Walker, L.13.6.; Ledger Merchant, L16.12.; Robert Fleming, L.18.0.; Saml. Richardson, L9.10.0.; Total, L144.1.1.   Peter Foster, Admr.

Colo. Thomas Tinsley's Certificate: I do certify that Zachariah Clarke, decd. joined Thomas Foster, decd., as his surety to Thos. Stuart, jr., of Augusta County in the sum of L3.15, payable the 15th May 1782, which sd. note was taken up by John Oliver, decd., of Bath Co. ... That a considerable part of said debt is still due from sd Oliver's estate to sd. Clarke's est., of which estate Peter Foster is exor. D. 21 Oct., 1808. - Commissioner's Office, Richmond, 4 Dec. 1808, Sworn to before Patk. Hendren, M. Commissioner.

William Lawrence, Surv. exor. of)
John Lawrence, decd., plt.)   U. S. Cir. Ct.
          against)
Edmund Taylor)   1811 (48)

Smith's exor)
          vs)   (In Hanover County - 1784)
Lawrence's ex)

Will of JOHN LAWRENCE, of HANOVER COUNTY, VIRGINIA.
Dated 7th day of May, 1778

In the name of God Amen, I John Lawrence of the Parish of Saint
Martin and County of Hanover do make and ordain this writing to be my
last Will and Testament in manner following. Item I desire that all
my just debts be first paid. Item my Will and desire is that the Land
I sold to Edmund Taylor whereon he now lives being part of the tract
of Land I purchased of Peter Lyons Gent. attorney for James Goldart
Esqr. of Liverpool, Bounded on the lines of John Day, Nelson Berkeley
Gent. Alsup Yarbrough, John Thornton thence along Goodall's line to
a corner Red Oak near Goodalls fence, thence along a new line made
agreeable to a survey made by Wm. Pettit surveyor of Louisa Containing three hundred nine and half acres more or less and the said Edmd.
Taylor not having a Deed or conveyance for said Land I will and desire
the above said Land to the said Edmd. Taylor and to his heirs and
assigns forever on condition that he the said Taylor's paying to my
estate the sum of fourteen shills. and seven pence Currt. Money with
Interest from October Seventeen hundred and sixty nine - Item my will
and desire is that John Bumpass hold and enjoy half my Mill which I sold
him to him and his assigns forever. Item all the remainder of My Lands
I Desire may be sold by my Exrs. and the money arising from such sale to
be equally divided with the remainder of my estate be it whatsoever
kind among all my Children namely John Lawrence, James Lawrence, Eliza.
Lawrence, Harry Lawrence, Nancy Lawrence, and Edmd. Lawrence, to them
and their heirs and assigns forever. Item my Will and desire is that
if any of my said Children shou'd die before they come of age or have
Lawful Issue that then the part of my estate given him, her or them,
shall be equally divided among those of my children then Living to
them and their heirs and assigns forever. Item Lastly I do appoint
my sons John Lawrence, William Lawrence and James Lawrence Executors
of this my last Will and Testament, making void all other Wills by me
before made. In Witness whereof I have hereunto set my hand and seal
this 7th day of May 1778

Witnesses   John Lawrence (Seal)
J. Thomson
Nelson Berkeley
Paul Woolfolk

Codicil to this Will

Item I give to my son William Lawrence one bay mare known by the name of Jenny.

Item I give to my son James Lawrence one bay mare Colt by the name of Sorrel Mares Colt

Item I give to my son Harry Lawrence one bay mare Colt known by the name of Jenny's Colt.

Item I give to my son Edwd. Lawrence Hampton's mare Colt and twenty pounds Currt. money

Witnesses   John Lawrence
Jno. Thomson
Nelson Berkeley
Paul Woolfolk

At a Court continued and held for Hanover County on Monday the 9th day of May 1791

This last Will and Testm. of John Lawrence deceased, was offered for proof by William Lawrence and James Lawrence executors therein named and was proved by the oath of Nelson Berkeley and Paul Woolfolk two of the Witnesses thereto and also by the oath of the said Execu-tors, and is ordered to be recorded

                    Test   William Pollard jr C H C

November 1805

            A Copy

                    Teste   Thomas Pollard D C H C

Inventory and appraisement of the estate of John Lawrence
decd. taken November 30th 1791 -

Negroes

Jeffery, Saunders	0 . 0.. 0	
Thornton L25, Dick L35	60 . 0 . 0	
Taylor L60, Judy L30	90 . 0 . 0	
Michael L60, Sally L45	105 . 0 . 0	
Fanny L, Betty L30	70 . 0 . 0	
Kezey L, Lisey L12.10	30 .10 . 0	
Harry Randolph 125/.	6 . 5 . 0	
David Anderson	6 . 5 . 0	
Cate L30, Amy L50	80 . 0 . 0	
Billey L45, Ralph L35	80 . 0 . 0	
Edmund L15, Alsey 125/.	21 . 5 . 0	654 . 5 . 0
Lucy L30, Dolly L45	75 . 0 . 0	
Aron L40, Frank L35	75 . 0 . 0	
Lewis L15, Thornton 125/.	21 . 5 . 0	
Milley L35, Jenny L35	70 . 0 . 0	
Phillis L10, Rachel 125/.	16 . 5 . 0	
Silah L45, Isbell L15	60 . 0 . 0	
Daniel L15, Molly L10	25 . 0 . 0	
Beck L45, Aggy 125/.	51 . 5 . 0	
Nanny L45, Isham L17.10	62 .10 . 0	456 . 5 . 0
Flora L35, Barnaba L50	85 . 0 . 0	
Armistead L45, Bob L35	80 . 0 . 0	
Solomon	25 . 0 . 0	
Marcia L40, Hanbury L20	60 . 0 . 0	
Eather L15, Charles L10, Joseph 125/.	31 . 5 . 0	
Sabina L45, Jack L35	80 . 0 . 0	
Leah L5, Matt	45 . 0 . 0	
Robin 125/., Sukey L45	51 . 5 . 0	
Charlotte	6 . 5 . 0	463 .15 . 0
		1574 . 5 . 0

Inventory and appraisement of the estate of John Lawrence:
(Continued)

1/2 Dozen Table & 1/2 dozen tea spoons	7 . 0 . 0
2 butter pots 4/6. 1 decanter 2/.	6 . 6
1 Copper kettle 70/. 1 skillet 8/	3 .18 . 0
A parcel of earthen ware	12 . 6
3 Sad Irons knives &C	6 . 0
6 Bottles	1 . 6
1 Sword 20/. 1 case rasors 6/	1 . 6 . 0
A parcel of old Iron	1 . 6 . 0
2 Cow hides	17 . 6
5 bee hives	1 . 7 . 6
78 Barrels Corn ε 8/	31 . 4 . 0
97 Treek (?) tops 1/	4 .17 . 0
2151 lbs. blades 2/6 pct.	2 .13 . 9
18 lbs wool 1/3	1 . 2 . 6
4/4 bus. pease 3/	12 . 9 57 . 5 . 6

Ł 1912 . 10 -

        In conformity to the annexed order of H. Court we the
subscribers being duly sworn have appraised the negroes and personal estate of John Lawrence, deceased, a list of which is herewith inclosed

        Certified this 30th November 1791

                                Thos. Price
                                Wm. Winston
                                John Day

                                William Lawrence exr
                                of John Lawrence decd

At a Court of monthly session held for Hanover county at the
courthouse on Wednesday the 15th of August 1798

        This Inventory and appraisement of the estate of John
Lawrence decd was returned and is ordered to be recorded

                Teste

                                William Pollard C. H. C.
        A Copy
                toste
                                Tho. Pollard D. C. H. C.

Inventory and appraisement of the estate of John Lawrence:
(Continued)

1 Bay Mare L9. 1 Ditto L15. 1 Ditto L10	34 . 0 . 0	
1 Blk Horse L8. 1 bay ditto L10	18 . 0 . 0	
1 Sorrel ditto	9 . 0 . 0	
36 Sheep 10/	18 . 0 . 0	
1 old steer 40/. 3 yearlings 36/	3 .16 . 0	
23 Cattle 35/	40 . 5 . 0	
1 Yoke Oxen	8 . 0 . 0	
39 Hogs 8/	15 .12 . 0	
1 Sow and pigs	1 .15 . 0	
29 hogs 18/	26 . 2 . 0	174 .10 -

A parcel of plantation utensils	7 .10 . 0	
A parcel of kitchen furniture	1 .15 .	
A parcel of Carpenters tools	17 . 6	
4 reap hooks	4 .	
4 Scythe blades and 3 cradles	1 . 8 . 0	
3 spinning wheels	10 . 0	
4 pr hames 10/. 1 pr Iron traces 12/	1 . 2 . 0	
A parcel of leather	1 .10 . 0	
A parcel of pewter	15 . 0	
Ox cart and chains	3 .10 . 0	
Tea kettle, Coffee pot &c	1 .10 . 0	
8 Casks 24/. A parcel ditto 15/	1 .19 . 0	
14 Geese	1 . 8 . 0	
Old chair carriage	3 . 0 . 0	
Old wheat fan and hhds	12 . 0	
1 Loom 25/ harness &c 18/	2 . 3 . 0	
1 Desk 80/. 1 bible 12/.	4 .12 . 0	34 . 5 . 6

1 Cask and 2 tubs	9 . 0	
3 Feather beds	13 .10 . 0	
1 ditto 160/. 1 ditto 160/	16 . 0 . 0	
2 ditto and furniture ea L10	20 . 0 . 0	
4 blankets and quilt 60/	3 . 0 . 0	
Old Desk	2 . 0 . 0	
8 lbs feathers a 2/6	1 . 0 . 0	
4 Tables 48/. 18 chairs 66/	5 .14 . 0	
1 pr scales and weights	7 . 6	
1 Case Lancets 2/6 1 gun 50/.	2 .12 . 6	
1 Case and bottles 8/ 1 Jug 3/	11 . 0	
1 Silver watch 80/ Spice mortar 12/	4 .12 . 0	
1 Chest 10/. 1 Jarr 6/	16 . 0	
1 Looking glass and dressing table	1 . 0 . 0	
1 Chest and trunk	12 . 0	72 . 4 . 0

Lawrences exors.   ) 1811 (48)
     vs   ) U. S. Circt. Ct.
Littlepage   ) 5th Circt. Va. Dist.

    At a Court held for Hanover County at the court house on
Thursday the 7th of February 1793
    William Lawrence and James Lawrence executors of John Law-
late Sheriff of this County decd., Plts.,   against
    Richard Littlepage late deputy Sheriff for the said John Law-
rence, Barttelot Anderson, Robert Page, Ciceley Anderson, administratrix of William Anderson decd. and Benjamin Toler exor. of John Jones,
decd. which said Barttelot Anderson, Robert Page, William Anderson,
and John Jones were securities for Littlepage's due performance of the
said office of Deputy Sheriff, Defds.

    Upon notices of motions to the December Court for Judgments
for all arrears of the revenue & certificate taxes due from the said
County of Hanover for the year 1785 and which were assigned to the said
Richard Littlepage for collection which notices were continued by consent of the parties from Court to Court until this time,
    This day came as well the Plaintiffs by David Bullock and Ed-
mund Berkeley junr their attorneys as the Defendant Littlepage by William DuVal, John Warden, Nathaniel Pope junr. and Matthew Page Junr. his
attornies. It is considered by the Court that the said motion as to the
Defendant Littlepage be dismissed and that the said Defendant Littlepage recover against the said Plaintiffs his costs in this behalf expended. And on motion of the Plaintiffs the said motion is dismissed
as to the other Defendants. A Copy   William Pollard C H C

    The Commonwealth of Virginia - To the Sheriff of Hanover Co.:
Greeting: We command you that of the goods & chattels of Richard Littlepage late deputy sheriff under John Lawrence late sheriff of Hanover
Co. in your bailiwick you cause to be made L1559.4.9.1 which William
Lawrence and James Lawrence exors. of the said John Lawrence late in
our District Court held at the Capitol in the City of Richmond recovered
against him for the balance due from him of the revenue taxes collected
by him in the said county of Hanover for the years 1735 & 1786 including the damages on said taxes according to Law with interest on L488..13
part thereof to be computed after the rate of 5 per centum per annum
from the 1st day of May 1786, and on L1071.4.7.½ the residue at like
rate from the 1st day of April 1787 till paid; & the further sum of
L1137.10.11 balance of certificate taxes collected by said Littlepage
in said county for the years 1785-1786, including damages, etc., with
interest on L510.14.7 thereof to be computed after the rate of 5 per
centum from the 31st of January 1787, etc.; also L3.1.1. the said
Richard Littlepage's proportion of the costs arising upon the executions
issued on behalf of the Commonwealth against the said John upon the
Judgments obtained against him for the revenue taxes of 1785 & revenue
& certificate taxes of 1786, also $5.06 costs in this behalf expended
whereof sd. Richd. Littlepage is convict as appears to us of record ...
Wit. John Robinson, Clerk of our said Court at Richmond the 18 June
1799, 23d year of our foundation -   sgd.   J Robinson

Overton   )1814 (#53)
  vs   ) U. S. Cir. Ct.
Honeyman & DuVal) 5th Cir. Va. Dist.
  (1801)

To the Honourable the Judges &c ... of the 4th Circuit,
Eastern District of Virginia -

  Your Orator Waller Overton who is an inhabitant of the State
of Kentucky sheweth that on or about the 24th of February 1780 he having engaged in partnership with Clough Overton for the purpose of lo-
cating & surveying lands on the Waters of the Ohio for such as needed
agents in such business on shares, undertook by bond dated the same day
to locate and survey for Doctor Robert Honeyman 3000 acres on the Ohio
or its branches they to have one fourth of the land so located ... That
about the Month of July 1782 Clough Overton was killed by the Indians
at the battle of blue licks and the business was afterwards commenced
and finished by your Orator ... the necessary papers for obtaining patents delivered to the said Robert Honeyman, who assigned them to William DuVal Esquire who obtained patents for the same ... Your orator believing himself intitled in Equity and also under the Law of Jointten-
nancy in force at the time of Clough Overton's death, to the one fourth
of the land so located and surveyed hath applied to the said Honeyman
and William DuVal for a conveyance of the same which they have refused
saying they do not think they can with safety make the conveyance without a decree of a Court of Chancery. In consideration whereof, etc...

ANSWER OF RICHARD OVERTON

  The answer of Richard Overton Heir at Law and one of the devisees of Clough Overton, Deced. ...that Clough Overton died unmarried without issue, Teste, but leaving seven Brothers towit, Richard Overton,
this Defendant his Eldest Brother, John Overton, James Overton (who is
since deceased without issue), George Overton, Dabney C. Overton, William Overton & Thomas Overton, and three Sisters, Mary Overton, Elizabeth
C. Overton, and Sarah B. Overton. Clough Overton appointed Waller Overton, the Complainant, Joseph Lindsay, Ebernezer Miller & William Stewart, Executors. Eben. Miller qualified. All the executors are since
dead except Waller Overton who never qualified as exec. This Defendant
doth aver that himself and agent hath been for nearly twelve years in
in the quiet and peacible possession of 500 acres a part of said 3000
a. divided as afsd. This Defendant whilst in that Country boarded in
the Complainant's House but never heard of the Claim until the filing of
the present Bill, long after this Deft. had settled in the State of N.C.
Sworn to in City of Richmond before Wm. McKim, Mag. 3 Nov. 1803.

  Va. Louisa Co. Sc.:18 Nov., 1802. Saml. Overton, Junr. made
oath before George Pottie, J. P. for sd. Co., that Richard Overton,
Mary Overton, Bath C. Lacy & Elizabeth his wife, formerly Elizabeth Overton, John, Dabney, George, William, Thomas and Sally or Sarah Overton
are not inhabitants of the State of Virginia.
  Fayette Co., Ky.15 Oct.,1803; Levi Todd, Clk. of Ct. Thos.
Wallace, J.P.: John Overton made oath that Clough Overton was killed on
the 19th day of August, 1782 by the Indians at the Battle of Blue Licks.
  Richmond,Va. 17 Nov.,1802. Samuel Myers, Mag. Wm. DuVal made
oath that Robert Honeyman transferred sd. 3000 a. to him and that he
trans. one-fourth part of same to sd. complt. & Clough Overton in 1797
while in Ky. This Deft. believes he left the deed with his son Saml. P.
DuVal of Ky. to deliver to the parties.

Hanbury's Exors.) 1815 (#55)
    vs   ) U. S. Circt. Ct.
Page   ) 5th Circt. Va. Dist.

Lloyd Exor. of Hanbury) 1852 (#137)
    vs   ) U. S. Circt. Ct.
Pages Adm. &C (1807)) 5th Circt. Va. Dist.

        To the honble the Judges, etc.... Humbly complaining sheweth,
Your Orator John Lloyd a British subject surviving acting exor. of Os-
good Hanbury who was surviving partner of Capel and Osgood Hanbury late
Merchants and partners of the City of London - That on the third day of
May in the year of our Lord 1768 Mann Page Esquire now deceased of
Mannsfield in the County of Spotsylvania being indebted to the said
Capel and Osgood Hanbury in the sum of L5742:8:4 Stg: with Interest ex-
ecuted a Deed of Mortgage conveying to them in Fee Simple a Tract of
Land in the County of Hanover whereof he was then seized called Mehixan,
containing by estimation 900 acres, also 87 slaves then on the said
Tract of Land, likewise 2000 acres in the County of King William on the
Pamunkey River called Claibornes neck ... also that the said Deed of
Mortgage should stand and be a security for any further advances made
by the said Capel and Osgood Hanbury to the said Mann Page with interest thereon ...That the said Capel and Osgood Hanbury received sundry
payments from said Page and made advances to him ... That the said Mann
Page died during the late war between Great Britain and America. That
he left a last Will whereof he appointed Mann Page of Mannsfield his
son Executor by which he devised large Estates in Lands and slaves to
the said Mann Page charged with the payment of the said debt ... That
the said Mann Page the Elder by his Will devised a part and perhaps the
whole of the Mortgaged slaves and the said Mortgaged Lands to Robert
Page one of his sons. That the said Robert Page is since dead having
left Issue two sons towit Chas. Carter Page and Mann Page & by his last
Will & Testament devised all the mortgaged property which had been devised him aforesaid by his father to his said sons ... That Mann Page
the Executor of Mann Page the Elder was originally chargeable with the
greater part of the said Debt and that the same was to be apportioned
between him and the said sons of Robert Page but he having been Exor.
also of the said Robert Page and Guardian to his said Children and having been for a number of years in full possession of all the property
real and personal and in the receipts of profits thereof they being
still Infants under his Guardianship he made repeated assurances of providing for the payment of the whole and in conformity with these assurances considerable payments were made from time to time. That Mann Page
sold a valuable Estate in the County of Prince William for the purpose
of paying the amount of a Decree which was entered on the 19th day of
December 1800 for a foreclosure of said mortgage... That the said Mann
Page departed this life about the year --- and Robert Patton Esqr. adm.
on his estate and took possession of his slaves and personal property
which was of great value and the Bulk of which had come into his possession by the death of said Mann Page the Elder ... Your Orator further sheweth that the payments made by the said Charles Carter Page and
Mann Page the Younger as they allege amount to more than they ought to
be charged with by virtue of the Estates held by them even if the said
Mann Page the Executor had not been legally indebted to them ... and

your Orator's Agent believing that the Estate of the said Mann Mage the
Exor. ought to be charged with the whole of the said Debt is unwilling
to proceed against them unless it should appear that the debt cannot be
charged on the said Mann Page the Executor ...

WILL OF ROBERT CARTER PAGE OF HANOVER CO.
D. 25 November, 1780 - P. 4 April, 1782.

    In the name of God Amen I Robert Carter Page of the county of
Hanover do make this my last will and testament-
    After all my just debts are paid I give and grant to my two
sons Mann Page and Charles Carter Page all my lands lying in the counties of Hanover & King William, together with all my negroes stocks &c
thereon except such as may hereafter be excepted to be between them
equally divided in such manner as their guardians may think most proper,
the division not to take place untill my son Mann Page comes to the age
of twenty one years, during whose minority I desire the estate may be
kept in one body and the profits arising from it to be equally divided
between them, after paying the expences of a liberal education, cloath-
ing &c.
    I give to my daughter Elizabeth Page the sum of fifteen hund-
red pounds of Money to be paid in gold or silver or in paper money an
equivalent to the aforementioned sum to be paid out of the estate left
my sons Mann and Charles Carter Page - my daughter to be maintained out
of the estate as her guardians may think necessary I also give to her
the girl Mary that waits upon her, with her issue and any two girls of
the age of twelve she shall choose out of my estate either when she marries or comes to the age of twenty one years. I also desire her fortune may be paid at the above mentioned time provided the profits from
the estate will admit of it; if not to be paid as soon as possible. I
could wish in the division of the said land &c. in the counties aforesaid, that the house which is now building with all my furniture, should
fall to my son Mann Page I also give to my son Mann the maid Sarah with
her issue exclusive of the division of the rest of my negroes - To my
son Charles I also give the girl Sally with her issue. Ned I particularly request my brother Mann Page to take charge of as a waiting man to
my son Mann, and his wife to make & mend all my children's clothes I
give to my son Mann my gold watch - I give to my son Charles Carter
Page my silver watch - to my daughter Elizabeth I give her mother's
gold watch and any trinkets that might have belonged to her. I give to
my brother Mann Page my horse Oscar, and Jenny Dismal. I do hereby appoint Mann Page, John Page, Charles Carter, Benjamin Harrison, and
George Baylor esquires as guardians and exets. to all my children - I
desire that before any division shall be made of my negroes, that the
agreement entered into with my brothers John & Mann Page to make provision for my brothers Gwynn & Matthew Page be fully complied with -
    In witness whereof I hereunto set my hand and seal this twen-
ty fifth day of November one thousand seven hundred & eighty
Test: Mann Page   Ro. C. Page (Seal)
Thomas Hughes, George Baylor

At a Court held for Hanover county on thursday the 4th day of Apr 1782
This last will & testament of Robert Carter Page gentn. deceased was
offered to proof by Mann Page & Benjamin Harrison esqrs. executors

therein named and was proved by the oath of Thomas Hughes a witness thereto and also by the oath of the said executor, whereupon it is ordered that the said will be recorded as to the personal estate thereby conveyed and that the same should be certified as to the real estate

May 1798   A Copy   Test   W. Pollard Junr   C. H. C.
                  teste   Tho. Pollard   D. C. H. C.

LIST OF LOTS SOLD AT HANOVER TOWN BY MANN PAGE EXOR. OF MANN PAGE, DECD. 17 Feby. 1785

No.	Price	Names of Purchasors	No.	Price	Names of Purchasors
27	£23.00	Doctor Read	34	£38.00	Malcolm Hart
28	11.	do.	23	38.	ditto
40	37.	John Tinsley	12	15. 5.	ditto
39	25.	(Saml. Tinsley	63	24.10.	Mann Sawterhite
.		(Saml. Crutchfield	101	17.	Jos. Brand
33	47.	James Parker	122	36. 5.	Micajah Crew
72	75.	Robt. Johnston	100	15. 5.	Jos. Brand
51	16.	Ed. Clarke	82	12. 5.	Cary Wyatt
71	48.	Thos. Tinsley	37	16. 5.	Wm. Thornton
68	12.	Doctr. John Quinlan	119	21.	Joseph Brand
132	13.	Doctr. Read) J.K.Read	118	15.	ditto
133	14.10	Clods. Veal)	83	13.	Mann Page
148	14.	do.) C.V. bought	24)		
149	12.	do.) for T.Garland	35)		
67	13.10.	Edmd. Clarke	36)	250.	Crutchfd. Insp.
50	20. 5.	do.	47)		Mann Page
73	57.10	Mordecai Booth	48)		
66	13.	Edmd. Clarke	49)		
84	14.5	Geo. Wiley	15	9.	Saml. Bird
104	55.	John Christian	14	8.	Wyatt Yancey
1&2)			11	23.	Zacheriah Clarke
7&8)	460.	(Pages Inspn.	98	11. 5.	Cary Wyatt
9&10)		(Mann Page	6	12.	Wm. Cook
105	55.	John Christian	123	24.10	John Timberlake
38	15.	Saml. Tinsley	85	17. 5	Geo. Wiley
88	55.	Edmd. Clarke	65	18. 5	Wm. McClure
89	50.	Wm. Dabney	64	18.10	Mann Savterhite
17	31	Mann Page Jno Garland			

57 lots sold for £1846:10:0

Terms of the above sale
the bonds are to carry interest
from the date if not punctually
paid

A copy   Tho. Tinsley

John Murdock & Company   ) 1807 (#37)

vs   ) U. S. Cir. Ct.

Parke Goodall and Thomas Tinsley,) 5th Circt. Va. Dist.

securities, &C   )

Murdock & Co.   ) 1808 (#57)

vs   ) U. S. Cir. Ct.

Pearson's Heirs   ) 5th Circt. Va. Dist.

John Murdock and Company, Plaintiffs, against Parke Goodall and Thomas Tinsley, securities to the administration of John Hicks, administrator of Samuel Pearson, deceased, and Peter Crutchfield, deputy Sheriff, to whom was committed the estate of John Hicks, deceased, and Edmund Pearson, John Pearson, Elizabeth Pearson, Susanne Pearson, Maria Pearson, Sarah Pearson, Rebecca Pearson, Fanny Pearson, James Pearson and Livinia Pearson, children and devisees of the said Samuel Pearson, deceased, Defendants.

WILL OF SAMUEL PEARSON

Dated 9 July, 1790

Recorded 3 July, 1794

In the NAME OF GOD AMEN I Samuel Pearson of the county of Hanover being unwell but of sound mind and memory, do make this as my last will & testament disposing of my estate in manner following –

Imprimis my will and desire is, that after the payment of my just debts, then all my estate both real & personal, I give to be equally divided Between all my children, when they shall come to the age of twenty one years. Lastly 1 do appoint my good nds (sic) John Hicks & Robert Duncan executors of this my last Will & testament & do revoke every other will or wills by me heretofore made. In Witness whereof I have hereunto set my hand & seal, this 9th day of July 1790

Sealed & Published   Saml. Pearson (Seal)

In the presence of

John Pendleton

Josias Bingham

Sarah Pendleton

At a Court held for Hanover county at the Courthouse on Thursday the 3d. of July 1794

This last will & testament of Samuel Pearson deceased was offered for proof by John Hicks an executor therein named & was

John Murdock & Co. vs
Park Goodall & Thomas Tinsley, cont.:

Proof of Will of Samuel Pearson, cont.:

and was proved by the oath of John Pendleton & Josias Bingham, witnesses thereto, & also by the oath of the said executor & is ordered to be recorded –

November 1802   A Copy   Test   William Pollard C.H.C.
teste   Tho. Pollard D. C. H. C.

BOND OF SAMUEL PEARSON

I Samuel Pearson of Newcastle, Hanr. County do promise to pay to John Murdock & Company of Glasgow Merchants or their Assigns ... £29 Current Money on or before the twenty fifth Decenr. next ensuing... Eleventh day of May Anno Don. 1774
Wit. John Hicks   Samuel Pearson (Seal)

LAND OF SAMUEL PEARSON

William Mann, being duly sworn, etc., saith that Samuel Pearson died seized and possessed of a tract of land in the county of Hanover on Pamunkey river near the Buck   creek ford, and on which the said Samuel resided at the time of his death – November term 1807.

INVENTORY OF ESTATE OF SAMUEL PEARSON, DECD.
16th day of July 1794

4 works steers @ 80/.	£ 16.	
6 Cows & 3 Calves @ 50/.	15.	
8 Other Cattle	10.	
25 head of sheep & lambs	12.	10
2 Colts	15.	
1 Sorrel mare	2.	
1 Bay mare	15.	
1 Grey horse	8.	
1 bay mere	15.	
Peter a negro man	60.	
Ephram a do. do.	60.	
America a do. do.	30.	
Jemmey a do. do.	30.	
Ben a do. do.	45.	
Hannah a negro woman	25.	
Esmah a do.	45.	
Daphney a negro child	20.	
Philby a do. do.	15.	

John Murdock & Co. va
Parke Goodall & Thomas Tinsley, cont.:

Inventory of Estate of Samuel Pearson, decd., cont.:

	£ s. d.
Isham a negro boy	£ 50.
Billy a do. do.	35.
Ben a do. do.	28.
Bevely a do. do.	18.
6 hogs @ 20/.	6.
7 shoats @ 9/.	3. 3.
2 Sows 6 shoats & 6 pigs	3. 18.
1 Ox Cart	6.
1 X Cut saw	1. 5.
4 Grubbing hoes	10.
5 Axes 12/. Sundry tools 19/6	1. 11. 6
4 Trowel hoes & 1 Colter 12/.)	1. 4.
5 Syth blades 12/)	
3 Sythe Cradles @ 4/	12.

£591. 13. 6

Amo: brot. over   £591. 13. 6

	£ s. d.
1 Bed Mattress & furniture	12.
1 Dressing table & glass	1. 5.
16 Small pictures @ 2/	1. 12.
18 leather bottom chairs @ 12/.	10. 16.
3 Tables	4. 8.
1 Blk walnut desk & bookcase	8.
1 do. Corner Cupboard	5.
1 Looking Glass	1. 10.
2 Tea boards 12/. 1 Gunn £3	3. 12.
1 Table & 1 stand 42/. 1 Chest of Draws 70/	5. 12.
2 Beds Bedsteads	15.
2 Arm chairs 40/ 1 Corner Cupboard 20/.	3.
1 Looking glass 6/. 1 map 6/.	12.
2 Beds & furniture	12.
1 Table 10/. 1 Trunk 20/.	1. 10.
1 Pr. fire shovel & tongs	6.
1 Cradle 5/. 1 Table 20/. 3 Trunks 24/	2. 9.
1 Bed & furniture	9.
2 Chirs 4/. 2 Spinning wheels 10/.	14.
1 Mans saddle 24/. 1 flax wheel 12/.	1. 16.
2 Jugs 5/. 1 Pr. Saddle bags 15/	1.
3 Reap hooks 3/9. 5 Empty cask 12/	15. 9.
3 Stone pots 6/. 2 Pewter Basons 6/.	12.
1 Powter 2 qt. measure 3/	3.
5 do. Candle moulds 7/6	7. 6.
1 do. & 1 pt. measure	2.
1 Tin funnel 1/6 1 Rat trap 7/6	9.

Inventory of Estate of Samuel Pearson, decd., cont.:

5 Candle sticks, muffers & tray	£ 1.		
1 Old brass motor	. 15.		
1 Pr. scales & weights	1.		
1 Case & Bottles 20/. 1 Trunk 12/	1. 12.		
2 Cannisters	3.		
3 Stone Potts 8/. 2 Stone jugs 2/6	10.	6.	
1 Gallon Jug 1/6 2 Cannisters 2/6		4.	
1 Sive 3/. 5 Barrels 15/. 6 hoes 24/	2. 2.		
3 Wedges 12/. 1 narrow ax 2/6	14.	6.	
4 Iron Potts 24/. 2 Dutch ovens 6/.	1. 10.		
Sundry Kitchen furniture	1. 19.		
1 Pewter cullender 6/. 1 Spice moter 12/	18.		
1 Bell mettle skillet 6/. 4 Pewter basons 15/.	1. 1.		
2 Pr. flat irons 6/. 1 Coffee mill 7/.	13.		
7 Tubs & pails 7/. 1 Table 2/6	9.	6.	
2 Tin Coffee pots 2/6. 1 do. 1/6	4.		
4 Stone Pots 9/. 1 Pewter bason 3/.	12.		
2 Saddles & bridles 70/. 6 pewter dishes 18/.	4. 8.		
12 Pewter plates 15/. 2 doz: queens china do. 7/	1. 2.		
2 Diaper Table Cloths @ 18/.	1. 16.		
3 Oznbgs. do. do. @ 7/6	1. 2.	6.	
4 Silver Table Spoons @ 12/.	2. 8.		
6 Silver Tea Spoons	18.		
1 Pr. do. Sugar Tongs	9.		
Sundry Broken Silver	16.		
1 Pr. Sale Shovels	6.		
1 Pr. Glass salts	2.		
1 Japan waiter	2.		
1 China Mug 1 do. Bowl & 2 Glass Tumblers	7.	6.	
Sundry China & Delph ware	2. 10.		

£727. 1. 3

In obedience to an order of Court hereunto annexed, We the subscribers
being first sworn, have appraised all the estate of Samuel Pearson
deced as was shewn us by the executor. Certified under our hands this
16th day of July 1794

John Hicks   John Pendleton
                                          Josias Bingham senr.
                                          James Trevilian

Recorded 4th of September 1794 at a Court held for Hanover County
                            Test   William Pollard C H C
November 1802 A Copy   test   Tho. Pollard D C H C

Underwood & als) 1830 (#128)
vs) U. S. Circt. Ct.,
Underwood's Exors. &c) 5th Circt., Va. Dist.
(1826)

To the Honourable the Judges &c ... Your orator and oratrixes, Joseph R. Underwood, Lucy Ann Skiles (late Lucy Ann Underwood) and her husband, William H. Skiles, Louisa F. Gorin, (late Louisa F. Underwood) and her husband, Franklin Gorin, Malvina M. Underwood, Jane Underwood and Warner L. Underwood, the last three being infants, sue by their next friend the said Joseph R. Underwood, all being citizens of the Commonwealth of Kentucky and not residents within Virginia, sheweth, that Jane Underwood deceased late of Hanover county departed this life on the 13th of April 1821 having previously made and published her last will and testament a copy of which duly authenticated is herewith filed marked "A". That your complainants are the legatees mentioned in the said will - That James Underwood one of the executors mentioned in said will took upon himself the execution thereof and qualified as executor in due form of law in the County Court of Hanover County - That Thomas Pollard the other executor named in said will declined uniting with said James Underwood in the execution of the provisions of the said will consequently the said James was the sole acting executor of the said will ... who is defendant to this bill, the said James Underwood being a citizen and inhabitant of the State of Virginia.

Joseph R. Underwood, guardian for Malvina, Jane and Warner, rendered bond with Edmund and Thomas Rogers his sureties - Thomas Underwood deceased was the father of the defendant and also the second husband of the testatrix Jane Underwood deceased who previous to her intermarriage with the said Thomas was the widow of Nathaniel W. Dandridge, decd. The property in dispute belonged to and was the individual estate and property of the said Jane previous to her intermarriage with the said Thomas Underwood decd., and in part is the increase of such property. The marriage between the said Thomas and said Jane was solemnized in the year 1795. A few days previous to the marriage the said Jane and Thomas entered into a marriage agreement for the purpose of preventing either from claiming any interest whatever in the property of the other in consequence of the marriage and this was effected through the aid of a trustee to whom said Jane conveyed all her estate real and personal a copy of which marriage agreement is herewith filed. Thomas Underwood died on the 29th of January, 1815. Jane Underwood died on the 13th day of April, 1831. Immediately after the death of the said Thomas Jane took possession of all the property real and personal mentioned in the marriage contract and held possession of same until her death. James Underwood lived with the said Jane from the time of the death of the said Thomas until said Jane died, and was executor of the will of Thomas Underwood his father having qualified in the spring of 1815. Copy of will of Thomas hereto annexed marked "D".

Bill of Complaint, cont.:

  Shortly after the death of her husband Jane entered into a
very beneficial contract with said James the defendant, dated the 8th
day f March, 1815, by which he has received 700 or 800 acres of land
in the county of Hanover including the plantation on which the said
Jane and Thomas lived during their coverture and where said Jane continued to live until her death and which is the same land mentioned
in the marriage agreement aforesaid and on which the slaves mentioned
in the marriage contract were situated at its date and continued thereon until Jane's death -

  Jane's family consisted at the time of the death of the
said Thomas, of Malvina, then aged sixteen years and Jane and Warner,
then aged twelve years and Elizabeth Underwood sister of the defendant in addition to said Jane and your defendant (James Underwood).

  Thomas Underwood left 4000 acres of land in the State of
Kentucky, (copies of grants for the land in Kentucky are herewith
exhibited - G & H) who also left a personal estate worth a considerable amount. The defendant was offered $15. per acre for 2000 acres
for part of the Kentucky land but he failed to sell it ...

WILL OF JANE UNDERWOOD

of Hanover County, Va.
d. 16 day of Feb., 1818

  I Jane Underwood of Hanover do make this my last will and
Testament revoking all others. I give Joseph R. Underwood one negro
Boy Harry - I give Henry W. Underwood Two negroes Ben and Edmund - I
give Lucy A. Underwood one negro girl Aggie - I give Louisa F. Underwood one negro girl Nelly - My will is that if Lucy A. or Louisa F.
Underwood dies without heir, the other is to have her proportion of
my estate with the future increase. I give Malvina M. Underwood the
following slaves to wit, Sylvia, Bob, Anna and her Children, Sylvia
and Sam, Daphney and her daughter Patsy with their future increase,
one feather bed and furniture, one Beaureau and one Gold Ring.

  I give Jane Underwood the following slaves to wit, Lucy
and her children, Daniel, Mary, Richard, Rosetta and Lucy also Peggy
and her children, Isaac, Nelson and Dianna, and James and Ceaser with
the future increase of the females - One feather Bed and furniture,
one Bureau, one Mourning Ring I had for my sister Joanna and the
tumbler it is in -

Will of Jane Underwood, cont.:

     I give Warner L. Underwood the following slaves to wit,
Phillis and her children Jack, Nancy, Myres, Isham, Collin, William
and Thomas, Gabriel, Abram, Secily and Hannah with their future increase, one feather bed and furniture. My will is that as Jane and
Warner L. Underwood are Twins that if either dies without heir, the
other is to have his or her portion of my estate. My will is that
if Malvina Underwood dies without heir that Jane and Warner L. Underwood have her portion of my estate - I give Elizabeth Underwood the
following negroes to wit, Liewil, Moses, Rachel and her child Martha
Ann, with their future increase - I give James Underwood two negroes
Davy and Polley with the future increase of Polley -

     I appoint James Underwood and Thomas Pollard of Hanover my
Executors and request them to hire out my negroes before any division
thereof untill they raise the following sums of money to wit: Four
hundred Pounds which I request them to pay Col. Edmund Pendleton of
Caroline or his representatives, one hundred Pounds to Nancy Winston
for the use of herself and children and one hundred Pounds to Thomas
and John Meriwether to be equally divided between them for the use of
their respective families - I give my nephew Edmund Pendleton a pair
of Gold Buttons - I give Milly Page a brown silk gown and a pair of
stone buttons - I give Susan Harris and Sally Ann Alsop Ten dollars
to get mourning Jewelry. I give Malvina, Jane and Warner L. Underwood the balance of my clothes also my household furniture. I give
James Underwood my stock of all kinds, plantation Tools, and Kitchen
furniture - I appoint James Underwood Guardian for Malvina, Jane and
Warner L. Underwood and request him to have them well educated and
taken care of until they become of age or marry

     My will is that my friend Thomas Pollard be well paid for
his trouble as my Executor - My old woman Margaret is to go with
either of her children and the owner of such child to take care of
her - My will is that the crop on hand at the time of my death be
applied in discharging the money Legacies aforesaid - Witness my
hand and seal this 16th day of February 1818 -

Syned sealed and published   Jane Underwood   (Seal)
in presence of

Samuel Mosby
Garland Thompson
John S Mosby

At a Court of Monthly Session held for Hanover County, at the Courthouse on Wednesday the 22d of May 1821
This last will and Testament of Jane Underwood deceased was proved by
the oath of John S Mosby a witness thereto, and ordered to be recorded .
                    Test   William Pollard C H C
     A Copy   Teste   Tho. Pollard C H C

WILL OF THOMAS UNDERWOOD

Dated 26th Sept., 1813
Recorded 22nd Mar., 1815

Being tolerable well and perfectly in my senses, but calling
to mind the uncertainty of life, make this my last Will and Testament.
In the first place I direct my Executors hereafter named to sell so
much of my Kentucky land as will raise the sum of two hundred pounds,
which I request may be paid to my son James it being in consideration
of the several services he has rendered me - I give unto my said son
James a feather Bed & furniture which he commonly sleeps on   I give
to my son John & his heirs forever the one seventh part of all my estate which may arise from the sales of my stocks of every kind, my
crops or any other property I may be legally entitled to by inter-
marriing with my present wife - I also give in like manner to sons
Thomas and James the seventh part of like property to them and their
heirs forever, in like manner I give to my daughter Mary Dandridge and
to my daughter Ann Dudley each one seventh part of the like property
to them and each of them and their heirs forever. I give and bequeath
unto my Daughter Elisth. a Negro Woman Jane & her child Milly and her
future increase together with one sixth part of all my lands in the
State of Kentucky to her and her heirs forever - I give and bequeath
unto my sons Thomas and James each a sixth part of my Kentucky land
to them and there heirs forever   I give unto my daughter Mary Dandridge
1/6 th part of all my land in Kentucky

Item I give and bequeath to my Daughter Ann Dudley and her
heirs forever 1/6th part of my Kentucky land as my last mentioned
Daughter has a claim of long standing upon my estate in consequence
of a judgment obtained by Joseph Payne jr agst me and assd. by him
to her it being done by way of compromise and not because I thought
it could ultimately be recovered of me and not being more than I expected to be able to give to each of my other children - I did assent
to it yet should my said daughter or any other person claiming under
her right recover out of my estate the amount of sd judgment then in
such case I hereby revoke all & every clause in this will heretofore
made in her favour as it is my desire that my said Daughter Anna be
entitled to no more of my estate than 1/6th part of my Kentucky land
and one seventh part of my other estate not otherwise disposed of -
I give to my Daughter Elizabeth a feather bed & furniture which she
commonly sleeps on. I have in trust in the hands of my Executors the
one sixth part of my Kentucky land & the one seventh part of my other
estate not otherwise disposed of to be by them applied in the best
manner in their power for the benefit of my son Francis during his
life & his wife's life and after their death to go to his son Wm.
Underwood & his heirs forever - The sum of 200 Pounds given my son
James is in consideration of all demands he may have against me,

Underwood vs Underwood, cont.:

Will of Thomas Underwood, cont.:

which sum may be paid him out of my money that my executors raise out
of my estate so as to divide my Kentucky land in six equal parts between my children according to the tenor of this will - I appoint my
sons Thomas and James Underwood Executors of this my last will which
I have signed with my own hand & sealed this 26th September 1813

N. B.   It is my wish that all the   Tho Underwood   (Seal)
property given my Daughter Mary Dandridge
may go to her and her heirs forever
                    T. U.

         At a Court of Monthly Session held for Hanover County at
the Court House on Wednesday the 22nd of March 1815

         This writing purporting to be the last Will & testament of
Thomas Underwood Deceased was offered for proof by James Underwood one
of the Executors therein named & John Starke Charles P Goodall & William Ellett being sworn & examined declare that they are well acquainted
with the handwriting of the said Deceased & that they verily believed
that the said will was wholly written and signed by him & the same
being also proved by the Oath of the said Executor is ordered to be
recorded -

            Teste   William Pollard C H C

   A Copy   Teste   Tho. Pollard   C H C

                    MARRIAGE AGREEMENT
                        between
            JANE DANDRIDGE AND THOMAS UNDERWOOD

         THIS INDENTURE made this tenth day of January one thousand
seven hundred and ninety five between Thomas Underwood of the County
of Goochland, widower, of the first part, Jane Dandridge, of the
county of Hanover, widow, of the second part, and Thomas Pollard of
the County of Fairfax, Edmund Pendleton (son of John) of the County
of Caroline and William Pollard of the County of Hanover of the third
part, WHEREAS a marriage is shortly intended to be celebrated between
the said Thomas Underwood and Jane Dandridge each of whom is seized
of lands and possessed of slaves and other personal estate, the right
and title to which it hath been mutually agreed shall remain in him
and her respectively notwithstanding the marriage and that no claim

Marriage Agreement, cont.:

or interest shall by virtue thereof vest in either to any part of the
other's estate. Now THIS INDENTURE WITNESSETH that for carrying the
said agreement into execution & for the sum of five shillings to the
said Jane Dandridge paid by the said Thomas Pollard Edmund Pendleton
and William Pollard the receipt of which she doth hereby acknowledge
she the said Jane Dandridge hath given, granted, bargained, sold and
doth hereby give, grant, bargain, and sell unto the said Thomas, Edmund Pendleton and William Pollard, the survivors or survivor of them,
and the heirs, Executors or administrators of such survivor, all that
tract or parcel of land containing about seven hundred acres lying in
the said County of Hanover, which the said Jane holds under the
Jointure and will of her former husband Nathaniel West Dandridge, and
by conveyance of the remainder or reversion in fee simple from William
Dandridge, son, heir and devisee of the said Nathaniel West, all of
record in the said County Court of Hanover, with all the rights and
priviledges appertaining to the said land, also all the slaves of which
the said Jane is possessed and the stocks of all kinds and other personal estate now on the said plantation and the household goods at
present in the County of Caroline, but intended to be removed to the
said plantation, whether such slaves or other personal estate be such
as are the absolute property of the said Jane, or those held for her
life only under the said Jointure and will, with the future increase
of the Slaves, TO HAVE AND TO HOLD the lands slaves and other estate
hereby conveyed unto the said Thomas Pollard, Edmund Pendleton and
William Pollard the survivors or survivor of them and the heirs executors or administrators of such survivor IN TRUST to and for the following uses that is to say to the use of the said Jane Dandridge as
of her former interest therein, until the said intended marriage shall
take place and from and after the solemnization thereof IN TRUST out
of the annual profits of the said estate or by sale of part thereof
in case it be found necessary to pay all the just debts now due from
the said Jane, and to apply the residue of the said annual profits
to the maintenance of the said Jane and the necessary repairs and improvements on the said land and plantation, during the coverture and
in case the said Thomas Underwood shall survive the said Jane, then
in Trust for the use of such person or persons, being related by con-
sanguinity to the said Jane and in such parts or portitions as she the
said Jane by Deed executed in her life time or by her last will in
writing or any writing purporting to be her last will notwithstanding
her coverture, shall direct, limit or appoint, and in default of such
appointment, then to raise out of the said estate the sum of fifty
pounds current money for the use of Elizabeth Johnson, niece of the
said Jane and as to all the residue thereof to the use of Frances
Rogers, Elizabeth Meriwether and Millie Pendleton, sisters of the said
Jane, equally to be divided among them, to hold to each, a third part
thereof for her life, and at her death to pass to her descendants,
according to the laws of descent and distributions respectively.

Marriage Agreement, cont.:

But if it shall happen that the said Jane shall outlive the
said Thomas Underwood, then in trust to and for the use of the said
Jane as of her former interest therein, from and after his death,
anything herein contained to the contrary notwithstanding. And the
said Thomas Underwood, for himself his heirs Executors or Administrators doth covenant and grant to and with the said Thomas Pollard
Edmund Pendleton & William Pollard their survivors or survivor as
aforesaid, that in case the said intended marriage shall take effect
he or they shall not, and will not by virtue thereof, claim, demand,
or be entitled to any part of the estate of the said Jane hereby
settled, but shall and will suffer the same to pass and go according to the true intent and meaning of these presents, without hindrance or molestation from him his heirs Executors or administrators,
any defect herein found notwithstanding and the said Jane Dandridge
for herself her heirs Executors or administrators doth covenant and
grant to and with the said Thomas Pollard Edmund Pendleton and William Pollard their survivors or survivor as aforesaid that in case the
said marriage shall happen and she shall survive the said Thomas Underwood, she shall not and will not claim demand or be entitled to any
dower or other interest in the real or personal estate of the said
Thomas, but shall and will be barred therefrom by these presents, and
any defect in form or substance herein notwithstanding. In witness
whereof the said parties have hereunto set their hands and seals the
day and year first above written.

Sealed and mutually delivered
the words (in writing) first
interlined

In presence of us

Before executing this writing the aforesaid Jane Dandridge
hath thought proper to make the following change in the provisional
disposition of her estate in case she shall die before her intended
husband without making a Deed or will for such disposition according
to the power reserved in the Deed that is to say besides the fifty
pounds for her niece Elizabeth Johnson there shall by raised the sum
of five guineas for each of her sisters Sarah Pendleton and Anne
Taylor and her nephew John Taylor to purchase a ring or such other
memorial of her as they shall respectively chuse. And in case her
brother Thomas Pollard and the children of her late brother William
Pollard will collate and add to the residue of her estate the sum of
three hundred pounds (by an equal moiety from each family) being her
estimated value of certain negroes which they hold under the will of
their father, but which she thinks herself justly intitled to, in

Marriage Agreement, cont.:

that case the said Thomas shall be intitled to one fifth part of the
residue, including that augmentation, and her brother William's
Children equally amongst them another fifth part, each family to
receive as much more as with the one hundred and fifty pounds will
make their parts each equal to that of each of her three sisters named
in the deed, which in the event of this collation, is to be reduced
to one fifth part of the whole - And this is to be considered as a
provisional disposition in the same manner as if incorporated in the
Deed.

Jno Pendleton Jr   Tho Underwood   (Seal)
Thomas T Page   Jane Dandridge   (Seal)
Edmund Pendleton Sr   Edm Pendleton jr   (Seal)

        At a Court held for Hanover County at the Courthouse on
Thursday the 4th of June 1795 This writing or Deed of Trust indented,
was proved by the oath of John Pendleton, Jr. and Thomas T. Page
two of the witnesses thereto, and at a Court held for the said
County on Thursday the 3rd of December next following was further
proved by the oath of Edmund Pendleton, the third, the other witness
thereto and is ordered to be recorded -

                          Test   William Pollard   C H C

              A Copy   Teste   William Pollard   C H C

UNDERWOOD TO UNDERWOOD - DEED

        This Deed Poll entered into this 8th day of March 1815
Betwixt Jane Underwood relict of Thomas Underwood deceased of the one
part and James Underwood of the other part both of Hanover County
Whereas the said Jane is aged and is desirous of obtaining the services
of the said James to manage for her in all her affairs, for and during
her life and willing to make him a compensation therefor, And Whereas
also the said James has agreed to furnish a waggon and horses for her
use on her plantation, and to act and do for her as hitherto he hath
done for and during her life aforesed. NOW THIS DEED Witnesseth that in
consideration of the premises and of one Dollar in hand paid, the receipt whereof is hereby acknowledged, she the sd. Jane hath bargained
and sold to the sd. James the tract of land on which she now lives containing about 700 acres lying in the county aforesaid and bounded by
the lands of Samuel Mosby, Philip Woodson, William Woodson and others.

Underwood to Underwood, Deed, cont.:

To have and to hold the same to the said James forever reserving to
herself however her life in the sd. lands except as to fifty acres
to be laid off at some one corner of the sd. lands, which the sd.
James is to have an immediate right to. In Testimony whereof as well
the sd. Jane Underwood as the sd. James Underwood have hereunto set
their hands and affixed their seals the day and year first above
mentioned

Archd. B. Dandridge   Jane Underwood   (Seal)
Wm Underwood   Jas Underwood   (Seal)
Jno. Michie
Elizabeth Underwood

Hanover County towit,

              We Charles Thompson Junr and Chas P Goodall
Magistrates of the said County, do certify that Jane Underwood and
James Underwood parties to the within conveyance have duly acknowledged the same before us, on the 5th day of April in the year 1815,
and desired us to certify the said acknowledgment to the Clerk of the
County Court of Hanover in order that the said conveyance may be recorded. As witness our hands and seals

                                       Charles Thompson Jr   (Seal)
                                       C. P. Goodall   (Seal)

Hanover County towit,

              This conveyance, with the certificate of the ac-
knowledgment thereof, thereon endorsed, were this day delivered to me,
whereupon the said conveyance is admitted to record. Witness my hand
the 21st day of April 1815

                                       Tho Pollard   D C H C

        A Copy
                    teste

                                       Tho. Pollard   D C H C

INVENTORY AND APPRAISMENT
PERSONAL ESTATE OF
JANE UNDERWOOD, DECEASED
Dated July 30th, 1821

51 Slaves	$11,475.00
18 Spoons (silver)	25.00
Bowles Glasses Waiters Decanters	6.00
Carpets	5.00
Plates Dishes Coffee pots &c)	
Jugs Scales &c)	6.00
knives & forks	1.25
Carboys & bottles	2.50
Wash Buckets	.25
3 Chairs	1.00
Lott of Books	4.00
4 Beds Steads &c	90.00
1 Mahogany Table	12.00
2 Bureaus	18.00
1 Looking Glass	1.25
13 Table Clocks	16.25
7 Pair Sheets	21.00
18 Bedquilts & counterpins	54.00
2 Blankets	.25
4 Trunks	2.50
24 Towels & pillow cases	6.00
2 Curtains	2.50
Miscellaneous	4.00
Chair Cover	.50
4 Candle Sticks, 3 pr. Snuffers)	
Trivet & Toaster)	1.50
2 Pine Tables	1.00
2 Scrubbing Brushes	.25
Kitchen furniture	21.75
1 Churn	.50
12 Axes	8.00
10 Scythes	15.00
6 Spades	3.00
5 Large Cary ploughs	12.50
10 Small do. do. &c	25.00
7 Cowlter ploughs	7.00
2 Pair Wedges &c	1.50
	$ 11,852.25

THE DEPOSITIONS OF JOHN UNDERWOOD

The deposition of John Underwood, of lawful age, residing in the County of Goochland, taken at the tavern of William D. Taylor, at Goochland Ct House, on the 2nd day of May, 1827: This deponent ... saith, that in the years 1822 and 1823 his children, Malvina, Jane and Warner boarded with James Underwood; that Jane and Warner were twins born the 17th of August, 1808, and that Malvina was probably three years older. He further saith that Jane went to live with Thomas Underwood in the year 1808, and Malvina and Warner went a few years later. The greater part of certain household furniture which Mrs. Jane Underwood bequeathed to Malvina, Jane and Warner, was received by this deponent, the balance having been bought by James Underwood...

The deposition of John Underwood taken at the tavern of Allen Denton in the County of Hanover on the 11th day of May, 1827 ... This deponent saith that Nathaniel W. Dandridge the elder died in the year 1821.

Sworn to before And. Bowles and William Wingfield, Justices of the Peace of Hanover County.

THE DEPOSITION OF FREDERICK SHOEMAKER

The deposition of Frederick Shoemaker, taken at the tavern of Allen Denton, etc. ... This deponent saith that Malvina and Jane lived at Doctor Bates to go to school, the defendant taking them to and from home to school. He further saith that the farm of the Defendant was called "Gilliams".

THE DEPOSITION OF MISS ELIZABETH UNDERWOOD

The deposition of Miss Elizabeth Underwood, of the County of Goochland, of lawful age, taken at the tavern of William D. Taylor, Goochland C H ... This deponent states that she was a member of the family of Thomas Underwood, deceased, from the time of his last marriage until his death - and of Mrs. Jane Underwood's family from the time of the death of her husband Thomas Underwood untill her death - That the defendant, James Underwood, also lived with the said Thomas and Jane during that time except for one year, and that she had heard Mrs. Jane Underwood say many times that James Underwood had been very kind to her; that she had heard Mrs. Jane Underwood say she meant to educate Malvina M., Jane and Warner L. Underwood well, and that she got Miss Peggy Crew to live with her for that purpose, who continued there until the old ladie's death, having just commenced the school when the old Lady died. Warner was boarded out (to go to school) two years or

nearly so, one year at Mr. Mosby's & one year (or untill the school
master went away) at Mr. Webster's - Jane & Malvina boarded one year
at Mr. Bates's. They generally came home on friday evenings and returned on the Monday morning following, James Underwood sometimes
bringing them home on friday evenings when the servant was out of the
way but not often ... Mrs. Jane Underwood generally had five women
about the house to spin, & in bad weather there were more; whenever
the situation of the crops required they went out to work - several
little girls & boys were also about the house, the number I don't
recollect. Moses, a boy, waited in the house for some years and after
he was taken from home Spotswood, a small boy, was taken in the house
to learn to wait in the house - I don't recollect the others - Malvina, Jane and Warner's father kept a carriage there (at Mrs. Jane
Underwood's) for many years. They went across James River twice,
once to the defendant's wedding and once afterwards. The carriage
furnished by their father was there at that time and both times they
went over the River they went in that carriage. This deponent states
that she never heard anything about who paid the expenses of the plaintiff's going to Powhatan and back, for carriages &c, but suppose James
Underwood did. They (Malvina, Jane and Warner) used his gig and horse
to go to Major Alsup's one time and sometimes to go to Meeting on Sundays - Various purchases for the household were made of John M Price
and Price & Thompson for the household... This deponent also recollects hearing Thomas Underwood mention a debt due to old uncle George
Underwood ...

Sworn to before N. M. Vaughan, Benjamin Anderson and Tho. Curd. 3rd
day of May, 1827.

THE DEPOSITION OF MARY DANDRIDGE

          The deposition of Mary Dandridge taken at the tavern of Allen
Denton, in the County of Hanover, 11th May, 1827, who being sworn, sayeth that she lived with Thomas Underwood her father from the time of
his last marriage untill the deponent was married, - that she was very
often at the house of Mrs. Jane Underwood during the latter's last wid-
ownood, - that Mrs. Underwood lived very well during that time, and
entertained more than she, the deponent, ever knew in a private house.
The deponent further states that she had heard the children say the
defendant was very kind to them, and that they lived with the Defendant from the time of the death of the said Mrs. Underwood until they
moved to the home of Mrs. Mary Underwood.

THE ANSWER OF JOHN F. TODD

I John F Todd for myself and as agent for Joseph R Underwood,
Lucy Ann Skiles (late Lucy Ann Underwood) and her husband Wm H Skiles,
Louisa F Gorin (late Louisa F Underwood) & her husband Franklin Gorin,
Jane Wilson (late Jane Underwood) and her husband James W Wilson and
Warner L Underwood, and also for my wife Malvina M (late Malvina M
Underwood) do hereby in consideration of a decree of the United States
Court for the fifth Circuit Eastern District of Virginia, rendered on
the 11th of December 1830, in a suit in Chancery therein pending in
which said Joseph, Lucy Ann & her husband, Louisa F and her husband,
Malvina M, Jane and Warner L were plaintiffs, and James Underwood
executor of Jane Underwood deceased was Defendant , and for the purpose
of carrying said decree into full and complete effect, release, discharge & forever acquit the said James Underwood, his heirs, Executors
& Administrators of all actions, suits, arrests, quarrels, controver-
sies, and demands whatsoever touching or concerning the matters or
things put in controversy by the aforesaid suit in Chancery from the
Beginning of the world up to the 5th day of November 1828 being the
date of the award made by John Guerant & Benjamin Anderson and referred
to in the decree aftersaid   In testimony whereof I have in my own right
and as agent aforesaid hereto set my hand & seal this 12th August 1832 -

Attest   Jno. F. Todd   (Seal)

THE DEPOSITION OF HENRY M. UNDERWOOD

The deposition of Henry M Underwood residing in the county of
Goochland taken at the tavern of Wm D Taylor at Goochland Courthouse,
on the 2nd day of May 1827, before Benjamin Anderson, Tho. Curd and
John Martin, justices of the peace for the said county, - the deponent
speaks of his father John Underwood"who is father of the last three
named plaintiffs: Malvina M., Jane and Warner L."

Sulpoena dated 20 April, 1826: Sheriff's report: "James
Underwood lives near Allens Creek Church in Hanover".

LETTER: MRS. JANE UNDERWOOD TO JOHN UNDERWOOD

                                        Hanover, Sept. 14th 1817 -
Sir:
Your children particularly Malvina and Warner ought to be sent to
school the ensuing year, there will be a good school at Johnson's Spring
and they can if you choose to get them in there, come home every friday
and return on monday which will make it less expensive than boarding
them entirely from home, mending their clothes and washing may be done

Letter, Mrs. Jane Underwood to John Underwood, cont.:

at home, and the expense saved. If my situation would afford it, would
not call on you to aid me, but it does not - If you do not get them in
very soon they will be excluded as the school is nearly made up -
Isaac Curd and Mr. Mosby are the persons to apply to; I shall be glad
to see you on the subject, & if you cannot come down to see us, let me
hear from you - You will excuse me for reminding you of the duty of a
parent, your little dear children complain much of your absence, and
say you have forgot your children sometimes papa does not know he has
such children he has not seen us so long. I do not know how he looks,
&c, which makes me sorry as I am your and their real friend
John Underwood Esquire   Jane Underwood
         Goochland

ENTRY OF THOMAS UNDERWOOD, ESQR. & JANE, HIS WIFE
Land Office Treasury Warrant No. 992

          Decemr. 5th 1795 Surveyd. the entery of Thomas Underwood
Esqr. and Jane his wife in Hanover County, by virtue of a Land Office
Treasury Warrant granted to Jane Dandridge (who Intermarried with
the sd. Underwood before the making of the sd. entery) for twenty
acres of land the 19th day of December 1794, No. 992, and bounded as
followeth Viz Beginning at a cor. red oak on the road, thence along
George Bartlotts line of marked trees S 11½ degrees W 61 poles to a
corner white oak to William Childers, thence along Childer's line of
marked trees N 11½ W 59½ poles to a corner hiccory in Dandridge's
line, thence along Dandridges oald line N 79½ E 52 poles to the beginning, including fourteen and one quarter acres of Land

                              Pr John Street S H C.

Rec. 5th Sepr. 97
Gt. issd. 7th June /98
Thos. Underwood & Jane his wife
14½ acres
Hanover

John Murdock & Co.) 1824 (#112)
      vs   ) U. S. Cir. Ct.
Winston's devisees) 5th Cir. Va. Dist.

       To the Marshall of the District of Virginia, Greeting – You are hereby commanded to summon Francis Irvine surviving executor of William Winston deced. and the said Francis Irvine and Mary Ann his wife, Richard Curd, exor: of Edward Curd deced. who succeeded to the estate of, and survived his wife Elizabeth, Susanna Slaughter widow, in her own right and exx. of Lawrence Slaughter deced: Doctor William Cochran, Lucy Cochran & George Slaughter late the husband of Caty Cockran , which said William, Lucy and Caty are children & legal representatives of Lucy Cochran late Lucy Winston who survived her late husband, David Cochran, deced: William Littlepage exor: of Thomas Winston deced: William B. Winston, John Winston, Sarah Winston who married Doctor James Faulconer and is now dead & Gerard Banks and Ann his wife, which said William B., John, Sarah and Anne are the children of John Winston deced., John Curd and ―― Winston, exor. and executrix of William Winston, junr. deced., which said Mary Ann, Elizabeth, Susanna, Lucy, Thomas, John & William are devisees & legatees of William Winston deced: to appear before the Judges of the Court of the United States for the Fifth Circuit, Virginia District, at the City of Richmond the 2nd day of November next to answer a bill in Chancery exhibited against them by John Murdock & Co., subjects of the King of the United Kingdoms of Great Britain & Ireland ... 24 day of September, 1811, and the 36th Year of the Independence of the United States of America.

                                      Will Marshall, Clk.

WILL OF WILLIAM WINSTON, SENR.

       In the name of God Amen I Wm. Winston Senior of the Parish of Saint Paul and County of Hanover being low and weak of body but thank God of sound disposing mind and memory do make ordain and declare this my last Will and Testament in manner and form following First it is my desire that all my Just debts be discharged as soon as my Executors hereafter named can make it convenient – I some time past gave my son William Winston two hundred and fifty acres of Land to be taken off the Tract of Land whereon I now live at the lower end for which I gave a Deed, but to prevent all or any disputes that may arise between him and my son Thomas Winston after my death relative to the bounds of the said Land I think it proper here to mention it – beginning in the Fork of Totapotamoy Creek Thence up Creek as high as the mouth of a branch just below my mill, Thence up the branch to the head, thence up the bottom to the main Road, Thence up the road about three hundred yards to the head of another bottom, Thence down the bottom to the head of a branch Thence down the branch that leads to my old mill Thence down the old mill branch to the beginning, be the same more or less in ye said bounds. I give to him my son William Winston and to his heirs forever. Item I give and bequeath unto my son Thomas Winston all the remainder of my said Land whereon I now live to him and his heirs forever.- Item I give my Grist Mill and all things belonging thereto to my sons William & Thomas Winston to them and their heirs forever. Item I give and bequeath

unto my son Thomas Winston the foregoing Negroes to wit Tom, Phil, Abram
Forday, Nell wife of Tom and her child Tamor and Sangular child of Phillis to him and his heirs forever as also Tamars future increase Item I
give and bequeath all the remainder of my negroes & their increase to be
equally divided between my three daughters Elizabeth, Mary Ann & Susanna
Winston being at present Twenty two in number to them and their heirs
forever. Item I give and bequeath unto Elizabeth, Mary Ann & Susanna
Winston each a Bed & furniture to them and their heirs forever. Item I
give and bequeath to my son Thomas Winston my large looking Glass, my
desk & twelve Black Walnut chairs & two elbow ditto and my large Walnut
Table to him & his heirs Item I give & bequeath the remaining part of
my household furniture to be equally divided between my son Thomas &
three unmarried daughters - Item I give and bequeath my riding chair
& chair horses. to my three unmarried daughters Elizabeth, Mary Ann &
Susanna Winston to them and their heirs Item I give and bequeath unto
my son William Winston six head of cattle & six head of sheep to him
and his heirs - Item I give & bequeath to my son Thomas Winston all
the remaining part of my stock of Horses, Cattle, sheep & Hogs to him
and his heirs - Item I give to my son John Winston ten pounds P year
during his life, to be paid by my son Thomas & by him to be paid out
yearly in proper necessary's for said John Winston. I have already
given & made provision for all my other children not here mentioned &
I desire my Estate may not be appraised. Item I give & bequeath to my
son in law David Cockran whom I had not fully consider'd off before
the making this part of my Will a negro Girl named Rachel with all her
future increase, to him and his heirs woh negro Girl he has been in
possession off these two years & upwards - Lastly I constitute and appoint Mr. David Cockran, Francis Irwin & my two sons William & Thomas
Winston Executors of this my last Will & Testament - In Witness where-
of I have hereunto sett my hand & affixt my seal this Twenty third day
of February 1781 -
Sign'd seal'd & deliver'd
In the presence of   Wm. Winston   (Seal)
Thos. Austin
Jno. Richardson
J. C. Littlepage
Wm. Radford

At a Court held for Hanover County on Thursday the 5th day of April 1781
This last Will and Testament of William Winston Gentn. deceased was of-
fered to proof by David Cochrane, Thomas Winston & Francis Irwin Execu-
tors therein named & was proved by the oath of Thomas Austin & John
Carter Littlepage Witnesses thereto, and also by the oath of the said
Executors and is ordered to be recorded -

                          Test   William Pollard Junr C H C

September 1811   A Copy
                          teste   Tho. Pollard D C H C

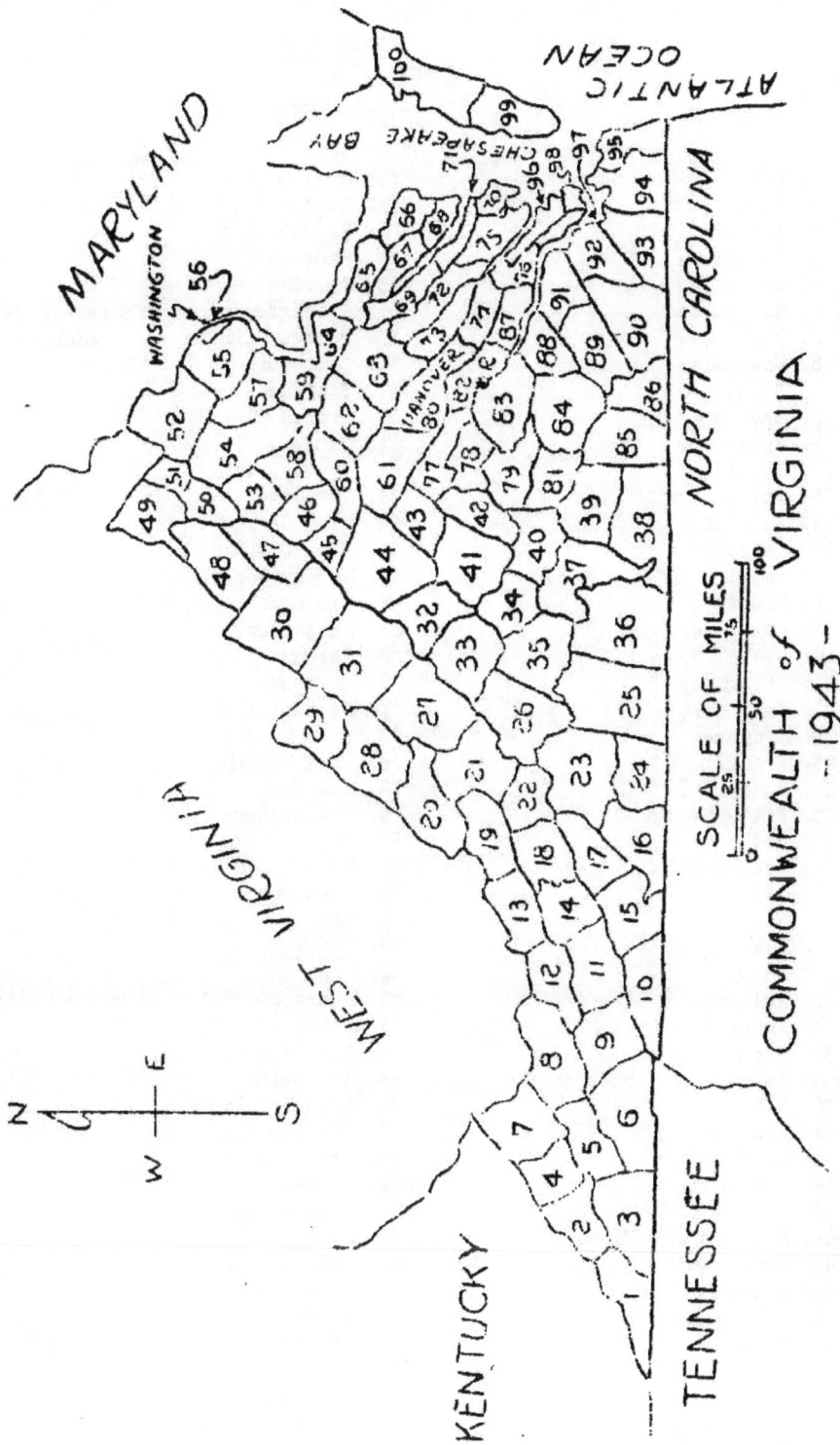

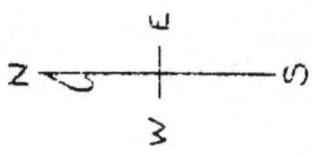

COMMONWEALTH of VIRGINIA -- 1943 --

1. Lee	51. Clarke
2. Wise	52. Loudon
3. Scott	53. Rappahannock
4. Dickinson	54. Fauquier
5. Russell	55. Fairfax
6. Washington	56. Arlington (Part of Dist. of Col.
7. Buchanan	57. Prince William included.)
8. Tazewell	58. Culpeper
9. Smyth	59. Stafford
10. Grayson	60. Orange
11. Wythe	61. Louisa
12. Bland	62. Spotsylvania
13. Giles	63. Caroline
14. Pulaski	64. King George
15. Carroll	65. Westmoreland
16. Patrick	66. Northumberland
17. Floyd	67. Richmond
18. Montgomery	68. Lancaster
19. Craig	69. Essex
20. Alleghany	70. Matthews
21. Botetourt	71. Middlesex
22. Roanoke	72. King & Queen
23. Franklin	73. King William
24. Henry	74. New Kent
25. Pittsylvania	75. Gloucester
26. Bedford	76. James City
27. Rockbridge	77. Goochland
28. Bath	78. Powhatan
29. Highland	79. Amelia
30. Rockingham	80. HANOVER
31. Augusta	81. Nottoway
32. Nelson	82. Henrico - "R" - Richmond (City)
33. Amherst	83. Chesterfield
34. Appomattox	84. Dinwiddie
35. Campbell	85. Brunswick
36. Halifax	86. Greensville
37. Charlotte	87. Charles City
38. Mecklenburg	88. Prince George
39. Lunenburg	89. Sussex
40. Prince Edward	90. Southampton
41. Buckingham	91. Surry
42. Cumberland	92. Isle of Wight
43. Fluvanna	93. Nansemond
44. Albemarle	94. Norfolk
45. Greene	95. Princess Anne
46. Madison	96. York
47. Page	97. Warwick
48. Shenandoah	98. Elizabeth City
49. Frederick	99. Northampton
50. Warren	100. Accomack

INDEX TO INTRODUCTION

SUBJECT INDEX

INDEX

VIRGINIA MIGRATIONS

HANOVER COUNTY

Volume II

-o-

1743 - 1871

WILLS, DEEDS, DEPOSITIONS, LETTERS, MARRIAGES
OBITUARIES, ESTATES FOR SALE, ABSENTEE LAND OWNERS
and
OTHER DOCUMENTS OF HISTORICAL AND GENEALOGICAL INTEREST

Compiled by

EUGENIA G. GLAZEBROOK
and
PRESTON G. GLAZEBROOK

Richmond - Virginia

PREFACE

The publication of Volume II of this series of Hanover County
records, planned to follow closely that of Volume I, has been greatly de-
layed by events connected with the recent war.

The object in compiling this material is to bring together as
much data as possible concerning Hanover County, its people and customs,
and thus supply information otherwise lost in the destruction by fire in
1865 of the Will, Deed, Order, Plat, and Bond Books, as well as the Marriage Registers, of that county. To do this the records from many sources
have been used, including suit papers, newspaper files, tax books, and the
marriage bonds now in the Archives Department of the Virginia State Library.

These documents shed much light on the movement of the people
from county to county, and from State to State. Such small bits of paper
as subpoenas frequently carry invaluable notations as to the death of a
person summoned to appear in court, or his removal from a particular community. Dates unobtainable elsewhere are frequently supplied in this way.
Orders of Publication, in stating that individuals connected with a given
suit were "No longer inhabitants of this Commonwealth", inform the reader
of a migration that had taken place prior to the date of the order. It is
possible that an examination of the tax books would disclose the State to
which this person moved, provided he owned real estate in Virginia after
his removal. Examples of this are to be found in this volume among absentee landowners.

In order to bring out clearly the personalities of those filing
bills of complaint, answers to such bills, wills, and deeds, these documents have been given in greater detail than would have been necessary
merely to supply the facts in each case. The phonetic spelling often used
furnishes an exact reproduction of the pronunciation of the person in question. In the letters of Col. John Syme and others will be seen a clear de-
lineation of the characters of the writers.

To Judge Leon M. Bazile, of the Fifteenth Judicial Circuit of
Virginia, the compilers are indebted for a most interesting introduction
to this volume, in which he has drawn generously on his wide knowledge of
the history of Hanover County, as well as that of Virginia.

Richmond, Virginia   Eugenia G. Glazebrook
August, 1949   Preston G. Glazebrook

TABLE OF CONTENTS

Page

INTRODUCTION

As the result of war and fire the court records of some of the eastern counties of Virginia have been destroyed. Of the counties that came out of York, York, Louisa, and Albemarle alone have almost complete sets of county records. The court records of the remaining counties formed from York prior to 1865 have to a large extent been destroyed. The records of King William County have twice been the victims of fire. About the end of the Revolution the interior of King William Court House was consumed by fire, "together with a number of its records", including suit papers and judgment dockets. (Lyons vs Gregory, 3 Hen. & Munf. 237-8, 1808).

So many court records were destroyed during the Revolution the General Assembly passed the Act of 17 December, 1787, for the relief of persons "who have been or may be injured by the destruction of the Records of County Courts". The preamble of the Act recited, "Whereas the records of several county courts within the Commonwealth, and other papers of consequence have been or may be destroyed by fraud, accident, or otherwise, to the great injury of citizens of this Commonwealth; For relief, therefore, of such persons whose estates, titles, or interests have been, or may be affected thereby; Be it Enacted," etc. Collection of the Permanent Acts of Virginia (1794) ch. xxxiii, pp. 42-43.

Later, on 19 January, 1885, the Clerk's Office of King William County was burned and the remainder of its court records were either wholly or partially destroyed.

Nearly all of the records of King and Queen County have been destroyed, as have the records of Gloucester. Caroline has most of the County Court Order Books and a number of Marriage Registers and Bond Books; but all of its early deed and will books are gone.

As noted in the introduction to the first volume of this series, the Hanover Court records, with few exceptions, have been destroyed.

Research in recent years has demonstrated, however, that an immense amount of Hanover material remains in existence. The sources are varied and scattered. Much of it is in private hands in Hanover County and elsewhere all over the United States. Large quantities of Hanover material are in the Archives Division of the Virginia State Library at Richmond, and in the Library of William and Mary College at Williamsburg, and the Library of the University of Virginia at Charlottesville. A very large quantity of Hanover material is in the Huntington Library, San Marino, California. An index to a large part of this last mentioned material is in Volume 30, of Fleet's Virginia Colonial Abstracts.

One of the richest sources of material of Hanover is found in the suit files of the United States District Court at Richmond, Virginia.

During the Colonial period and the early years of the Commonwealth Hanover County was the site of two large tobacco ports, located at Hanovertown and New Castle on the Panumkey River. Much of the trade of the colony with the Mother country was transacted from these towns. Many of the colonial merchants and planters became indebted to the British merchants with whom they dealt.

During the Revolution trade with and payments to subjects of the British monarch were suspended. By the Act of October 1777 the Federal Assembly of Virginia sequestered British property and authorized those indebted to British subjects to discharge such debts by paying same into the Loan Office. 9 Hening Stats. 377-380.

In the celebrated case of Carter Page, executor of Archibald Cary v. Edmund Pendleton and Peter Lyons administrators of John Robinson, et al. Wythe 211 (1793) Chancellor George Wythe held that a debt due to a British creditor was not discharged by payment in paper money into the Loan Office under the Virginia Act, which provided that such payments should have that effect; and that the right to money due to an enemy cannot be confiscated.

After the National Government was established the British merchants brought numerous suits in the Federal Court against citizens of Virginia.

Before the right of the British creditors was established one of the greatest contests in American legal history occurred in the case of Ware admr. of Jones v. Hylton et al. in which the British creditors were represented by John Wickham, William Ronald, John Baker and John Starke. The defendants were represented by Patrick Henry, John Marshall, Alexander Campbell and James Jones. After this case was finally decided by the Supreme Court of the United States in 1796, 3 Dall., 199, the British creditors were free to pursue their American debtors and as noted, many suits in the Federal Court in Virginia resulted. Included among the defendants were many residents of Hanover County, as we saw in Volume I of this series.

The present volume also shows that the Federal Court was resorted to by Virginians who sued British subjects, and by residents of other states who sued residents of Virginia. Included among these classes of litigants on one side or the other, and sometimes on both sides, were people who were or had been residents of Hanover County.

These suits being largely for the purpose of subjecting real estate to the payment of debts, deeds, wills, accounts, and the genealogy of the parties, all formed essential parts of the controversy, and in this way many Hanover wills, deeds, accounts, and plats were filed in these suits and are still preserved. Many depositions and interesting exhibits such as John Syme's letters are also filed among the papers of these suits, and furnish much information of interest to the historian and genealogist.

In this volume Mrs. Glazebrook has continued the work which she began with Volume I of this series and she has included in the first part of the volume the historical and genealogical parts of seven suits which are in the United States District Court at Richmond, Virginia. To these she has added a number of wills from the Richmond Chancery Court and one from Goochland County relating to the suits from the Federal Court or the people connected therewith. She has also included a very interesting Hanover will secured from the Clerk's office of Louisa County.

To these she has added a large quantity of genealogical information concerning residents of Hanover County consisting of orders of publication copied from early newspapers; an extensive list of Hanover marriages for the years 1777-1787, copied from documents in the Archives Division in the State Library; a list of Hanover marriages between 1831-1847, copied from the "Hanover Miscellany, 1727-1847," a book of photostats of Hanover documents in the Huntington Library, which is in the Archives Department of the Virginia State Library. To this she has added a number of Hanover marriages and obituary notices from early Virginia newspapers, the Virginia Gazette, the Richmond Enquirer, and Richmond Whig and Public Advertiser.

These lists, while not complete, are of the greatest interest to all persons who are concerned with Hanover genealogy, and in many instances are the only source where such information may be readily obtained.

Mrs. Clazebrook has also added a list of the non-resident land owners in Hanover County for the years 1814 and 1815, taken from the Land Books for those years. These lists for both parishes give the name of the land owner, his place of residence, the acreage owned, the names of the adjoining owners, and its distance and direction from the Court House. It is interesting to note that while the Commissioner of the Revenue for St. Paul's Parish described the tracts of land in his parish as being east, west, north, south, south-east or south-west from the Court House, the Commissioner of the Revenue for St. Martin's Parish invariably described every tract in his parish as being west from the Court House.

Many of these absentee land owners were natives of Hanover County who had moved elsewhere. Others were natives of adjoining counties, and at least one, Robert Morris, a citizen of Pennsylvania.

Included in this volume are advertisements of Hanover estates offered for sale, taken from the Virginia Gazette, beginning with 1767 and extending through 1779.

Of the suits from the files of the United States Court the first to be noticed is that of Backhouse v. J. Boswell's Exor. (p. 9), which supplements the previous Boswell material contained in Volume I of this series, (pp. 1-19). To this material has been added the will of John B. Johnson, as well as those of Chapman Johnson and George Nicholson Johnson, taken from the Will Books of the Hustings Court of the City of Richmond, now in the Clerk's Office of the Richmond Chancery Court.

John Boswell Johnson was the son of Thomas Johnson (minor) and Jane Chapman, his wife, and was, therefore, the brother of Chapman Johnson. He was born 14 September, 1771, and died in 1815. It is believed that he attended the classical school conducted by the Rev. Peter Nelson. Later he entered the College of William and Mary, where he was a student in 1798. He moved to Sumner County, Tennessee, where he died. He married Elizabeth

They had the following issue:

1. Thomas Johnson
2. Chapman Johnson, and
3. Maria Barclay Johnson

(26V206; his will, this volume, p. 10; and List of William and Mary Alumni 1693-1888, 1941).

Chapman Johnson was the son of Thomas Johnson (minor) and Jane Chapman, his wife. He was born in Louisa County, Virginia, probably at Boswell's Tavern, on 15 March, 1779, and he died at his residence in the City of Richmond, Virginia, 12 July, 1849. He studied for two years at the classical school conducted by the Rev. Peter Nelson, probably at "Wingfield" on the Little River, in Hanover County. From this school he entered William and Mary College in 1799, and graduated therefrom in 1802. Shortly thereafter he began the practice of law in Staunton, Virginia, qualifying as a lawyer on 1 July, 1802. He qualified in the Virginia Court of Appeals in 1805. In 1824 he moved from Staunton to Richmond, Virginia, where he became one of the leading members of the bar. John Randolph Tucker classed him with Benjamin Watkins Leigh and Robert Stanardas the three ablest lawyers at the Richmond bar in the decade 1830-1840.

Describing him Mr. Tucker said:

"Mr. Johnson was a great logician. Starting with primordial principles he moved with majestic tread and with great deliberation to his almost irresistable conclusion. So subtle was his induction that it required great acuteness in his antagonist to detect his departure from the right line of reasoning in the successive stages of his progression; and, in the United States Bank v. Steenberger, so successful was his powerful argument as to disturb the balances of the judgment of Judge Smith, who presided at the trial at nisi prius. His celebrated antagonist, General Walter Jones, watching with impatience his triumphant march with an acumen of which he was master, said to one of his colleagues: 'He is a great sophist. It is impossible to answer by following him; he can only be met by reversing his reasoning and by proving his conclusions, final and successive, to be errors, because contrary to established decisions and to principles settled by authority. This will prove the radical fallacy of his reasoning which cannot be well exposed by following his steps!'

I have often heard him when I knew nothing of law, and often I came to the bar. He impressed me, as he did his compeers, as a noble type of a powerful advocate, an honorable man and learned lawyer."

He was elected Commonwealth's Attorney for Augusta County and served as such from 1809 to 1612. He represented the senatorial district composed of the counties of Augusta, Rockingham, Rockbridge, Shenandoah, Pendleton, and Bath, later Augusta, Rockbridge and Pendleton, in the Virginia State Senate for the sessions 1810/11; 1811/12; 1812/13; 1813/14; 1814/15; 1815/16; 1816/17;1818/19; 1819/20; 19120/21; 1821/22; 1822/23; 1823/24; 1824/25 and 1825/26.

In the Convention of 1829/30 he, with Briscoe G. Baldwin, William McCoy, and Samuel McD. Moore, represented the Fifth District composed of the counties of Augusta, Rockbridge, and Pendleton. From the beginning he took an active and prominent part in the proceedings of the Convention. He was a member of the important Committee to take into consideration the Legislative Department of Government, of which James Madison, former President of the United States, was chairman, and John Tyler, later President of the

United States, and John Randolph, of Roanoke, were members. On Wednesday,
11 November, 1829, after the Convention went into a committee of the whole,
he began what was one of the very great addresses made in the Convention.
This speech on the basis of representation occupied all of that day, all of
the following day, and more than half of Friday, 13 November, 1829.

In the session of 1834/35 he represented the City of Richmond in
the House of Delegates, and in the sessions of 1846/47 and 1847/48 he represented Augusta County in the House of Delegates.

He was the captain of a volunteer company in the War of 1812, and
also served as an aide to General James Breckenridge.

He was a very handsome man, as indicated by his portrait by
St. Memin. He always dressed well, and had a noble and commanding presence.
He was endowed with winning manners and conversational talents of the highest order. It has been said that his speeches in court "were long and loud,
but always very able". He was a friend and admirer of Jefferson, and he was
a Visitor of the University from 1819 to 1845, and Rector from 1835 to 1845.

He married Mary Anne Nicholson, the daughter of George Nicholson,
and Margaret, his wife. They had the following issue:

1. George Nicholson Johnson
2. William Boswell Johnson
3. Mary Anne Johnson, who married Adolphus Frederick Gifford; and
4. Carter Page Johnson

(29V155-6; 35V161-163,168,246, et seq.; 25V155-6; 26V206; his
tombstone in Shockoe Hill Cemetery, Richmond, Virginia; List of William and
Mary Alumni (1941); Virginia Migrations, Volume I, p. 4; 1 Va. L. Reg.
appendix 23; Register of the General Assembly of Virginia, 1776-1918;
Debates of the Convention of 1829/30, 3, 6, 16, 21, and 257-294; Peyton's
History of Augusta County 378-9; and this volume p. 11.)

George Nicholson Johnson was the son of Chapman Johnson and Mary
Ann Nicholson, his wife. He was born in Staunton, Virginia, circa 1807, and
died in Richmond, Virginia, in 1855. He was educated for the law, and was
associated with his father in the practice of his profession. The Honorable
John Randolph Tucker, in his address on the Richmond Bar, made 7 February,
1895, describes George Nicholson Johnson as the "able and worthy" representative of his great ancestor. He married Margaret Menzies, the daughter of
Adam Menzies, of Kentucky, and Elizabeth, his wife. They had the following
issue:

1. Mary Ann Johnson
2. Margaret Howard Johnson
3. Chapman Johnson
4. Arthur Nicholson Johnson; and
5. Caroline Gifford Johnson

(Peyton's History of Augusta County, 378-9; 1 Va. L. Reg., appendix 25; and this volume, p. 12.)

The first suit in this volume is Smith's Exors. v. Garland Anderson &c. This is an interesting suit concerning a partnership which existed and was dissolved prior to the American Revolution.

Garland Anderson, the defendant, is believed to have been the son of Bartelot Anderson, a distinguished attorney of Hanover County, and Mary Cosby, his wife. He was born in 1742 and died 8 March, 1811. He was a large land-owner in the upper part of St. Martin's Parish, Hanover County, and across the North Anna of the Pamunkey in Caroline County. Anderson's Bridge across the North Anna, so frequently mentioned in the history of the Revolution, was named for him, his real estate lying on both sides of the River at this point. He was a member of the County Court of Hanover, and he represented Hanover in the General Assembly, sessions of 1776; 1777; 1779; 1783; 1784/5 and 1785/86. He was one of the Personal Property Assessors for St. Martin's Parish in 1786. He was also a member of the Vestry of St. Martin's Parish, Hanover County.

It appears from the papers in Smith's Exors. v. Garland Anderson &c, that he was a merchant in partnership with Charles Smith, and that the partnership was dissolved in October, 1767, and the business apparently continued by Anderson thereafter.

By deed of 1 September, 1789, he conveyed his real estate in St. Martin's Parish, Hanover, and in Caroline County, to his son, John B. Anderson, receiving a life estate therein for himself and family.

He married Marcia Burbridge according to the bill filed by Frederick Harris in the suit of Smith's Exors. v. Anderson (this volume p. 5). They had the following issue:

1. John B. Anderson
2. William Anderson
3. Garland Anderson
4. Elizabeth Anderson
5. Mary Anderson, who married --- Anderson, and died before August, 1816, leaving one child, Mary Quarles Anderson, an infant in 1816.
6. Nancy Anderson
7. Maria Anderson, who died prior to February, 1817
8. Burbridge Anderson
9. Armistead Anderson; and
10. Genet Anderson

(W. P. Anderson's Anderson-Overton Genealogy (1945) 31, 49; Register of the General Assembly of Virginia 1776-1915; Personal Property Books for St. Martin's Parish, 1786; Anderson's Early Descendants of Wm. Overton and Elizabeth Waters, 34; this volume 1-8, especially 5, and St. Paul's Vestry Book, 477 and 499.)

The litigation under the style of Smith's Exors. v. Garland Anderson appears to have been begun in the High Court of Chancery with the bill filed by Christopher Smith, of Louisa County, exor. of Charles Smith, deceased, against Garland Anderson. Later Robert Boyle, who was a British subject, sued Anderson and Smith in the United States Court, and this appears to be the manner in which the Federal Court acquired jurisdiction over the controversy between Smith's Exors. and Anderson. It appears from the papers in the

cause that prior to the Revolution Garland Anderson and Charles Smith, partners, engaged in business as merchants in Hanover County. In October, 1767,
they dissolved the partnership, Anderson assuming the payment of the debts
and agreeing to pay Smith £1200. To secure this obligation Anderson executed
a deed of trust dated 8 October, 1773, by which he conveyed to John Snelson,
as trustee, 894 acres of land on the North Anna in Caroline County, including
the mill known as Anderson's Mill, as security for the protection of Charles
Smith against default in Anderson's undertaking. It was claimed that Anderson failed to pay Smith or the debts of the partnership, and one of the
British creditors having sued Anderson and Smith's Executors in the Federal
Court, the controversy between Smith's Executors and Anderson appears to
have been litigated in that Court.

One of the most interesting suits in this volume is Roots v. Gist,
(pp. 13-43). While the suit relates primarily to the Smith family of
Gould's Hill, on the Pamunkey River in lower Hanover County, and contains
deeds, wills, and documents containing much hitherto unknown information of
great interest, the chief historical find is a heretofore unknown legal opinion written by Patrick Henry in February 1770. This is believed to be the
earliest letter of Patrick Henry thus far published, and it is a most important Henry document. Samuel Gist, who was in London at the time, had consulted the celebrated Charles Yorke, later Lord Chancellor of England, who
had given him an opinion as to his, Gist's, rights in the matter in controversy with Joseph Smith of Hanover. Patrick Henry took issue with Yorke's
conclusion and clearly states his reasons for so doing.

This suit was begun in the United States Court by Thomas Reade
Rootes v. Samuel Gist, long after the death of the last Smith.

It appears from the papers in this suit that John Smith of Gould's
Hill, Hanover County, died in 1747, leaving a will, a widow named Mary, and
two sons, Joseph and John Smith, and apparently two daughters, Elizabeth and
Sarah Smith. (See the will of John Massie, p. 23.)

John Smith was a merchant and appears to have had his store at
Gould Hill. He was also a member of the County Court of Hanover. It appears
that he married Mary Massie, who was the sister of John Massie, of Goochland
County. (See the extract from John Smith's will, p. 22, and John Massie's
will, pp. 23-25; and V. Ex. Journal of the Council, p. 108.)

Samuel Gist, who later became one of the wealthiest and most powerful citizens of Hanover County, in his youth was the storekeeper for John
Smith. After John Smith's death he married his widow, became the guardian
of her infant sons, and according to the allegations made by Thomas Reade
Rootes in his bill, possessed himself of the wealth left by John Smith. (See
his bill pp. 13-17). These charges were vigorously denied by Samuel Gist in
his answer (pp. 18-22).

Unfortunately the copy of John Smith's will, said to have been
filed with the bill, appears to have been lost. All that has been located
is an extract from the same (pp. 22-23).

The will of John Massie, of Goochland County, which was an important exhibit in this suit, was probated in the General Court on 26 April,
1746, and by reason of the destruction of the records of that Court, this is
probably the only official copy of this will now in existence.

Of the children of John Smith, his son John Smith died unmarried.
His elder brother, Joseph Smith, married Martha Jacqueline Rootes, of Middlesex County, Virginia, who was Martha Jacquelin Smith, and the widow of Thomas
Reade Rootes. The plaintiff in this suit was the son of this last mentioned
union. The union between Joseph Smith and Martha Jacqueline Rootes resulted
in one son, Edward Jacqueline Smith. Edward Jacqueline Smith died in 1792,
about the time he reached his majority. His father, Joseph Smith, who was a
member of the County Court of Hanover County, died in 1773. By reason of
the death of his half-brother Thomas Reade Rootes claimed to have succeeded
to what had been the Smith fortune, or what was left of it.

There are a number of Court records relating to Gist's transactions
with reference to this estate (p. 25). The bond of Jacqueline Ambler as guardian of Edward Jacqueline Smith, and the marriage agreement between Joseph
Smith and Martha Jacqueline Rootes will be found in this suit (p. 26); also
the marriage bond of Thomas Reade Rootes and Martha Smith, the daughter of
John Smith, of Middlesex County, dated 8 February, 1763 (p. 27).

The deed from Joseph Smith to Samuel Gist, dated 17 September, 1765,
conveying a grist mill on Crump's Creek known as Smith's Mill, is of much
interest. Peter Lyons, who represented the Reverend James Maury in the Parson's Cause, in which Samuel Gist was the principal witness, and who was the
second President of the Virginia Court of Appeals, was a witness to this deed.

Seven letters written by Samuel Gist to John Smith and Joseph Smith
between 1768 and 1770 are included among the exhibits in this suit.

John Smith, of Gould's Hill, Hanover County, is believed to have
been the son of David Smith, and Elizabeth, his wife. (St. Peter's Parish
Register, p. 391.) If so, he was born in St. Peter's Parish, New Kent
County, Virginia, circa 1686, and was baptized 24 October, 1686. He died at
Gould's Hill, Hanover County, in 1746. He had been a member of the County
Court of Hanover County prior to 1742 and for some reason, unknown at this
time, had ceased to be a member of the Court. On the 15 December, 1742, he
was again appointed a member of the Court, and it was directed by the Gover-
nor and Council that he be put into his former place. (The bill in Rootes v.
Gist; this volume, pp. 13-17; V. Executive Journal of the Council, p. 108;
and the will of John Massie, this volume, pp. 23-24.)

John Smith II, of Gould's Hill, was the son of John Smith, of
Gould's Hill and Mary Massie, his wife. He was born circa 1744, and died
in Hanover County in 1774. He was a merchant in that County and was one of
the signers of the Association respecting the importation of British goods
entered into Friday, 22 June, 1770, by the members of the House of Burgesses
and the Body of Merchants Assembled on that day in the City of Williamsburg.
With Patrick Henry he represented Hanover County in the House of Burgesses
in the session of 1772. He was a member of the Committee of Public Claims,
and served with Patrick Henry and others on two special committees during
that Session. He was not a member of the House in 1773, and as noted, died
the following year. He was also a member of the vestry of St. Paul's Parish,
and was one of the church wardens of the parish. It appears from the Gist
correspondence that he looked after Samuel Gist's business interests in Hanover County after Gist moved to London. He died unmarried. (The bill in
Rootes v. Gist, this volume, p. 13; Journal of the House of Burgesses 1772,
pp. xxx, 143, 158, 170, 194, and 202; and the Letters of Samuel Gist, this
volume, pp. 28-36, and Vestry Book of St. Paul's Parish, pp. 498 and 499.)

Samuel Gist, it is believed, was born in England and came to Virginia when quite young. According to the bill in Rootes v. Smith he was the storekeeper for John Smith at Gould's Hill prior to 1746 and he appears to have been one of the executors named in John Smith's will. He also qualified as or acted as the guardian for Smith's infant sons. He is first mentioned in the Vestry Book for St. Paul's Parish 30 September, 1751, when the vestry ordered the processioning of the land of "John Smith's Orphans which Samuel Gist holds". Later he was one of the processioners for the Parish. Shortly after John Smith's death he married his widow, Mary Smith, and this and the control over the Smith estate which he acquired appears to have been the foundation of his subsequent fortune. He became one of the leading merchants of the country and was the chief witness offered on behalf of the Reverend James Maury in his unsuccessful action in the County Court of Hanover County in December, 1765, known as the Parson's Cause. He was a member of the County Court of Hanover County and one of the Quorum in 1764. He purchased Dundee and Woodberry on the River Road in Hanover County, Virginia

In 1750 Samuel Gist was authorized by the Council together with John Hiscox and John Griffin, of Bristol, Merchants, Benjamin Watkins, George Nicholas, John Buchanan, William Thompson, junr., and others to patent one hundred thousand acres of land on the New River, and they were allowed four years to complete the surveys.

He was one of the wealthy men of the county, having in addition to his real estate more than eighty slaves. He imported Bulle-Rock, the first Arabian race horse in the English colonies in America, "a distinction of which the Old Dominion is properly proud", said Fairfax Harrison in his delightful article on the Equine F. F. V.'s in the Virginia Magazine of History and Biography.

In October, 1765, he left Hanover County and returned to England "on account of the bad state of his health", he says in his answer in Rootes v. Gist. He evidently recovered his health after his return to England, as shortly thereafter he became established as one of the leading London merchants engaged in the Virginia trade. In March, 1769 he was one of the signers of the Merchants' Address to the King, for which he was severely criticised by the colonists in Virginia. He attempts to justify his action in signing the Address in his letter of 30 August, 1769, to John Smith. On the outbreak of the Revolution he was charged with being a British subject and in order to prevent the escheat of his property his daughter, Mary, the wife of William Anderson, applied to the General Assembly of Virginia to vest his estate in her, the wife of a loyal Virginian. By the Act of May, 1782, this was done. After the Revolution in some way Gist recovered his property in Hanover County. He died in 1815 leaving a very long will, a copy of which is in the State Archives. In this will he emancipated his slaves.

As noted above, he married Mary Smith, the widow of John Smith, of Gould's Hill, Hanover County. They had one daughter, Mary Gist, who married first, William Anderson, of Hanover County, and second, Martin Perks, of London.

(The Bill, Answer and Exhibits in Rootes v Gist, this volume 13-36; 37V338-9½ 15V346-7; Letter of 30 August, 1769, this volume, 36; V. Ex. Journal of the Council of Colonial Virginia, 326; The Vestry Book of St. Paul's Parish, 312, 339, 340, 374, 376, 400, 489 and 557; and 11H54.)

William Anderson was the son of David Anderson and Elizabeth Mills, his wife, the youngest child of Nicholas Mills and Anne Clopton. He was born in Hanover County, Virginia, circa 1736, and died in England in 1796. On 24 February, 1778, he was appointed commissioner for the estate of Samuel Gist, Esquire, in Amherst, Goochland, and Hanover Counties, pursuant to the Act of Assembly for Sequestering British Property. Later by Act of May, 1782, this property was vested in his wife, Mary, who was the daughter of Samuel Gist, as stated above. In the receipt of Thomas Smith, (p. 38) he is referred to as Captain William Anderson, which indicates that he was a militia officer prior to the Revolution. He furnished horses for the Revolutionary Army. After the Revolution he moved to England where he became a merchant engaged in the Virginia trade, and acquired a considerable fortune. A copy of his will is in the State Archives. He died without issue. (Anderson Family Records, 9-10; II Journal of the Council of the State of Virginia, 90 and 305; and 11H54.)

Among the papers of this suit is a very interesting deposition made by John Austin in 1807 (p. 38); two letters from William Anderson to Thomas Reade Rootes (pp.38-39), and the papers in a suit brought before 1760 against Gist and his wife (pp. 39-40) which indicates that his wife may have been named Sarah. If so, her name must have consisted of a combination of the two names, since John Smith in the excerpt from his will (p. 22) refers to her as Mary, and Samuel Gist in his answer (p. 18) admits that he married John Smith's widow, and further states (p. 19) that he left Hanover for England in October 1765, and that his wife died in Maryland "soon afterwards". The answer signed by Samuel Gist and Sarah Gist was filed some time prior to April, 1760 (pp. 39-40). Therefore, the name of Mrs. Gist must have been Mary Sarah or Sarah Mary.

Thomas Reade Rootes, the plaintiff in this suit, was the son of Thomas Reade Rootes and Martha Jacqueline Smith, his wife. He was born 20 February, 1764, in Middlesex County, Virginia, and died in Gloucester County, Virginia, 3 January, 1824. Shortly after his birth, his father sailed for England where he died when his son was only eighteen months old. His mother married circa September, 1767, Joseph Smith, of Gould's Hill, Hanover County, Virginia, and young Rootes was brought to Gould's Hill where it appears that he was raised. He was a student at William and Mary College in 1779. He was a prominent lawyer of his day and appears to have been a wealthy man. He moved to Caroline County some time prior to 1793 and in that year represented Caroline in the General Assembly of Virginia, and in the Sessions of 1794 and 1795. In 1817 he purchased Federal Hill in the City of Fredericksburg where he resided for a time. Later he moved to White Marsh, in Gloucester County. He was twice married, first to Sarah Ryng Battaile, and second to Mrs. Mary M. C. Prosser. The second marriage was without issue. The issue of the first marriage were as follows:

1. Thomas Reade Rootes, born 18 January, 1785, and died 2 November, 1820.

2. Martha Jacqueline Rootes, born 28 September, 1786, who married first, 8 May, 1810, Howell Cobb, a distinguished member of Congress from Georgia; and second, Doctor Henry Jackson, professor of Philosophy and Chemistry in the University of Georgia.

3. Mary Robinson Rootes, who was born 21 November, 1788, and died 29 January, 1811. She married, 10 December, 1809, William Fitzhugh Gordon, a distinguished lawyer, member of the General Assembly of Virginia, member of the Convention of 1829/30, and member of Congress.

4. Sarah Robinson Rootes was born 20 September, 1792, and died 21 November, 1855. She married 11 April, 1812, Colonel John Addison Cobb, of Georgia.

5. Laura Battaile Rootes, born 4 July, 1797. She died unmarried, 25 October, 1817.

6. Serena Ryng Rootes, born 5 October, 1802, and died in 1889. She married Henry Clinton Lea, of Georgia, who later moved to Alabama; and

7. Edward Jacqueline Smith Rootes, born 27 January, 1804, and died 20 July, 1840.

(4V208-211; information furnished by George H. S. King, 12-6-46; Swem, and Williams Register of the General Assembly of Virginia 1776-1918; Fox v. Rootes, E. F. 97, Fredericksburg, and Battaile v. Wilkinson, E.F.19, Fredericksburg.)

Another suit of almost equal interest with that of Rootes v. Gist is Warre v. Syme, and Hoops v. Syme, in the first of which Colonel John Syme, of Rocky Mills, was the defendant.

Warre v. Syme was a suit instituted by a British creditor against John Syme. The chief interest of this suit consists of twenty-one letters written by Colonel John Syme between 9 June, 1753 and 14 March, 1774. This is by far the largest collection of Syme letters which has been discovered to this date. A number of his letters relating for the greater part to matters pertaining to his duties as County Lieutenant for Hanover County during the Revolution have been published in the Calendar of State Papers. With this exception the present volume contains all of his letters thus far available to the public.

This suit also contains an interesting deed from Colonel John Syme to Thomas Walker, conveying 1650 acres of land lying near the Turkey Run Mountain, "formerly in the County of Hanover, now Albemarle", and a deed from Capt. John Syme, junr., to William Crenshaw, confirming the conveyance of 300 acres of his mother's land lying in Louisa County.

The last paper in this suit is the will of Adam Hoops, who was the father of Mrs. Sarah Syme, the second wife of Colonel John Syme, of Rocky Mills.

Adam Hoops was a citizen of Pennsylvania, resident of the Falls, in the County of Bucks. As his will indicates, he was a very wealthy man. His daughter, Sarah Hoops, married Col. John Syme sometime after the death of his first wife. On her marriage to Colonel Syme, Adam Hoops turned over to him ₤4000 current money of Pennsylvania, for his daughter, Sarah. Later he turned over to Colonel Syme ₤553:17:1 for his granddaughter, Elizabeth Syme, who was the eldest child of Colonel Syme and Sarah Hoops, his second wife.

It appears from the deed of 18 August, 1790, executed by Colonel John Syme to John Warden, of the Parish of St. David, in King William County, as trustee, that on 15 March, 1768 a marriage then being contemplated between Col. Syme and Sarah Hoops, Col. Syme entered into a contract with Adam Hoops, her father, by which in return for the payment of ₤2000 Sterling, evidenced by the bonds of Benjamin Harrison and William Byrd and the marriage, Colonel Syme agreed to convey Rocky Mills in St. Martin's Parish, Hanover County, together with fifty slaves, to the use of John Syme and Sarah, his wife, during their joint lives, with remainder for life to the survivor, with remainder in fee to the children born to them. On 1 April, 1768, after the marriage had taken place, Adam Hoops delivered over to Col. Syme the bonds, and confirmed the same by his will. Colonel Syme, as appears from the papers relating to him which have come to light, was very inattentive to his business, and neglected to perform his part of the bargain until 18 August, 1790, when he executed the deed to John Warden, as Trustee, to carry out his agreement with Adam Hoops. This deed was executed twenty-two years after it should have been executed.

The letters written by Colonel Syme and published in this volume throw much light on life in the Colony of Virginia and Hanover County between 1755 and 1774. The letter dated 24 April, 1755, speaks with sanguine hope about the results expected of the ill-fated Braddock expedition. Col. Syme and his neighbor in later life, Colonel Nathaniel West Dandridge, served as captains with the Virginia troops in this war.

These letters show that Colonel Syme lived extravagantly and was always in debt which seemed to increase each year. One would rather judge from the correspondence that Messrs. Lidderdale, Harmer & Farrell were probably not so honest in their dealings with Colonel Syme. Nevertheless he appears to have continued his extravagance and to have trusted too much to the merchants with whom he was dealing.

Many names of persons well known in Virginia of this period appear in this correspondence, - George Webb, Isaac Winston, junr., Col. John Henry, Peyton Randolph, Francis Jerdone, Dr. John Shore, Capt. John Darracott, Capt. Meux, Colonel Lewis, Col. Nathaniel West Dandridge, Anthony Winston, L. Pope, and many others.

These letters show that Col. Syme imported race horses, including the famous horse, Juniper. They also show that the early mill stones used in Hanover came from England.

On the whole these letters present a continued picture of colonial life in Virginia from 1753 until March, 1774. They speak of the French and Indian War, the Stamp Act, and the beginning of the American Revolution; of business and lack of business on the part of Colonel Syme; bad crop years and family afflictions, all interwoven into a most interesting whole.

With the exception of the Letter Books and Ledgers of Francis Jerdone in the William and Mary College Library it is believed that the Syme letters in this volume are the largest single collection of such Hanover material of this period thus far brought out of concealment. Their perusal will amply repay any one interested in Colonial History.

The first case of Hoops v. Syme (71) establishes the fact that Colonel Syme's daughter by his first marriage, Mildred Syme, married David Hoops; that Mildred Syme died circa 1778, leaving two sons, who also died prior to 1804. This is a matter of some interest since William Wirt Henry, in the appendix to Volume II of his <u>Patrick Henry</u>, states that Mildred Syme died unmarried.

The second case of Hoops v. Syme (72-76) was against the son of Col. Syme, Captain John Syme.

In this suit is an interesting deposition given by Nicholas Syme, one of Colonel John Syme's sons by his first marriage (p. 74).

Mrs. Glazebrook has also added to this collection the will of Nicholas Meriwether dated 12 December, 1743, and probated in Goochland County 26 November, 1744 (pp. 68-70). He was the great grandfather of Mildred Meriwether, the first wife of Col. John Syme. Mrs. Glazebrook has included also the will of Martha H. Syme, dated 12 June, 1820, and probated 18 October, 1824 (pp. 77-79). This last will shows that the testatrix had no love for her brothers-in-law, Doctor John T. Swann and Lemuel Riddick.

Colonel John Syme was the son of John Syme and Sarah Winston, his second wife. He was born in October or November, 1728, at Studley, in St. Paul's Parish, Hanover County, in the same house in which his half-brother, Patrick Henry, was later born, and he died at Rocky Mills in St. Martin's Parish, Hanover County, Virginia, on 25 November, 1805, at the age of 77 years and 11 months. With Col. John Chiswell he was elected to the House of Burgesses for the session 1752, but on a contest by Henry Robinson their election was declared void, and a new election ordered. When the new election was held he was defeated by Henry Robinson. He was elected to the House of Burgesses for the sessions of 1756-58; 1758-61; 1761-65; 1766-69, and 1773-75. He was one of the representatives in the Convention of 1776, and a member of the House of Delegates of Virginia, sessions of 1776, 1777, 1778, 1781-2, and a member of the State Senate in the sessions of 1784-85, 1785-86, 1786-87, and 1787-88. (J. H. B. 1752-55, vii. N14, 62).

He served as a captain in the French and Indian War, and was a County Lieutenant for Hanover County during the American Revolution, in which cause he devoted his whole time and a large part of his personal fortune, and that of his children.

He married first Mildred Meriwether, the daughter of Nicholas Meriwether, the younger, and Mildred, his wife. She died when quite young, circa 1761, leaving four children:

1. John Syme, junr., who was born circa 1755 or 1756.

2. Nicholas Syme

3. Sarah Syme, who married Colonel Samuel Jordan Cabell.

4. Mildred Syme, who married David Hoops.

He married second, Sarah Hoops, the daughter of Adam Hoops and Elizabeth, his wife. They had the following issue:

1. Elizabeth Syme, who married George A. Fleming, of Goochland County.

2. Jane Isabella Syme, who married first, John Thompson, and second, Doctor John T. Swann.

3. Anne Maria Syme, who married Lemuel Riddick.

4. Martha H. Syme, who died unmarried. She was blind.

(The Virginia Argus, 4 December, 1805; Journals of the House of Burgesses, 1756-1775; Swem & Williams's Register of the General Assembly of Virginia 1776-1918; 10V108; The Calendar of State Papers; Gwathmey's Virginians in the Revolution; Eckenrode's Colonial Soldiers of Virginia; 8H54-55; Nelson v. Suddarth, 350-351 (1807); Syme v. Johnson, 3 Call 560; II W. W. Henry's Patrick Henry, Appendix xi, 633-634; Hoops v. Syme, this volume, pp. 72-76.)

Much confusion exists in the printed records as to the dates of the Syme births and the death of Mildred Meriwether Syme. The date of her birth is established with a fair degree of accuracy by the Act October, 1764, (8H54-57). It is there stated that her father's will was dated 4 December, 1738, and that she had been conceived on that date but was unborn. She was, therefore, born some time after that date, probably in the early or middle part of 1739. In Brown's The Cabells and Their Kin, it is stated that she was born 19 May, 1739, and died in 1764. The first date would appear to be correct, but it also appears that she died before 1764. Judge Fleming states in the opinion in Nelson v. Suddarth, 1 Hen. & Munf. 359 (1807), that she was the wife of Colonel Syme in 1755, and at that time was fifteen or sixteen years of age. It would appear from the Act in 8H54-57 that she was sixteen years of age in 1755. Judge Fleming further states in his opinion in Nelson v. Suddarth, supra, that Mildred Meriwether Syme died "about the time she came of age", which would indicate that she died circa 1761. It has been stated that her eldest son, Captain John Syme, was born in 1752 (W. P. Anderson's Anderson-Overton Genealogy 215, and Anderson's Early Descendants of William Overton and Elizabeth Waters, 126). In view of the established date of his mother's birth it would seem that 1752 would be much too early for the birth of her son.

John Warden in his argument in Nelson v. Suddarth (1Hen.& Munf.357) states that Mildred Meriwether Syme died in infancy, which, if true, would place her death in 1759 instead of in 1760. He further states that John Syme, her oldest son, was then "only three years old". He follows this with the statement that Captain John Syme was born in 1752 and came of age in 1773. It seems impossible to reconcile these statements. If he was only three years old at the time of his mother's death he was born circa 1756. When it is considered that there were three additional children it would seem probable that Captain John Syme was born circa 1755.

It is definitely established that Sarah Syme, the daughter of Col. John Syme and Mildred Meriwether, was born 5 November, 1760. Her mother evidently died shortly thereafter. This indicates that Mrs. Syme reached the age of twenty-one before she died, the statements in Nelson v. Suddarth, supra to the contrary notwithstanding. (The Cabells and their Kin.)

When Nicholas Syme was born is unknown. He was a student at Donald Robertson's school in King and Queen in 1771 (34V232,236). If we can assume that his brother, Captain John Syme, was born in 1755 or 1756, it is probable that he was born the following year. He died circa 1812 (Ans. Dr. Wm. Cochrane in The Cochrane Family, 28). His sister Mildred Syme, who married David Hoops, was probably born between 1758 and 1759.

The will of John Thomson (pp. 80-83) is one of the earliest of the destroyed Hanover wills that has thus far come to light. It was executed in July 1758 and probated in June, 1759.

It is later than the will of William Morris found in the John Blair Dabney manuscript, pp. 36-38; but it is earlier than the wills of Isaac Winston (1760) and that of Barbara Overton Winston (1764) found in 4 The Valentine Papers 2371 and 2376. It is of earlier date than any of the very interesting wills found in Virginia Migrations, Vol. I, Hanover County. Mrs. Glazebrook's first volume of this series, and the earliest will in point of date and probate found in this volume.

There are a number of earlier wills in Hanover Deed Book 1734-1705, in the Archives Division of the Virginia State Library, and it is possible that some earlier Hanover wills will in the course of time come to light.

This will was found by the Deputy Clerk of Louisa County and called to the attention of the author of this introduction. He secured a copy of it and furnished it to Mrs. Glazebrook for inclusion in this volume.

A certified copy of this will is filed in the Louisa suit of Thompson v. Thompson E. F. 1819 (August S-Z) judgments.

It appears from the will that John Thomson was a merchant, probably at New Castle. The plat of New Castle made in 1738/39 by John Henry, surveyor for Colonel William Meriwether, as copied in June, 1754, shows John Thompson bought lot No. 20 in the Town of New Castle which was then occupied by Duncan Graham, and that he occupied Lot No. 36 in the said town which had been originally sold to Ed. Littlepage. It appears from St. Paul's Vestry Book that in October, 1731, he owned a farm somewhere in the vicinity of New Castle (Vestry Book p. 300, No. 22; Id. 310, No. 22; Id. 353, No. 19, and Id. 388, No. 18). It appears from the Processioners' Report, district No. 18, made subsequent to 19 November, 1759, after the death of John Thomson, that his land adjoined that of John Street, who owned Santee on the Old Church Road below New Castle. This land appears to have belonged to his estate in November, 1763, and April, 1764, as it was then processioned in his name (Vestry Book pp. 421-22). It was still owned by his estate in 1767-68 (Id. 456). Another tract of land was processioned in the name of his heirs in 1767 (Id. 459-60). His lands were again ordered processioned in 1771 (Id. pp. 482, 487), and again in 1779 (Id. pp. 551 and 556, Nos. 6 and 15).

His wife's name was apparently Keren-happuch. According to the King James version of the Bible Job 42:14-15: "He had also seven sons and three daughters; and he called the name of the first Jemima; and the name of the second Keziah; and the name of the third, Keren-happuch". "And in all the land were no women found so fair as the daughters of Job; and their father gave them inheritance among their bretheren."

The translation of the Douay version of the Bible varies as to the

13th and 14th verses 42 Job:

"And he called the name of one Dies, and the name of the second, Cassia, and the namo of the third, Cornustibii."

"And there were not found in all the earth women so beautiful as the daughters of Job; and their father gave them inheritance among their bretheren."

It is apparent that her name was taken from the King James version of the Bible, and that the clerk who drew the certificate of probate was more familiar with the Book of Job than was the draughtsman of the will, since the former spelled the name correctly and the latter did not.

Available sources fail to disclose who were the parents of John Thomson and his wife. His will shows that he and Keren-happuch, his wife, were the parents of the following children:

1. Mary, who married James Brown, who appears to have been held in very poor esteem by the testator, notwithstanding his affection for his daughter and her children.

2. Margaret, who married the Presbyterian minister, the Reverend James Todd, who graduated from Princeton in the class of 1749; was a member of the Louisa Committee of Safety of 4 December, 1775; a strong advocate of religious freedom in Virginia; and a trustee of Hampden-Sydney College from 1775 to 1790. He died 27 July, 1790. (6V174; 7V33; 5W(1)106 and 15W(1)252.)

3. Joseph Thomson, and

4. Elizabeth Thomson.

The latter two were infants at the time of John Thomson's death.

It appears from the suit of Thomson v Thomson above referred to, that Joseph Thomson married and had a number of children. The name of his wife is not disclosed. The names of his children are given as follows:

1. Elizabeth Thomson, who married James Shelton, and died leaving one child, John Shelton, who was an infant in 1815.

2. Susanna Chiles Thomson, who married Miller Brown.

3. Mary W. Thomson.

4. James Thomson.

5. Margaret Thomson.

6. Archibald Thomson.

7. John T. Thomson.

8. Nancy Thomson, and

9. Sarah Thomson.

The last seven of the children named above were infants circa 1815.

The next suit, Mercer & Wife v. Selden, while not relating directly to Hanover people, contains a deed to Hanover land, and was included in
this volume because it recites much information about the Watson family of
that county. (This volume, pp. 84-86)

The rest of the suit relates to the Page family of Gloucester, and
while long and interesting, can better be included in a volume "At Large",
than in one for a specific county.

The deed in question, from John Watson and wife, to Edmund Logwood,
concerns a tract of land devised by John Watson to his son, Joseph, containing 650 acres of land. On Little Allen's Creek is Edge Hill, on the south
side of the South Anna of the Pamunkey, which is just west of Gold Mine, and
in the general neighborhood of Rocky Mills, Mount Brilliant, and Colonel
Nathaniel West Dandridge's plantation on Great Allen's Creek. According to
this deed Edge Hill was the home of John Watson, Sr., in January, 1762,
when he made his will.

I am at this time unable to identify the tract of 1046 acres which
was partly in Hanover and partly in Goochland, lying on the waters of Tuckahoe. Probably examination of the records of Goochland may disclose the location of this land.

This deed also shows that Edmund Taylor was sub-sheriff of Hanover
County in 1773, a fact hitherto undisclosed in any known record.

Bayne v. Street, admr. of Winston et-al: In this suit Richard
Littlepage, having a letter of attorney from John Meux, conveyed Meux's land
to William Overton Winston, who in turn sold the same to George Bayne, who
sold the land with deed of warranty. Meux, on proof of these facts, recovered
the land, and Bayne repaid the purchase price to the purchaser from him. The
suit was against Winston's administrators and heirs. The bill gives the
names of William Overton Winston's children, and the names of some of his
grandchildren.

These suits are followed by the Hanover marriages which have been
heretofore mentioned. The list extends from page 88 through page 94, and
lists one hundred and forty three marriages.

These are followed by Hanover obituaries from the Virginia Gazette
and other newspapers (pp.95-97). This list contains thirty-eight obituaries,
all of which are of interest.

This is followed by the very interesting list of Absentee Land
Owners in Hanover County, 1814 and 1815, which was copied from the Land Books
for those years. This list (pp. 98-106) is a most interesting document.

Next comes an extremely interesting list of Hanover estates (107-
108) advertised for sale in the Virginia Gazette between 1767 and 1779. Advertisements of Newington, in King and Queen County, and Piping Tree Ferry,
and West Point, in King William County, advertised with Hanover land, are
also included.

The last item (p.109) is an order of publication at the direction of the Circuit Superior Court of Law and Chancery for the County of Hanover in February, 1837. This gives the names of the heirs of Nathaniel Bowe, deceased, late of Hanover County. Many people of distinction in Hanover County and the City of Richmond of this day are descended from the persons mentioned in this suit. For additional information as to this suit, the members of the Bowe family, and the wills of Nathaniel Bowe, John Bowe, and William Bowe, see Cocke's Hanover County Chancery Wills and Notes, 20-22.

On the whole it may be said that this book has sustained the high standard set by Volume I of this series, and it is to be hoped that other volumes will follow which will supply additional information as to Hanover County, its people and plantations. All of us who are interested in the history of Hanover County are deeply indebted to Mrs. Glazebrook for the work she has done to make available so many of the source records of Hanover County, the originals of which have been lost.

Leon M. Bazile

20 May, 1948

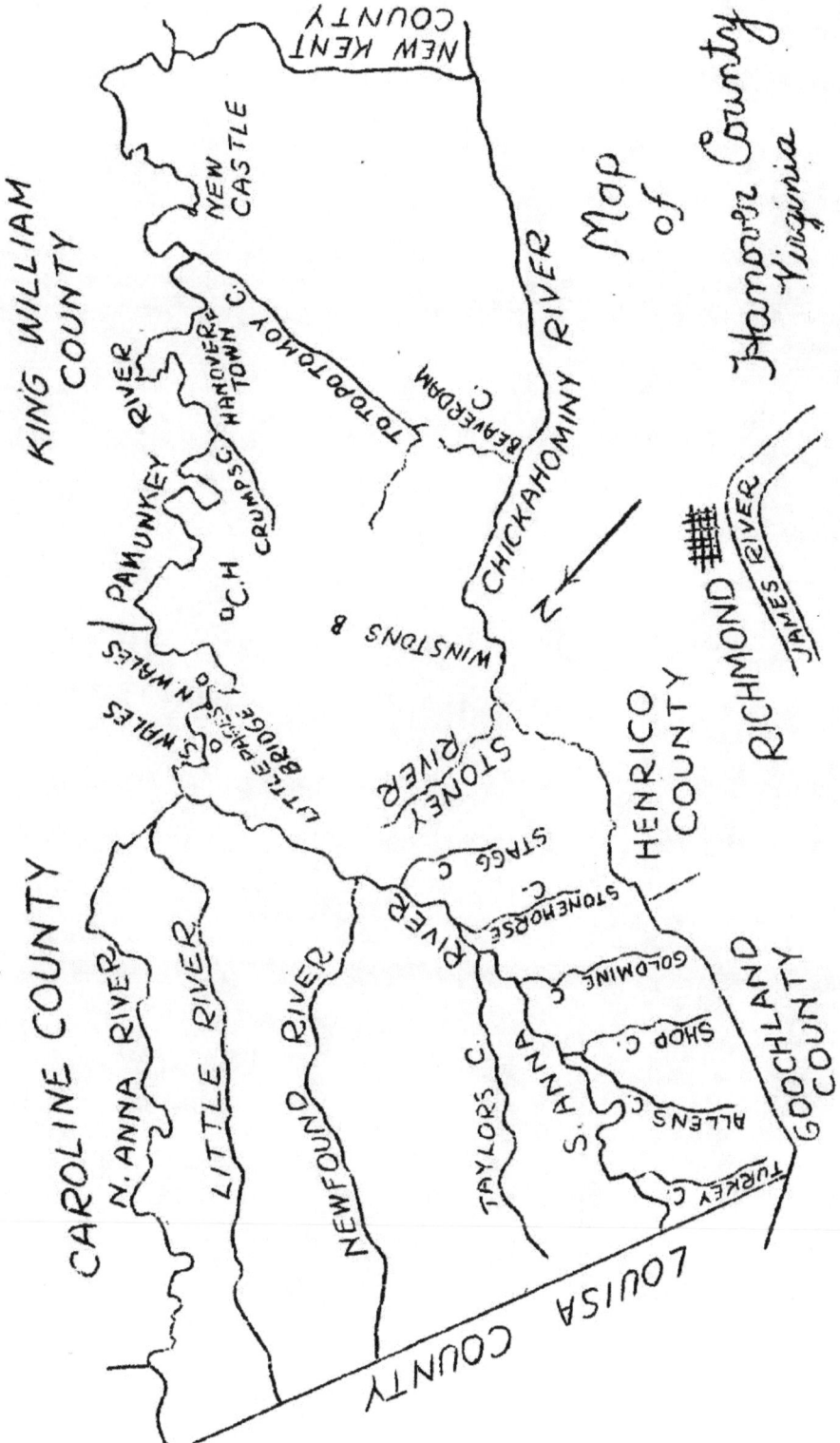

Map of Hanover County Virginia

KING WILLIAM COUNTY

NEW KENT COUNTY

NEW CASTLE

PAMUNKEY RIVER

HANOVER C.

CRUMPS C.

O.C.H.

TOTOPOTOMOY

N WALES

N WALES

LITTLE BRIDGE

CHICKAHOMINY RIVER

BEAVERDAM C.

WINSTONS B

STONEY RIVER

N

CAROLINE COUNTY

N. ANNA RIVER

LITTLE RIVER

NEWFOUND RIVER

S. ANNA RIVER

TAYLORS C.

STAGG C.

STONEHORSE C.

GOLDMINE C.

HENRICO COUNTY

SHOP C.

ALLENS C.

TURKEY C.

RICHMOND

JAMES RIVER

GOOCHLAND COUNTY

LOUISA COUNTY

ANDERSON
Smith

Smith's Exors.	)	1818 - Box 62
vs	)	U. S. Cir. Ct.
Garland Anderson &c	)	5th Cir. Va. Dist.
		Filed April, 1811

     To the Honble the Judges of the Circuit Court of the United States, 5th Circuit, District of Virginia -

     Charles Smith exor of Christopher Smith, decd., a Citizen and inhabitant of the State of Virginia, ... sheweth unto your Honors

     That prior to the late Revolutionary war between the United States and Great Britain your Orator's Testator Charles Smith was engaged in a commercial business with a certain Garland Anderson under the name and firm of Smith & Anderson, which was principally under the direction and management of said Anderson, as your Orator believes and therefore charges. That in the month of October in the year of 1767 a dissolution of the copartnery took place, whereby it was agreed that the said Garland Anderson should pay all the debts of the concern, and moreover pay to your Orator's said Testator the sum of ₤1200 equal to four thousand dollars, and the said Garland Anderson to secure the said Smith against the claims of the creditors of the said concern and also the payment of the said twelve hundred pounds, agreed and did on the 8th day of October in the year 1773 by his certain Indenture of trust convey to a certain John Snelson after reciting the said partnership and dissolution, and that he had agreed to pay all the debts then due or to become due from the said partnership in the first place, and before any of his private debts then due or to be due as also the said ₤1200, a certain tract or parcel of land, together with a water-grist mill lying and being in the County of Caroline, containing 894 acres, bounded as in the said Indenture set forth. Also 20 negro slaves, particularly named in the said Indenture... In Trust that the said John Snelson his Heirs, etc., should whenever it should become necessary dispose of so much and no more of the said thereby conveyed lands and slaves as should be sufficient and thereout pay and discharge the partnership debts so that the said Charles Smith shall be saved harmless therefrom. That by the terms of the dissolution the ₤1200 to be paid as aforesaid to the said Charles Smith was a debt due him from said partnership and was intended to be secured thereby ...

     That there remains due from said Anderson to his Testator Charles Smith, dec., about ₤1000 of the said ₤1200 with interest thereon since the 6 day of June, 1768 .

     Christopher Smith, who was much more intimate with the affairs of the said Charles Smith, dec., instituted a suit in the late High Court of Chancery against the said Garland Anderson, for recovery of said debt due his Testator in which he stated the death of the said Snelson and that the said Charles qualified as his executor, but before proceedings were had the suit abated by the death of the said Christopher.

Smith vs Anderson, continued:

   That a certain Robert Bogle a subject of the King of the United
Kingdom of Great Britain and Ireland, has instituted a suit in this Honorable Court against the said Garland Anderson and your Orator. The said
Bogle demands a considerable sum against the said concern due by a bill of
exchange which by the terms of the dissolution aforesaid should be paid by
the said Anderson.

   That your Orator is anxious to have an account from the said concern ... that trust estate be sold to pay the such of the partnership debts
as remain unpaid as also the balance due your Orator's Testator, the said
Charles Smith, decd., but your Orator has no means of inforcing the same
your Orator now being a Representative of the said John Snelson, decd., but
by the aid of this Honble Court.   To the end therefore ...

         Bill of Complaint of
         CHRISTOPHER SMITH

To the Honble George Wythe Judge of the high Court of Chancery, -

Humbly complaining sheweth to your Honour,

   Your orator Christopher Smith of the County of Louisa executor of
the last will and Testament of Charles Smith deceased who was executor of
John Snelson - that said Charles Smith and Garland Anderson having been concerned in a partnership in trade it was agreed between them that the said
Charles should give up his share of the partnership debts in consideration
whereof said Garland Anderson agreed to pay to said Charles Smith the sum
of L1200 and moreover to indemnify him and his legal representatives from
all partnership debts ... executing a deed of trust on the 8th day of October, 1773, conveying to said John Snelson a tract of land, etc., in Caroline
county containing about 895 acres ,..

   That the said John Snelson having died said Charles Smith who was
named his executor took on himself the burden of the execution of his will,
and the said Charles Smith being now dead your orator is his executor and
residuary devisee and the sole representative of the said John Snelson ...

   That your orator has been frequently called upon for the payment
of the debts and apprehends he shall be compelled to pay them unless the
trust property is applied to the discharge of them. That he has frequently
requested said Garland Anderson either to discharge said debts or to permit
him to sell so much of the trust property as would enable him to do it...
But the said Garland Anderson has refused to comply with his request.

   In tender consideration whereof ...

Smith vs Anderson, continued:

Deed of Trust
ANDERSON, SMITH, SNELSON
8 October, 1773

      This Indenture Tripartie made this 8th day of October, 1773, be-
tween Garland Anderson of the County of Hanover of the first part, Charles
Smith of the County of Louisa of the second part, and John Snelson of the
third part, WHEREAS the said Garland Anderson and the said Charles Smith
have hereunto been concerned as Merchants and Partners in Trade in Merchandize and have dissolved their Partnership on the following Terms to wit
That the said Garland Anderson has undertaken first to pay all debts then
due or to come due from the said Partnership in the first place and before
any of his private debts then due or to be due, and further the said Garland Anderson had undertaken to pay the said Charles Smith the sum of £1200
current money at certain times fixed for the payment thereof in consideration of which undertakings of the said Garland Anderson the said Charles
Smith had agreed to give up and did relinquish all the right and claim that
he had in and to the debts due to their partnership a part of which sum of
is paid, but there still remaining considerable debts due and unpaid from
the said Partnership the true intent and meaning of these presents is to
secure the said Charles Smith in the premises in such manner that neither
his person or his property shall or may be seized on or distressed in any
manner in case the said Garland Anderson shall not fulfill his contract.

      NOW THIS INDENTURE WITNESSETH that the said Garland Anderson for
and in consideration of the sum of five shillings to him in hand paid by
the said John Snelson the receipt whereof he doth hereby acknowledge ... by
these presents hath granted, etc., to the said John Snelson his heirs, etc.,
one Tract of Land together with a water Grist Mill lying and being in the
County of Caroline containing 894 acres, bounded by the lines of Samuel
Chewning, Philys Carpenter, and William Dickason and also twenty Negro
Slaves (mentioned by name), to have and to hold, ... unto the said John
Snelson, his heirs, etc. And the said John Snelson for himself, his Heirs,
etc., doth covenant, ... to and with the said Garland Anderson, his Heirs,
etc., that the said John Snelson, his Heirs, etc., or some of them shall
well and truly whenever and as soon as it shall become necessary dispose of
so much (and no more) of the said herein above conveyed as shall be sufficient to discharge the Partnership Debts aforesaid so that the said Charles
Smith shall be saved harmless and indemnified as aforesaid, and make and
execute any Deed of Revocation, Release or Acquittance that shall be reason-
ably required by the said Garland Anderson, his Heirs, Executors, etc.

      IN WITNESS whereof the parties to these presents have hereunto
set their Hands and Affixed their Seals the Day and Year first above written.

Wit.: Jane Bailey   Garld. Anderson (Seal)
Elizabeth Anderson   John Snelson   (Seal)
Edward (X) Shepherd   W. Bowden   Charles Smith   (Seal)
Samuel Hargrave   John Thilman
J. Meriwither   D. S.

Smith vs Anderson, continued:

The Answer of
GARLAND ANDERSON
to
Bill of Christopher Smith

This defendant admits that such contract was made with Complainant's Testator as in the Bill Charged - and that he executed a deed of trust as stated by Complainant for the purpose therein expressed - That this defendant hath fully paid and satisfied the said Complainant's testator in his life the £1200 the consideration of the said Testator's share of the partnership Debts in specie or its value previous to the commencement of the late American War and that this defendant _ been compelled to receive in depreciated paper money many of the debts due to said partnership his share of which the said Testator had by the contract aforesaid and transferred to this defendant one half of the loss of which but for the contract aforesaid, the said testator would have sustained.

This defendant hath never been informed by the Complainant that any other claim besides the judgment alluded to in his Bill hath been exhibited against him on account of the partnership Debts nor has any other demand been exhibited against this defendant.

The judgment to which the defendant supposes the complainant alluded is a judgment obtained against the partnership in the County Court of Hanover in the year 1774 by Starke Cross & Co., and to recover a scire facias hath been lately issued against the Complainant as Executor of the said Charles and this Defendant, which is now depending and from which this Defendant is advised both himself and the Complainant will be exonerated, that until a Decision shall be had upon the said sci: fac: this defendant humbly conceives that no sale of the property in the Deed of Trust expressed ought to be made especially as the decision is generally expected in favour of the complainant of this defendant, and as the sale might unnecessarily subject this defendant to very great inconveniency and loss.

This Defendant Prays to be hence dismissed with costs etc ...

Nicholas for Deft.

City of Richmond to wit:

Sworn to before Wm. DuVal, a magistrate for said City

A Copy Teste   Wm. W. Hening Cl C. R. D.

Subpoena for

Garland Anderson and John Claybrook, executor of William Claybrook, to answer bill in Chancery against them and others by Mark Starke and William Cross, surviving partners of Stark Cross & Company. Dated 20 December, 1807, 32nd year of Independence of the United States of America -

Wm. Marshall, Clk.

Smith vs Anderson, continued:

Bill of Complaint of
FREDERICK HARRIS
Dated August, 1816

To the Honble the Judges etc.

Your Orator Frederick Harris admor. de bonis non with will* annexed of Charles Smith the elder decd., and admr. de bonis non with will* annexed of Charles Smith the Younger deceased, sheweth

That the said Charles Smith the younger decd. (as exor. of Christopher Smith, who was executor of said Charles Smith the elder) in his lifetime exhibited a bill in Chancery in this honourable Court against a certain Garland Anderson and Robert Bogle pending which suit the said Charles Smith the plaintiff and the said Garland Anderson the defendant departed this life That your Orator is the personal representative of both the said Charles Smith the younger and Charles Smith the elder.

That John B. and William Anderson are the administrators of the said Garland Anderson, deceased, and the same John B. and William Anderson, with Garland, Elizabeth, Nancy, Maria, Burbridge, Armistead, Genet, and Mary Quarles Anderson (infant child of Mary Anderson), are the heirs and distributees of the said Garland Anderson.

In tender consideration whereof your Orator Prays that ... the suit aforesaid may be revived in your Orator's name and behalf against said Robert Bogle, and said heirs and distributees of said Garland Anderson in the same plight in which it stood at the time of the death of said Garland Anderson.

May it please your honours, etc. ...

Subpoena for heirs and distributees of Garland Anderson
dated 18 February, 1817, 41st Year of Independence of U. S.

Memo on above subpoena: "Maria Anderson has departed this life."

Sgd.   Ben: Mann D. M. for
A. Moore, M. V. D.

Order of Publication, carried in "The Enquirer", March 11, 1817 -
After stating the names of Plaintiffs and Defendants in above Bill:

"The defendants Robert Bogle, Burbridge and Armistead Anderson, not having entered their appearance, etc., and it appearing to the satisfaction of the court that said defendants are not inhabitants of this District, it is ordered that said defendants do appear here on the 1st day of the next term to answer the plaintiff's bill. A Copy, Teste, Richard Jeffries, Clk."

---

* Wills not found among these suit papers.

Smith vs Anderson, continued:

The Affidavit of
<u>FRANCIS HODGES</u>

Caroline County to wit:

          The affidavit of Francis Hodges taken before me, Fleming Terrell,
Justice of the Peace for the County aforesaid is as follows:

          This affiant being duly sworn saith that he, this affiant, is a·
subscribing witness to a receipt and agreement made and entered into between
Charles Smith and Garland Anderson, bearing date the Seventh day of October,
1767, and that John Epperson and Matthew Anderson were subscribing witnesses
also ... Further that he was a subscribing witness also to an account of the
said Charles Smith against the said Garland Anderson dated June 6th, 1768,
and that Sam Nuckols and David Davenport were also subscribing witnesses ...

          Given under my hand and Seal this 1st day of April 1817

                              Signed   Frank Hodges   (Seal)

- - -

Bogle   ) 1819 - Box 85
   vs   ) U. S. Cir. Ct.
Anderson's Heirs) 5th Cir., Va. Dist.

          Thursday, December the 14th, 1809.

          Robert Bogle,   against
          Garland Anderson and Charles Smith, Executor of Christopher Smith,
who was Executor of Charles Smith, deceased, Defendants.

The Answer of
<u>GARLAND ANDERSON</u>

          Who saith that on the 13th day of Augt. in the year 1766 Robert
Bogle & Scott commenced an action on the case against him in the County
Court of Hanover - After various continuances on the 4th day of November
1773 the plaintiffs conscious of their inability to maintain their suit dismissed it at their costs, as will more fully appear by the record.

          The defendant insists on the staleness of the demand; the plea of
limitations and the iniquity of harrassing him through a period of forty
years and upwards for the same demand; artfully shifting the name of the
firm, at each step, that a defeat in the first suit may not be pleaded in
bar of a second ...

City of Richmond to wit:

          Sworn to before me an Alderman for the said City

Nov 22 - 1809   Cr Tompkins

Bogle vs Anderson's Heirs, continued:

ORDER OF COURT

On the motion of the Plaintiffs by Counsel the Court setting
aside so much of the order made in this cause of the second day of December in the last year as conflicts with what followeth; Doth adjudge order
and Decree that the Defendants do render before one of the Commissioners
of this Court an account of the Real and Personal estate conveyed by Garland Anderson to John Snelson by the Indenture of the eighth day of October in the year 1773 ...

A Copy Teste Will. Marshall, Clk.

Commissioners Office Fredericksburg
4th November 1812

In obedience to the foregoing order your Commissioner, on the
9th of April 1812, the period when the same was brought to this office,
issued Notice to the parties, and appointed the 19th day of May following,
... but the parties did not attend, ... therefore other notices were issued ... On the 16th day of September following the parties appeared and
the Defendant John B. Anderson declared to the Commissioner that he was
not then prepared to go into the statement ... Adjournment was made to the
30th day of October when the said Anderson again appeared and exhibited
sundry papers, and having carefully examined the same your Commissioner
begs leave to make the following Report -

John B. Anderson exhibited upon oath a statement denominated
"Inventory and Appraisement of the Personal Estate of Garland Anderson,
deceased", containing such part of the personal estate as was made over
in trust to John Snelson for the safety of Charles Smith, to be of the
value of £1593, and he declared that the Land mentioned in the Deed of
Trust is still in the possession and occupancy of his mother, the widow
of his father, Garland Anderson ... That the said John B. Anderson and
William Anderson are administrators of Garland Anderson, deceased, and
that the said John B. Anderson acknowledged the notice on behalf of his
Brother William Anderson, the other Administrator...

Benjm. Parke
Commiss. in Chy.

- - -

Bogle and Scott   ) 1806 - Box 34
       vs   ) U. S. Cir. Ct.
Smith's exors &c (1801)) 5th Cir., Va. Dist.

To the Honourable the Judges, etc., Your Orators, Robert and
Robert Bogle & Scott prior to the year 1771 had considerable dealings with
Garland Anderson & the Testator of the Defendant, ... who carried on trade
under the firm of Smith and Anderson. Some time after this (July, 1771)
the said Smith departed this life, having first duly made and published
his last will and Testament in writing and thereof made his son Christopher his Executor.

Bogle & Scott vs Smith's exors., continued:

The Answer of
GARLAND ANDERSON

    ... Who saith that he "was a Partner with Charles Smith in the Trade of Merchandize and that they carried on such Partnership having equal shares thereof, from the year one thousand seven hundred and sixty one, until some time in the year one thousand seven hundred and sixty seven ..." That his Books and Papers being destroyed by part of the British Army during the War of the Revolution, he cannot refer to the entry ... That he (Anderson) conveyed certain Property in the County of Caroline to one John Snelson of the County of Hanover as an indemnity to the said Charles Smith against Debts of the Partnership ...

    Sworn to on the 9th Day of April, 1805, before Wm DuVal, one of the Magistrates of the City of Richmond.

- - -

Bill of Complaint *
BOGLE vs ANDERSON &c
May 25, 1807

To the Honourable the Judges, etc ...

    ... Wherefore your Complainant prays ... that he may have the benefit of the said Deed of Trust, that the property conveyed by said Deed, or so much of it as may be necessary may be sold and your Orator paid his Debt, Interest and Costs of Suit (the said John Snelson the Trustee having long since departed this life and hath now no legal representatives except the aforesaid representatives of the said Chas. Smith, who was the heir and executor and (sic) * the said John Snelson...

---

*Should this "and" have been "of"? Note the relationship here implied between Charles Smith and John Snelson. - E. G.

JOHNSON

Backhouse   ) U. S. Cir. Ct.
  vs   ) #157 - 149
J. Boswell's Exor.) (1806)

To the Honourable the Judges, etc., Your Orators

Humbly complaining shew unto your Honours your Complainants John Backhouse and Jane Backhouse admr. and admx. de bonis non of John Backhouse decd., subjects of the King of Great Britain ...

That a certain John Boswell late of the county of Louisa, a citizen of Virginia being in his lifetime indebted to John Backhouse decd. in a considerable sum of money and being possessed of a considerable estate real and personal did duly make and publish his last will and Testament in writing thereby devising in said will, a copy of which is hereto annexed * (after payment of his just debts) his said Estate to certain persons ...

He also devised the plantation on which he lived to be sold for payment of his British debts, and appointed Thomas Boswell, Thomas Johnson (minor), John Bourne, and Boswell Thornton, Executors, of whom Thomas Johnson (minor) alone took upon himself the burthen and Execution thereof ...

THE ANSWER OF JANE JOHNSON
Dated 25 April, 1807

This respondent is entirely ignorant of the claims against the estate of John Boswell, set forth in the Plaintiff's bill.

This respondent is the daughter of Thomas Johnson (minor), the executor of John Boswell, and a sister and co-heir of Rich'd Johnson, the executor of Thomas Johnson (mr) ...

She believes she is possessed of no property which ever belonged to John Boswell ... The slaves which were specifically devised to her by her father received their freedom and are no longer retained in bondage. No division of her father's personal property, she is informed, has ever been made, nor has any settlement of his estate ever been made ...

This respondent was entitled to none of the real estate of her father under his will.

Her brother Richard died intestate and without wife or children, and she is advised that she is entitled to an equal share of the estate which he was possessed of or had a right to ...

Louisa County: Sworn to before Ludlam Bramham, J. P.   25 April, 1807.

---

* See Virginia Migrations, Hanover County, Vol. I, page 1, for will of John Boswell. - E. G.

Johnson, continued: *

WILL OF JOHN B. JOHNSON
Dated February 12, 1815

I, John B. Johnson, of the State of Tennessee, Sumner Co., being
very sick but thank God in perfect mind and memory, do make this my last
will and testament ...

To my brother Chapman Johnston of the State of Virginia, I bequeath
the following Negroes ... in trust for my sister Ann Parrish to be applied
to her sole and exclusive use, benefit and behoof.

To my wife Elizabeth Johnson all the residue of my estate for her
use and that of my children until my second son Chapman, who was ten years
old the 21st of last October, comes of age, at which time it is my desire
that the estate real and personal be equally divided between my said wife and
three children Thomas   Chapman   and Mariah.

The executors are authorized to sell the estate if they think ad-
vantageous to the family, in which case the proceeds are to be put out at
interest and proceeds (sic) to be applied to the use of said wife and children until said second son Chapman become of age, then to be equally divided
between wife and three children, Thomas, Chapman, and Mariah.

Executrix, wife, Elizabeth Johnson and executor, brother, Chapman
Johnson, of the State of Virginia.

                              (Signed)   John B. Johnson

Wit.: S. or L. Hunt, William
Bloodworth, Mark C. (x) Holeman   Rec. Sumner Co., Tenn. Aug. Term, 1815

Chapman Johnson qualified as executor.

On motion of Chapman Johnson, of Staunton, Virginia, by Lion (or
Sion) Hunt his attorney it is ordered to be certified that by the last will
and testament of John B. Johnson, of Sumner County, proven in this court and
now duly recorded, there are devised to said Chapman Johnson in trust for
the benefit of his sister Nancy the following slaves, - Phillis and her children.   24 March, 1854.

Recorded in the Hustings Court held for the City of Richmond,
15 May, 1851. - Will Book No. 13, p. 95.

Authenticated copy of the last will and testament of John B. Johnson, late of Sumner County, Tenn., was this day produced in court and ordered
to be recorded at the instance of George Nicholson Johnson, and Chapman Johnson, the executor who qualified on said John B. Johnson's estate being dead,
George Nicholson Johnson made oath and entered into bond with Carter P. Johnson, surety, and received letters of administration on the estate of John B.
Johnson.

_____

* The wills of John B. Johnson, Chapman Johnson, and George Nicholson Johnson are not a part of the suit, Backhouse vs Boswell's Exors., but are here
included because of their obvious interest in connection with the Johnson
family of Hanover County. - E. G.

Johnson, continued·

WILL OF CHAPMAN JOHNSON
Hustings W. B. 12, p. 306
City of Richmond, Virginia

... "Whole estate to wife for her comfortable support and next that of her sister Mrs. Ellzey during her stay in Richmond, and lastly to the use and benefit of my children, George Nicholson, Mary Ann and Carter Page.

To son Nicholson whole of my law library including law books held in name of C. and C. N. Johnson."

Business and partnership of C. and C. N. Johnson to be regarded as settled and balanced between the partners ...

"To son William to whom I have already given a full share of my real estate I give one-fourth of my slaves, one-fourth of my maps and books other than law books and the whole of my kitchen and household furniture at "Bearwallow"* except piano forte subject to his mother's use of such furniture for her life."

"To son Carter, my gold watch and $500.00 to aid him im supporting himself with books and professional instruments ..."

"To daughter Mary Ann the piano forte at Richmond with the musick, musick-stand and musick-stool that goes with it, and the furniture usually kept in the room which she occupied as her bedchamber till her marriage, and which she usually sleeps in when on a visit to me except during its temporary occupation by Carter and his wife. After her mother's death I give her my profile by St. Memin; and her minature by Saunders I give to her husband Mr. Gifford."

"At my wife's death I give the piano-forte that usually stays at "Bearwallow" to Nicholson's eldest child Marianne."

"The residue of my estate both real and personal to be divided into three equal parts, one for Nicholson, one for Carter, and the third for Mary Ann, except only that such slaves as may fall into her division be vested in Nicholson and his executors forever for the separate use and benefit of Mary Ann forever."

Executors: three sons, Nicholson, William and Carter, each in succession according to seniority without security.

"Done at Richmond in my own handwriting, and duly published as my last will and testament this 8th day of January, 1847."

"C. Johnson"

Proved in the Hustings Court, City of Richmond, 13 August, 1849

---

* "Bearwallow" was in Augusta County, Virginia, according to an inventory of Chapman Johnson's estate, Hustings W. B. 13, p. 26, Richmond, Virginia. See also History of Augusta County, Virginia, by J. Lewis Peyton, p. 378.

Johnson, continued:

WILL OF GEORGE NICHOLSON JOHNSON

I, George Nicholson Johnson, of the City of Richmond, now being in the City of Washington on my way to visit the States of Kentucky and Indiana, do make and ordain my last will and Testament as follows - never having before made any will.

... To my brother William such of my law books as he may desire not exceeding $100.00 in value.

... To my sister Mary Ann the portrait of my great grand-mother Atcheson.

... To my son Chapman my father's gold reading spectacles and their shagreen case.

... To my brother Carter any of my miscellaneous books he may desire not exceeding $50.00 in value.

I bequeath to my dear wife (whom I pray God may bless and console) such of my personal property as she may select, not exceeding $500.00 in value, together with such books, clothing, jewelry, furniture and fixtures as may have been at any time presented to her by myself or others to have and to hold as her absolute property.

I desire that my executors convert the residue of my property real estate and personal in Virginia, Kentucky or elsewhere, into money and to invest that money in stock of the State of Virginia which stock shall belong to my said wife during her life for her own use and the support and education of our children, and at her death shall belong to such of our children as shall then be alive and the descendants of such as may then be dead, leaving issue ...

As my brother William will in case of my death have the care of the administration of my father's estate, I appoint my brother, Dr. Carter P. P. Johnson and my friend Andrew Johnston, (son of Robert Johnston, deceased) my executors without security.

Whereunto I hereby set my hand and seal this 19 day of August, 1849.

(Signed) G. N. Johnson

Codicil. 19 August, 1949. I give to my dear mother, if she be living at my death, $100.00 as a mark of my affection.   (Signed) G. N. Johnson

Probated in the City of Richmond at a Hustings Court held at the State Courthouse 9 April, 1855. Hustings W. B. 16, p. 589.

There being no witnesses to the foregoing will A. D. F. Gifford, R. T. Daniel and R. R. Hourson were sworn and severally deposed that they were well acquainted with the handwriting of the said George N. Johnson deceased ... and Carter P. Johnson, one of the executors in said will being dead, Andrew Johnston entered into bond in penalty of $16,000.00, and certificate was granted him for probate.   Teste Ro: Howard. Clk.

SMITH
Rootes-Gist

Rootes)   1825 - Box 116
  vs   )   U. S. Cir. Ct.
Gist   )   5th Cir. Va. Dist.
)   Filed 1805

        To the Honble the Judges of the Court of the U. S. for the
fifth Circuit in the Virginia District sitting in Chancery

        Humbly complaining sheweth unto your Honors your Orator Thomas
R. Rootes administrator de bonis non of Joseph Smith and John Smith both
deceased, late of Hanover County in the State of Virginia that John Smith
the Father of the said Joseph and John departed this life some time in the
year 1746 having first made and published his last Will and testament a
copy* of which duly recorded and certified is hereto annexed as part of
this bill, No. 1, in which said Will the said John among other devises gives
his widow Mary Smith one third part of his Lands and slaves for life and
one fifth part of his personal Estate forever and directs after the Death
of his said wife the negroes so lent her for life should be divided (except
some particularly named) between his two sons Joseph and John Smith with a
proviso that in case the Will of a certain John Massie (then disputed)
should be established in that case all the slaves, so lent to his said wife,
should be the property of his Eldest son Joseph all which will more fully
appear reference being had to the said Will and your Orator avers that the
Will of the said John Massie was established as will appear by a copy thereof hereto annexed which is properly recorded and certified and which he
prays may be taken as a part of this bill, by which said will a considerable
Estate was devised to said John Smith the second son of the testator John
Smith, as will appear reference being had to the said Will, No. 2.

        Your Orator states that the first named John Smith directed by
his Will aforesaid that no inventory or appraisement of his Estate should
be made and appointed John Martin and John Darracot his Executors, and his
wife Mary Executrix, which said Darricot took upon himself the burthen
thereof and has departed this life without returning any account of his
executorship of the said Estate and has left his Executors whom your Orator
prays may be made Defendants to this bill.

        Your Orator further states that some time in the year --- a
short period after the death of the said John Smith his widow intermarried
with one Samuel Gist who had been storekeeper of her late Husband, who had
been and was at the time of his Death a Merchant Dealing to a considerable
extent having on hand goods to a considerable amount besides cash and outstanding debts to a large amount, all of which fell into the hands of the
said Samuel Gist (his said wife being Executrix to her Husband) who now
resides in the City of London, is a subject of the King of Great Britain
and whom your Orator prays may be made a Defendant to this bill.

Rootes vs Gist (continued):

        Your Orator states that at the time of the intermarriage aforesaid
the children of the said John Smith, particularly the two sons were Infants
of tender age, Joseph being four or five years old and John about two years
old. That immediately after the said intermarriage the said Defendant possessed himself of the whole estate of the said John Smith deceased and of
the estate of John Massie, of whom the said John Smith was the only Executor,
in consequence of his said wife (long since Deceased) being named as an Executrix in the will of her said Husband John Smith, for though no bond can be
found on the record where Mrs. Smith or the said Defendant actually qualified as Exx or Exr to the said Will yet an Order of Hanover Court is found
bearing date the 4 day of June 1752 and hereunto annexed as part of this
bill (No. 3) in which the said Defendant calls himself Executor of the said
Will and in that capacity comes into Court to obtain a Division of the Estate agreeable to the said Will and the Law.

        Your Orator further states that at the same time the said Defend-
ant took upon himself the guardianship of Joseph and John Smith and entered
into bond with the aforementioned Darricot and one Thomas Booth copies of
which bonds are hereto annexed (No. 4) and (No. 5), and at the same time
became guardian for the other child of Mr. Smith as will appear hereafter by
which means he still retained the possession of the whole Estate of the said
Smith and Massie both of which were large and valuable lying in the counties
of Hanover and Goochland. The amount of Massie's may be estimated in some
Measure by the inventory and appraisement hereto annexed (No. 6).

        The amount and value of John Smiths Estate still remains unknown
the said Defendant having destroyed every clue leading to a discovery of the
same for your Orator avers that notwithstanding the order of Court obtained
in 1752 (many years after he had enjoyed the whole estates) to Divide the
Estate of John Smith no division thereof ever was made or returned to the
said Court by the Defendant or any other person as will appear by a Certificate of the proper Clerk annexed ... Although the Defendant Gist resided in
this country until the year 1765 he never executed the order for the division obtained in 1752 nor did he during that period ever settle the Guardianship account of Joseph Smith's Estate tho: thereto frequently ordered by the
Court of Hanover as will appear by copies of two orders made respecting the
said Defendants Guardianship aforesaid hereto annexed (Nos. 7 and 8), nor
did he ever settle any account for his ward John Smith except one for the
years 1764 and 1765 a copy of which is hereto annexed (No. 9), by which in
some Measure the value of the Estate may be ascertained and some conjecture
made respecting the profits of such an Estate during the long minority of
John Smith all which remains to the present time unaccounted for except the
sum of L362:18:1 as by a receipt hereto annexed was paid to Joseph Smith who
was appointed guardian to his Brother John in 1765 which receipt (No. 10) and
Guardians bond (No. 11) are hereto annexed.

Rootes vs Gist, continued:

      Your Orator states that the Defendant Gist not content with re-
ceiving and enjoying the profits of the aforementioned Estates for nearly
25 years did after the death of his wife the widow of the said John Smith
retain a great number of the slaves of the said John Smith's Estate being
those lent to Mrs. Smith during her life which said slaves and their increase he holds and retains possession of to this day or those hold them
who claim under him as will be hereafter explained.

      Your Orator states to your Honors that it is with great Diffi-
culty he is able to appear in Court with even a shadow of title against
the Defendant Gist there having been the strangest combination of circumstances in the progress of the aforementioned events that perhaps ever existed to enable one set of persons to deprive others of their Estates the
Defendant Gist in the first instance intermarried with the widow who was
left an Executrix and by that means and by becoming Guardian to the Children he obtained the possession of the whole Estates as before stated.
About the time of Joseph Smith arriving at age about 1765 the Defendant
(leaving his Wife behind him who soon after Departed this Life) removed to
the Kingdom of Great Britain where he has remained ever since and carried
with him every book or paper respecting the foregoing Estates or destroyed
them for your Orator who has been intimate in the affairs of the Estates
for nearly thirty years (the said Joseph Smith having married your Orator's
Mother when your Orator was an Infant of three or four years of age) has
never yet seen or heard of any books or papers respecting the said Estates,
but equally unfortunate for your Orator soon after the Defendant left this
Country some time about the year 1773 Joseph Smith departed this life and
William Anderson (who married Mary Gist the Daughter of the Defendant who
is now Mary Perks, the said Anderson having departed this life, which said
Mary and Martin Perks her present husband your Orator prays may be made defendants to this bill) administered upon the Estate of the said Joseph
Smith who left only one son, an Infant of two or three years old and in the
course of one year after the Death of Joseph Smith John Smith departed this
Life unmarried without issue, and the said William Anderson was the only
acting Executor to the said John so that if any paper respecting the Interests of the Estates aforesaid had escaped the ravages of Gist and time they
fell into the hands of his soninlaw Anderson, but your Orator in justice to
the Memory of William Anderson avers that in his opinion the Defendant Gist
had trusted nothing behind that could rise in judgment against him. However it is an extraordinary fact that the Defendant Gist who had been at
enmity with his said soninlaw from the time of his marriage with his Daughter and would not see either of them when in England or communicate with
them after they came to this country did immediately after the death of the
two Mr. Smiths reconcile himself to Wm. Anderson and remain on the most
friendly terms with him during the remainder of his life.

      Your Orator states that William Anderson did not institute any
suit against the Defendant Gist as in duty bound but did on the contrary
actually petition the Legislature of this State during the revolutionary
war for the Estates of Mr. Gist in consequence of marrying his Daughter a
copy of which petition is hereto annexed (No. 12), that the whole Estate
called Gists in this country to be the acutal property and Estate of Gist
tho: he ought to have known otherwise (by Documents to be hereafter presented) that there was a dispute about the Negroes and that Mr. Gist had

Rootes vs Gist (continued):

only a life Estate in part of the Goochland Land the Negroes being claimed
by Joseph Smith to whom he was administrator and the reversionary Interest
in the Land belonging to Edward Jaquelin Smith the only son of Joseph Smith
then an Infant and the ward of the said William Anderson as appear by a copy
of his Guardian bond hereto annexed (No. 13).

And to prove the knowledge of the fact respecting the Negroes
Your Orator hereto annexes a copy of a Letter of the Defendant Gist (No. 14)
in which he offers to give up one half of the Negroes which letter bears
date the 20 March, 1770 and is in the handwriting of the said Gist which
must have been well known to the said Anderson.

Also a letter from the late Patrick Henry directed to the said
Joseph Smith advising him not to take one half for the whole of the Negroes
were his by Law under his Father's Will which letter (No. 15) is hereunto
annexed as part of this bill which two letters were in actual possession of
the said Anderson and found a short time ago among a bundle of papers he delivered the late Jaquelin Ambler Esq. who was appointed Guardian of Edward
J. Smith about the year 1778 and who delivered the bundle to your Orator as
papers said to be of little value.

Your Orator states in addition to these circumstances that Edward
Jaquelin Smith departed this life in 1792 an Infant or if of age not 22
years old and that in consequence of the aforesaid events the claim has lain
dormant to the present period at which time your Orator avers the sums due
from the said Gist to your Orator as administrator of Joseph and John Smith
must be considered independent of the hire of the Negroes so retained by him
that the Negroes have increased to a number unknown to your Orator but from
1746 or 1747 when he received them to the present period your Orator supposes they amount to one hundred at least the said Defendant having upon the
Estates formerly called Gists and now said to be the property of the Defendants Perkins (sic) and Wife a great number of Negroes all proceeding from
the Negroes belonging to the Estate of the first named John Smith.

That the said Defendant Gist is also indebted to your Orator in
a large sum for the rent of 500 acres of land in the county of Goochland
which he possessed himself of in consequence of the marriage aforesaid and
has ever since retained it claiming it for life. Your Orator states that
he is also indebted to him in a large sum for the profits of Massies Estate
and for the Estate of John Smith the Younger the said John having devised
his Estate to the late Edward Jaquelin Smith to whom your Orator is Heir
Executor and residuary Legatee as will be seen by Copies of both Wills hereto annexed as part of this Bill.

William Anderson now deceased removed to the Kingdom of Great Britain some years before his Death and by his last Will and Testament among
others made Gist one of his Executors who has qualified accordingly, by
which means he has possessed himself of all the books and papers of Joseph
Smith and John Smith as your orator believes.

Rootes vs Gist (Continued):

Since the passage of an Act of Assembly to vest the Estate of
Samuel Gist in Mary the Wife of William Anderson her husband ... the said
William Anderson and Mary his Wife during the life of the said William were
possessed of the whole Estate of the said Gist in this Country including
the Negroes and Land aforesaid, and the Defendant Mary Perks since the
death of the said William until her intermarriage with Martin Perks has
been possessed of the same, and since the intermarriage of the said Martin
and Mary they have holden and still continue to hold possession of the same.

Your Orator also states that a certain Benjamin Toler who he
prays be made a Defendant to this bill, has been for many years the Manager of the said Estates for all the Defendants and still remains the Manager and Director of the same.

Your Orator states that he has in a friendly manner called upon
the said Samuel Gist to settle his Executorship account of the first named
John Smith to show and discover his books of accounts and to render a full
account of what goods cash and debts were on hand at the time of the death
of the said John Smith also to render an account of the profits of the Estate from the time of his intermarriage with the widow until the year 1752
when he became guardian of the Children as aforesaid, to render a particular account of the Negroes on the estates in Hanover and in Goochland at
the time of the Marriage aforesaid and also to render an account of the
same in 1752 when he was appointed Guardian as aforesaid, distinguishing
the increase from the original. Also render an account of the Negroes retained and claimed by himself in right of his Wife with a list of their
names ages sexes and supposed value; also a list of those that remain at
present and their increase, etc. That he would also render an account of
the profits of the said 500 acres in Goochland and that he would state and
set forth the lines and boundaries of the same so that it may be known and
designated from the remainder of the estate ... that he would render an account of the profits of John Massies Estate from the time he took possession
of the same untill 1752 and from that period render an account of the estate of John Smith the Younger and that he would deliver up to your Orator
the Negroes aforesaid and their increase and pay him hire and that he would
pay and satisfy your Orator such further other sums of Money as he should be
found indebted upon the other claims aforesaid and that he would deliver
up the said Land and pay the amount of the profits thereof and your Orator
has in the same way applied to the other Defendants to deliver up the said
Land and Negroes and pay the profits and hire of the same for the time they
have been possessed thereof, and to the Defendant Benjamin Toler to render
to him a list of the Negroes on said Estate in order to enable your Orator
to distinguish the same but now so it is May it please your Honors that the
said Defendants confederating how to injure and oppress your Orator in the
premises have refused to accede to any of the foregoing Just and Equitable
propositions ...

In tender consideration, etc.

Rootes vs Gist, (continued):

THE ANSWER OF SAMUEL GIST

Dated 29 October, 1805

    This Defendant Answereth and saith he believes it to be true that John Smith the Father of Joseph and John Smith all in the said Bill Named departed this Life some time in the year 1743 (?-torn) having first made and published his last will and Testament, but this Defendant believes that the said Will was not to the purport or Effect set forth in the said Bill, the said Testator as well as this Defendant recollects and believes having given to his Wife forever 1/5 of all his Estate except his Houses and Land in Hanover County of which he lent her 1/3, however this Defendant saith for greater certainty as to the contents of the said Will he craves leave --- (torn) thereto when produced.

    This Defendant further answering saith that the Will of John Massie in the said Bill named was established and he admits it to be true that some time after the Death of the said Testator John Smith ---ow (torn) intermarried with this Defendant, and that this Defendant has been in the early part of his Life Storekeeper of the said Testator and that the said Testator was at the time of his Death Factor for a very respectable Merchantile House at Bristol in England and had goods belonging to the said House in his hands and he believes that the said Goods were after the said Testator's Death sold by John Darracott and John Martin two of the Executors and the proceeds thereof were duly accounted for by them to the said House at Bristol, but this Defendant saith he does not believe that the said Testator was at the time of his Death a Merchant dealing to any considerable extent and this Defendant believes the property which the said Testator left was not considerable, and he further saith that all the ready money and other property of the said Testator which this Defendant became possessed of on the Occasion of his Marriage with the said Testator's idow was duly accounted for by this Defendant.

    This Defendant further admits that at the time of his Marriage with the Widow of the said Testator two Children of the said Testator were Infants of tender Age and that he conceived it to be his Duty and it was his wish to take care that the property left to them by their said Father should be properly managed and with that View and with the concurrence of the other Executors of their said Father he took upon himself the principal Management thereof and of the property left to the said John Smith by the said John Massie and that meaning to act to the utmost of his power for the benefit of the said two Children he took possession of as much of or (sic) belonging to the said two Estates as he was able but he does not believe that he possessed himself of the whole of the two estates and he denies that he claimed to hold the same as Executor of the said Testator though he admits that his Wife being Executrix he as representing her was --- (torn) though improperly Executor as in the Document in the said Bill in that behalf mentioned.

    This Defendant admits it to be true that he took upon himself in conjunction with the Executors of the said Testator the Guardianship of the said Two Children but denies that the Order so appointing him Guardian was obtained with any sinister view whatever ... and he denies that he never executed the Order for the Division obtained in the year 1752. On the con-

Rootes vs Gist (Continued)

trary this Defendant ... saith that the Division of the said Testator's
property was fairly and duly made under the said Order and that he also
settled the Guardianship account of the said Joseph and John Smith the
said accounts having been examined by Order of the Court for the County
of Hanover in Virginia aforesaid where this Defendant then resided by
some of the most respectable Gentlemen in the said County who this Defendant does not doubt made their Report of such Investigation to the
said Court as it was their Duty to do.

And this Defendant denies that any part of the property of the
said Joseph Smith or John Smith remained unaccounted for by him and he
saith that before he quitted Virginia he duly settled all his Concerns
with them and that the said Jospeh Smith was a very improvident Man and
became embarrassed in his Circumstances and was at the time this Defendant
quitted Virginia indebted to this Defendant after paying him for the Mill
in the said Bill mentioned and making him large allowances in the Sum of
Three hundred pounds. That the property that the said John Smith acquired
under the Will of his uncle the said John Massie and which constituted almost the whole of his Fortune was much incumbered with Debts at the time
this Defendant took possession of the same and that this Defendant in the
course of his Management of the said property paid off all the Debts and
Incumbrances thereon and much improved the same and delivered up the same
to his Guardian Joseph Smith his Brother on this Defendants quitting Virginia aforesaid in a very improved state with a Crop of Tobacco then housed
and coming into the House of the value of about L200 Sterling and also paid
to his said Guardian by the Direction of the said Court of Hanover and with
the approbation of the said John Smith a balance due to him of L362:18:1 upon
the final settlement of accounts between him and this Defendant.

This Defendant denies that he ever retained any Slave of or belonging to the said Testator John Smith's Estate or that he holds or to
his knowledge or belief they who claim under him hold any of the said Slaves
or their increase or that he has in any manner deprived the said Children
of any part of their Property.

But this Defendant saith that being obliged by the bad state of
his health to come to England he in the month of October 1765 quitted America leaving his family there who it was his intention should follow him
when he had provided suitable accommodations for them in England and that
this Defendant's Wife died in Maryland soon afterwards and this Defendant
saith he has been informed and verily believes that soon after the Death
of his said Wife the said Joseph Smith and some other persons whom this
Defendant has not been able to discover seized certain Negro slaves amounting to 8 or 10 or thereabouts which on the said Division had been allotted
to this Defendant's Wife and which then were on a distant Plantation belonging to this Defendant and that the said Joseph Smith retained them until
his Death one old Man excepted who as this Defendant has been informed and
believes ran away from the said Joseph Smith and returned to the said plantation of this Defendant and that the said Complainant on the Death of
the said Joseph Smith retained the possession of the said Negro Slaves and
still retains the possession thereof as this Defendant has been informed.

And this Defendant denies it to be true that he on his removal
to Great Britain carried with him every Book or Paper respecting the es-

Rootes vs Gist (continued:

the Estates in the said Bill mentioned or any of them or in any manner
destroyed any such Book or paper. On the Contrary he left all Books and
papers in any manner relating to his affairs or concerns behind him in
America and that it was necessary that he should do so for the purpose
of collecting Debts to a considerable Amount then due to him there and
this Defendant apprehends and believes that all the Books and papers respecting the said Estates are yet in America at least this Defendant saith
he has not the same or any of them in his custody or power.

And this Defendant saith he did not leave America in a private
manner but gave notice in the Virginia Gazette for nearly twelve months
before of his intention of going to England and thereby requested every
person to whom he might be indebted to apply to him for payment of their
respective Demands.

And this Defendant saith that he apprehends and believes that
the said Joseph Smith would at that time have complained to this Defendant
of this Defendant's Conduct towards him and would have sought redress
against this Defendant in case he had conceived that either he or his
said Brother had been wronged by this Defendant. But the said Joseph Smith
made no such complaints and was to the knowledge and belief of this Defendant quite satisfied with the Conduct of and Management of his and his said
Brother's property by this Defendant.

And this Defendant saith that he does not recollect that any Demand has been made upon him by any person in America since he left that
Country save and except the Demand made by the said Complainant's said Bill.

And this Defendant denies that any quarrel or reconciliation between
him and William Anderson in the said Bill named was in any manner influ-
enced by or had any thing to do with the affairs of the said Guardianship
as in the Bill falsely and maliciously insinuated.

And this Defendant denies it to be true that he in indebted to
the said Complainant for any Sum of Money for the Rent of the 500 a. of
Land in the County of Goochland in the said bill mentioned or any other
Land for this Defendant saith he conceives and believes that he is entitled
to the said Estate in the said County for his life the same having belonged
to his said late Wife and he having had issue by her but this Defendant
insists that the said Complainant has not any Title to the said Estate or
to any Rent for the same even if this Defendant should not be entitled to
the said Estate for his life as aforesaid the said Complainant as this Defendant is advised not being Heir to Edward Jaquelin Smith in the said Bill
named.

And this Defendant denies that he is in any manner indebted to
the said Complainant for any Sum of Money for any profits of Massie's
Estate or the Estate of John Smith the Younger.

And he admits it to be true that the said William Anderson appointed him this Defendant one of his Executors and that this Defendant proved his
Will but he denies that he thereby or by any means possessed himself of
any paper or Book of Joseph Smith or John Smith and that this Defendant

Rootes vs Gist (Continued)

has not in his power at this Distance of time to state the several parti-
culars required of him by the said Bill the said Guardianship accounts
having been long ago settled and the said Joseph Smith and John Smith
having been as this Defendant believes quite satisfied with or at least
having during their lives entirely acquiesced in the same and all Papers
and Documents relating thereto having been long considered by this Defendant as of no further importance.

     And this Defendant therefore cannot in any manner set forth what
the Estate of the said John Smith consisted of or state particularly the
Goods, Money, Debts, Negroes, or Stock, or name the said Negroes then or
their Increase now it being forty years since this Defendant left Virginia.

     ... That the Books of account of the said Testator John Smith
remained in America and that he the Defendant settled all accounts for
Joseph Smith's and John Smith's property in the proper way but when or
where he cannot at this Distance of time recollect nor when the Division
in the said Bill was made but believes it to have been made soon after the
Order of the Court for the purpose Neither does he recollect what Negroes
were allotted to the Widow or their names Ages Sexes or their increase
but he believes they did not exceed 9 or 10 in no. together with a Mulatto
Woman Servant and her Child whose servitude was so near expiring that this
Defendant set them free.

     He denies that the Estate of Joseph Smith was a large or profit-
able one but he admits that he wrote the letter in said Bill in that behalf
mentioned and was induced for the sake of Peace and Harmony to offer the
division therein alluded to.

     He saith he does not believe any of the Negroes now on the Estates
in Virginia aforesaid formerly called his have proceeded from any Negroes
retained by him or at any time belonging to the Estate of the said Testator
John Smith the Elder, Negroes formerly belonging to his Estate and allotted
to the Widow in the said Division having been seized by the said Joseph
Smith as aforesaid and this Defendant saith that either he or the persons
managing the said Estates have placed thereon Negroes purchased by him or
them or obtained by other means than those in the said Bill mentioned, but
this Defendant cannot at this distance of time set forth from whom purchased
or when or from whom obtained or where. And this Defendant saith he actually paid the said Joseph Smith the sum of £362:9:1 in cash on account of the
said John Smith's Estate and that he purchased from the said Joseph Smith
in the said year 1765 for the sum of £111:13:4 a Water Grist Mill and paid
to him the said sum of Money as the consideration for the same.

     This Defendant saith that he cannot at this Distance of time in
any manner set forth what were the proceeds of the said John Massie's Estate
until he this Defendant qualified as Guardian to the said John Smith, but
he saith he was acting Executor to the said William Anderson and was and is
now as he believes in possession of divers papers belonging to him before
his Death but that for many years past he has not considered the papers of
any further importance the matters to which they relate having been long
ago settled and whether he at any time was in possession of all the papers
of the said William Anderson this Defendant cannot set forth.

Rootes vs Gist (Continued):

        This Defendant saith that he never held any of the Negroes claimed
by the said Bill or their Increase and he submits to the Judgment of this
Honorable Court that at this distance of Time and after the matters and transactions enquired after by the said Bill have been so long finally settled and
closed and after the persons who were most interested in calling this Defendant to an Account in case they had conceived they had been wronged by
this Defendant are long since dead without having instituted any proceedings
against this Defendant this Defendant ought not to have been called on to
make any answer to the said bill or have been made a Defendant thereto ...
That if these matters are now opened much Injustice necessarily must be done
or arise to this Defendant in consequence of the loss of Vouchers and papers
relating to the same and he therefore --- (torn) the benefit of any Statute
or Act of Limitations of Actions or Suits in force in the United States as
if he had pleaded the same in bar of the said Complainants said Bill ...

        And this Defendant saith that the said Joseph Smith and John Smith
the Younger were at the times of their Deaths respectively considerably indebted to this Defendant ...

        And this Defendant humbly prays to be here dismissed with his
reasonable Costs and Charges in this behalf most wrongfully instituted.
                                                     (Benj. Winthrop)

                        Signed   Samuel Gist

        Sworn at the Public Office in Southampton buildings Chancery Lane
London this twenty ninth day of October 1805 before me one of the Masters
of the High Court of Chancery in England
                                        J. S. Harvey

                        WILL OF JOHN SMITH, SENIOR
                           D. ---; P. --- 1746
                             (Extract only)*

        ... Wife, Mary, one-third part of my Lands and Slaves for life, and
One-fifth part of my personal Estate forever; after death of said wife Mary
the negroes so lent to her for life are to be divided (except some particularly named) between my two sons Joseph and John Smith, provided that in
case the will of John Massie, now in dispute, should be established, in that
case all the slaves so lent to said wife Mary are to be the property of my
eldest son Joseph Smith. No inventory to be made of estate. Executors, John
Martin and John Darracott; Executrix, Wife, Mary...

        ————

        *The quotation from the will of John Smith, Sr., taken from the bill
of complaint of Thomas R. Rootes is here included for the convenience of the
reader. The will, said to have been attached to the bill of complaint, was
not found among the suit papers. - The daughters, Sarah and Elizabeth, devisees of John Massie, are not mentioned in the bill of complaint. - E. G.

Rootes vs Gist (Continued)

WILL OF JOHN MASSIE, of GOOCHLAND CO.
d. 26 October, 1743; p. 26 Apr.,1746
in the General Court

IN THE NAME OF GOD AMEN I John Massie of the County of Goochland being very infirm att this present but praised be God of sound memory, and knowing the uncertainty of this life, do ordain, constitute and appoint this my last will and testament in the manner and form following -

First I recommend my soul to god whom first created me trusting for mercy through the meritorious passion and sufferings of my Lord and Saviour Jesus Christ and what worldly estate it hath pleased God to bestow on me I give devise and bequeath in the manner and form following

Imprimis - I give and bequeath to my loving brother Peter Massie ten pounds current money to be paid out of my estate yearly during his natural life by my exr, hereafter named and further my desire is that the said money shall not go to discharge any debt or contract my sd brother Peter shall make or have made in my lifetime but my meaning is the said sum of ten pounds given yearly shall be to support him in clothes and other nessarys for life -

Item - I give and bequeath to my loving brother James Massie ten pounds currt. - (Upon the same conditions as in bequest to Peter Massie).

Item - I give and bequeath to my loving Nephew Thomas Darricot the sum of fifty pounds current to be paid to him at the age of twentyone to him and his heirs forever.

Item ... to loving niece Elizabeth Smith two hundred pounds currt. to be paid out of the produce of my estate (not selling and land or negroes) ...

Item ... to loving niece Sarah Smith (bequest similar to that of Elizabeth Smith).

Farther my will and desire is that if either of my two nieces Elizabeth and Sarah Smith should dye without issue or before the age of eighteen then my desire is that the sd sum be paid to the survivor of them.

Item I give to my loveing nephew Joseph Smith the sum of one hundred pounds currt to be paid to him at the age of twenty one out of the produce of my estate (not selling any land or negroes)to him and his heirs ...

Item (Similar bequest to nephew John Pinchback), for fifty pounds.

Item - ... to loving niece Ann Pinchback fifty pounds currt. to be paid out of the produce of my estate, etc.... to be delivered to her at the age of eighteen.

... My meaning in not selling any land or negroes is that the money given to the foregoing legatees be raised out of my crops of tobacco, corn, cattle, hogs &c yearly not selling two near the stock ... to each legatee in proportion as the money can be raised.

Rootes vs Gist (continued): - Will of John Massie

     I give and bequeath to my loveing nephew John Smith all my land in Goochland County containing 200 acres more or less and likewise all my land in Henrico County containing 200 acres more or less to him and his heirs forever.

     Item I give &c to my above mentioned loveing nephew John Smith all my negroes big and little now situated on the above given land in Goochland and Henrico or elsewhere them and their increase with the stock of cattle, hoggs, horses, etc., on said plantation to him and his heirs forever.

     Item I give &c to my loveing nephew John Smith all the remaining part of my estate real or personal of what nature or quality soever either in England or here to him and his heirs forever.

     And lastly I do hereby appoint, constitute and make my loveing brother John Smith whole and sole exr. of this my last Will and testament revoking all others heretofore made by me and this I have hereunto set my hand and seal this 26th day of October Anno Donini 1745 -

Wit.: Samuel Tschiffeli   (Signed) Jno. Massie (LS)
     James Massie

Virginia Sct. At a General Court held at the Capitol 26 April 1746

     Upon hearing this day as well Peter Massie heir at law of the within named John decd. as John Smith the executor named in this will and examining upon oath divers witnesses produced as well on behalf of the said Peter Massie as on behalf of the said executor the Court were of opinion that the within writing doth contain the true last Will and testament of the said John Massie decd. and ordered the same to be recorded. And on oath of the said John Smith certificate was granted him for obtaining a probat thereof he having given bond ...

                      Teste Ben: Waller Cl: Cur
            A Copy   Teste Wilson Allen C G C

Virginia Sct.

     At a Court held in the Courthouse in Williamsburg 21 Aprill 1748

     The writing purporting to be the last Will and testament of John Massie of the County of Goochland deceased was this day again contested and on consideration of the Depositions taken concerning the same and the arguments of the Counsel as well in behalf of Peter Massie brother and heir at law of the said John as on behalf of the executor named in the said Will, this Court is of opinion that the said writing doth contain the true last Will and testament of the said decedent and doth accordingly judge and order that the same be confirmed and established as such and that the Depositions aforesaid be recorded in this Court with the said Will

                   Teste Ben Waller   Cl: Cur
          A Copy   Teste Wilson Allen C. G. C.

Rootes vs Gist (Continued)

ESTATE OF JOHN SMITH, GENT., DECEASED
Ordered to be Settled

On motion of John Darracott & Samuel Gist two of the executors of the last Will & testament of John Smith Gent. deceased, it is ordered that Thomas Jones, Thomas Booth, John Bickerton & John Syme, Gentlemen, or any three of them, do settle the estate of the said decedent according to law; and that they divide that part of the said estate which lies in this county according to the will aforesaid, of the said decedent, and that John Boswell, John Wingfield, Thomas Bowles & Samuel Mosby or any three of them do divide that part of said decedents estate that lies in Goochland County according to his said Will.

Hanover Co. Court 4th June 1752   A Copy Teste Tho. Pollard D C H C

I do hereby certify that it does not appear from the records of the County Court of Hanover that any Report of the division contemplated in the above mentioned Order has been returned to the said Court.

November 22d. 1803   Tho. Pollard D C H C

SAMUEL GIST'S GUARDIANSHIP ACCOUNTS

Samuel Gist guardian of Joseph, John & Sarah Smith, not having yet rendered an account of the estates of the said wards, It is therefore ordered that he be summoned to appear at the next court to be held for this county, to render such account.

Hanover County Court Aug. 6, 1752 - A Copy Teste Tho. Pollard D C H C

SAMUEL GIST'S GUARDIANSHIP CERTIFIED

I do hereby certify that it appears from the records of the County Court of Hanover that Samuel Gist became guardian to Joseph Smith and John Smith, Orphans of John Smith, Gent., decd., on the 4th day of June 1752 ...

Hanover Office - Nov 1807   Tho. Pollard D C H C

SAMUEL GIST'S GUARDIANSHIP SETTLEMENT

Sept. 23, 1765. Then received of Samuel Gist Ⱡ360;18;1, being the balance due to my Brother Mr. John Smith when the said Gist settled the Acct. of his Guardianship with the Hanover Court this month.
Test - Thomas Smith   Jos. Smith

At a Court held for Hanover Co., Thursday, 30 October, 1765 This receipt was proved by oath of Thomas Smith, witness thereto, & recorded.

Test Wm. Pollard D C H C

Rootes vs Gist (continued)

MARRIAGE AGREEMENT BETWEEN
JOSEPH SMITH, GENT., and MARTHA JACQUELIN ROOTES

ARTICLES OF AGREEMENT, dated 27 August, 1767, between Joseph
Smith, of Hanover County, Gentleman, of the first part, Martha Jacquelin
Rootes, of the County of Middlesex, widow, of the second part, and John
Smith, of the same County of Middlesex, Esquire, of the Third part.

WHEREAS a Marriage is intended shortly to be solemnized between
the said Joseph Smith and Martha Jacquelin Rootes, These Articles Witness
That for and in consideration of the said intended Marriage, the said Joseph Smith and Martha Jacquelin Rootes, transfer, assign and make over unto
the said John Smith, his Exors., admrs., and assigns, all the Estate and
Fortune of the said Martha Jacquelin Rootes, whether the same consists of
Monies, Goods, Chattels, Slaves, Debts, Dues, or Demands, IN TRUST, to and
for the following, that is to say, to the separate use of the said Martha
for and during the intended marriage, and during her natural Life, and after
her Decease to and for the use of Thomas Reade Rootes, son of the said Martha. But in case of the Death of the said Thomas Reade Rootes in the lifetime of his said Mother, then to such use or uses as the said Martha shall
by her last Will and Testament or other Instrument in writing by her signed
and sealed direct and appoint, and the said Joseph Smith for himself his
Heirs Exors. and admors. doth for the Consideration aforesaid covenant, promise and agree to and with the said John Smith, his heirs and administrators
for and in behalf of the said Martha Jacquelin Rootes, her Heirs, Executors
and Administrators, that in case the said Intended Marriage shall take
Place, it shall and may be lawful for said Martha to receive and enjoy the
Profits of her said Estate to her separate use and also to dispose of said
Estate and Profits by her last Will and Testament or by any other instrument
in writing, by her to be signed and sealed notwithstanding her Coverture;
And further that in case said Martha shall survive said Joseph, she shall be
intitled not only to her own separate Estate, but also to her legal Dower
and Thirds of the Real, and Personal Estate of said Joseph Smith.

IN WITNESS WHEREOF the Parties to these Presents have hereunto interchangeably set their Hands and Seals this Day and Year first above written.

Recorded, Middlesex County Court at Urbanna, 6 October, 1767.

Teste   D. Ker,   Cl: Cur:

JAQUILIN AMBLER, GENT., GUARDIAN
of
EDWARD JAQUELIN SMITH

In Hanover County Court, February 5th 1778 On Motion of Jaquilin
Ambler, Gent. he is appointed Guardian of Edward Jaquelin Smith Orphan of
Joseph Smith Gent. deceased Whereupon the said Jaquelin Ambler together
with William Anderson Gent. of Dundee his security entered into and acknowledged a bond according to law, which bond is ordered to be recorded

Rootes vs Gist (Continued)

MARRIAGE OF THOMAS READE ROOTS
to
MARTHA JACQUELIN SMITH

1763, Feb. 8. Thomas Reade Rootes, of King and Queen County, to
Martha Smith, daughter of John Smith, Esq., of Middlesex County. Security,
Augustine Smith. Letter of John Smith consenting to "Mr. Thomas Reade Rootes'
marriage to my daughter, Martha Jacquelin Smith". *

. . ,.

SMITH TO GIST - GRIST MILL

This Indenture made this 17 September, 1765, Between Joseph Smith
of the County of Hanover, Gent., of the one part, and Samuel Gist of the
same county, Gent., of the other part, WITNESSETH, that the said Joseph
Smith for and in consideration of the sum of £111:13:4 by the said Samuel
Gist to him in hand paid ... hath granted, etc. unto the said Samuel Gist
and his heirs forever, all that water grist mill, called or known by the
name of Smiths mill lying on Crump Creek in the Parish of Saint Paul, in the
County of Hanover, and the ground whereon the mill doth stand, and one acre
of land thereto adjoining, for the use thereof, and also all the custom and
benefit of grinding, of all corn and grain whatsoever, and all and singular
the trees, wears, Ponds, Dams, streams, etc. ... hereditaments & appurtenances to the said mill & acre of land & premises aforesaid ...

In Witness whereof the parties to these presents have hereunto
interchangeably set their hands and affixed their seals the day and year
first above written

                                              Jos. Smith   (Seal)

Wit.: Petr. Lyons, Gregory Smith
      Robt. Walker, Wm. Grimes

Received the 17th of Septemr. 1765 of Mr. Samuel Gist the sum of
£111:13:4 being the consideration within mentioned to be paid by him to me

Wit.: Petr. Lyons, Gregory Smith   Jos. Smith
      Robt. Wathon, William Grimes

                                       Recorded in Hanover Co. Ct. 3 Oct.,1765
                                       Test William Pollard D C H C
            November 1803   A Copy   Teste William Pollard   C H C

Ref.: Middlesex Marriage Bonds. - See also Va. Mag. of Hist. and Biog.V.4,
p. 208, "The Rootes Family: Thomas Reade (2)Rootes married on Feb. 8, 1768
(Middlesex Co.), Maria (sic), dau. of John Smith, of 'Shooter's Hill', Mid-
dlesex Co., and had at least one son. Thomas Reade Rootes, Plaintiff in this
suit. John Smith, of 'Purton', Gloucester Co., Va., married on Feb. 17, 1680,
Mary, dau. of Col. Augustine Warner, of 'Warner Hall', Gloucester Co., Va.,
Speaker of the House of Burgesses, and Councillor, and died Apr. 17, 1698.
He was the grandfather of John Smith, of 'Shooter's Hill', who married Mary,
dau. of Edward Jacqueline, of Jamestown, and his wife, Martha, d. of William
Cary; gr.-dau. of Col. Miles Cary, of Warwick, also mem. of the Council.John
and Mary Smith were the parents of Maria (sic) who m. Thomas Reade Rootes."
Note - "Maria" should read "Martha". See bond above and mar.agmt. p.27.-E.G.

Rootes vs Gist (Continued)

PATRICK HENRY TO JOSEPH SMITH
Regarding Division of Estate
of John Smith, Senior

Dear Sir,   feby 16, 1770

   Having rec. yours by way of Richmond inclosing sundry papers but
being indisposed so as to be unfit for Business I had prepared an answer at
home; However meeting accidentally with Mr. Anderson at Mr. Woods I now
write this as crossing the River is now difficult. - Possibly it may be tho't
presumption in me to contradict Mr. York; But I presume he went on a mistake-
You may observe that he takes Notice of the division of yr ffathers Estate
when you were under Age at that Time, and altho' the Court did make an order
to divide the Estate, yet unless there was a suit in chancery prosecuted agt.
you such a division can't operate to ye prejudice of any right you derive
from the Will. Before I pronounce my opinion finally you must furnish me
with certain information whether there ever was a suit in chancery brot. to
obtain a division of the Estate whether you were not under age at the division? whether your Mother ever renounced yr ffathers will & sought for
her dower? - This much I can say that I am clear the Negroes are yrs under
the Will & are so still unless some subsequent proceeding has alter'd the
property in them By applying to the Clerk of Hanr. you will get full information of all the proceedings that have been had relative to this matter
Copy of which I must beg to see. In the meantime 'till you are further informed I advise you by no means to con--tent (torn) any compromise like that
offered in Mr. Gists Letre the ---ile (torn) & matter of which are a little
singular I keep the ---(torn) me 'till I have a copy of the records above
from Henr. & then I shall give my opinion submitted with my name which may
possibly be right altho contrary to Mr. York's. In the meantime I have to
beg Yr Excuse for the form of this Epistle & that you believe me to be

       Yr mo hble sert.

To Mr. Joseph Smith   P. Henry Jr.
 by Mr. Anderson

SAMUEL GIST TO JOHN SMITH, JR.
Regarding Division of Slaves

D Sir -   London Oct 12 1769
   The Inclosed is Copy of my last, since wch. I am without any of
your Favors ...

   I have lately wrote to your Brother & inclosed him a Copy of Mr.
York's opinion on your Fathers will (the original I have sent to Mr. Lyons)
& notwithstanding he, & the other Lawrs. (I have Consulted) are clear the
Negroes in dispute are my property, yet out of respect to him & to put an end
to all the differences between us, I have again offer'd to pay him half what
the Negroes may be valued at, by Hones' indifft. Men, chosen between us, the
valuation to be deducted from his Debt, if you do not pay the whole, (if you
do) & he accepts this Proposal, please pay him in any way that is most agreeable to him, if you take his whole Debt upon you, wch. I understand by your
Letter you do, please let me know what Sum to charge you with, & from what
time, this Debt being secured, if it is more agreeable to your Brother.

Rootes vs Gist (Continued)
Letter from Samuel Gist to John Smith, Junior, continued:

I am willing to divide the Nigroes fairly between us, as thereby we shall
both save expence, for let who will recover, the extra expence wch. cannot
be recover'd, will amo. to half their Value, as I am ditermined, if I am
cast in Virginia to appeal, if your Brother recover, as Mr. Pendleton &
his other Lawyers think to pay me the difference between 1/3 & 1/5 of their
Labour, from the time of your Fathers to the time of your Mothers Death,wch.
is 20 Years, the diffce will greatly exceed half their Value if he loose
them, as Mr. Yorke (who is the first Lawyer in this Kingdom) is clear he will,
the consequence will be his entire ruin, and by this mode he may gain, but
cannot loose. I shall therefore forbear to make any further observations
to you upon it, nor indeed should I have mentioned it, at all, but to desire you to pay him the Money if he accepts the Proposal, it being the last
I shall ever make him.

        I have a letter from T. Smith wherein he makes the Goods delivered
you amo. to £161.1.6-3/4 Stl.   I am Sir   Your very hbbl. St.
                                                              S. G.
To Mr. John Smith, Mercht., Hanover Town Va -

                        SAMUEL GIST TO JOSEPH SMITH
                        Regarding Division of Slaves.
                                                London Mar 20 - 1770
Mr. Joseph Smith
    D Sir
        I recd. your favor of the 13th Decemr. I thought I had sufficient-
ly explained myself as to the difference between the 1/3d & 1/6d part of the
Negroes mentioned in your Father's will, and if you will give it a little
serious attention I am sure you will think so, & that you may no further be
led into error for want of proper information abt. the Division of them, L
inform you that Coll. Snelson & Majr. Bickerton by order of Court divided
the whole Nigroes & gave me 1/5 of which they will inform you -

        You did not send me Martin's opinion on yr. Fathers will but I had
it by me, & have taken several opinions upon it, & they all agree that it
could have no weight in any Court, nor would he if living have been admitted
to give evidence in such a Cause the reason is that it would open a Door to
numberless Frauds a worthless man for a Fee or from Malice being admitted
to explain a Dead mans meaning as to his will agst record might set every
will that ever was made aside & which if you will take advice abt. any Lawyer of Common Sense will inform you, as also that when a Person accepts 1/5th
of anything instead of 1/3d it must be for a valuable consideration, & it is
on this Doctrine of yr. Mothers becoming a Purchaser is Founded & on wch Mr.
York the late Lord Chancellor was so clear You no doubt will Act on the best
advice, but as the Law is expensive (& the best men are sometimes mistaken)
& recovery let it be of wch. side it will, will be attended wth. an expense
nearly equal to their value & that you might gain but could not loose I was
induced to offer you a Division wch I shall urge no further as you do not approve of it, but the event will show who is Right.

        I am with Respectfull Compts. to Mrs. Smith & Yr little Family,
D Sir
                    Your affect.   hllr St
                                        Saml. Gist

Rootes vs Gist　(continued)

LETTERS OF
SAMUEL GIST to JOHN SMITH

London　Jan 26th 1768

Mr. John Smith
　　　D Sir:

　　　　Yours of the 6th of Novr. & 12th Decr. by Lilly are just come to
hand & Note the Contents -

　　　　I never doubted your Honor or Honesty　if I had I should not have
entered into the engagements with you wch I have done, but do not let my
Zeal to serve you lead you into Error.　Honor and Honesty are not the only
Necessary essentials for a Man of Business　it requires many others. Particularly the nicest Inspn. into a Man's Books to see what he receives from
his Trade & the earliest & Quickest remittance without wch Business must
drop, or at best Languish in such a Manner that it had better be dropt, now
in this I think the undermentioned Calculation must show you have not attended sufficiently thereto.

　　　　I shall think myself happy to save myself by Donaldsons Cargoe
notwithstanding all that is said about the short crop for the People at
Glasgow have just sold 1500 Hhds @ 2-3/8 at Bristol last week 500 Hhds was
sold at 2½ with the usual allowances notwithstanding that I think it was
right to fill the ship by Purchase but that should have been done as soon
as you Drew on me as I should thereby have gained much time to the Ship &
saved a great deale in the Price of the Tobacco especially if you had Bt on
Js. or Rappk. Rivers　the Preference indeed is due too York if it could have
been Bt. at near the same Price or if it had helped of my Goods wch it was
intended to do & I never before knew it fail of, but I have said enough
abt. it. You　must therefore allwys. take in yr. Tobo. in the Store as yr.
Neighbours (who are good Men) do, & some Lattitude must be allowed else
Business cannot be carrd. on to advantage. You　were falsely alarm'd abt
Byrd's Bill　it was noted for want of advice, but on receipt of Yr. Letter
was duly Paid & of wch. the holder had immediate Notice - had Byrd or Adams
in his behalf failed complying with his engagement I should by this Method
had both Drawer & indorser in my Power & thereby have saved you -

　　　　I will let part of my Ship on Charter, if I can, but I much
Question if it will be in my Power.

　　　　I am　D Sir
　　　　　　　Your most Obed. So.
　　　　　　　　　　Saml. Gist

P. S.　　　receive of T. Smith wt. Money he from time to time recvs. wch. if
you can lay out in good heavy upland Tobo. a 22/6 do, or dry light stemd.
or (?) it will help you Purchase as you must give some Cash to your Cusrs.
wch. will save drawing so much ---(torn).

Rootes vs Gist (Continued)
Letters of Samuel Gist to John Smith, continued:

POSTSCRIPT ON PRECEDING LETTER

Feby 1st

D Sir

The Glasgow People have Sold 6000 Hhds --- (torn). I have got a
Charter on my Ship from Mr. Hunt & Capt. Hubbard comes out in her but do
you nevertheless get all you can from Your Store Debts & with Goods. I am
afd. the Price (from the orders that are given) will be 25/ but do you do
the best you can. I hope you and Mr. Atkinson managed Yr last Orders well
a good deale will depend upon it, there is no fear of our gettg. Trs. for
what Hubbard dos. not bring.

Yr. Sister and Anderson are returned from Scotld. where they were
married ... I am told they talk of going to Virga. I have not seen her &
sincerely hope I never shall as she has allmost killed me by this act of
unditifullness.

S. G.

To Mr. John Smith
Mercht. Hanover Town Virginia
P. Capt. Outran

- - -

London, June 19, 1768

Mr John Smith
                D Sir -

By Capt. Mitchell who is arriving from York River I am advised
of Hubbards arrival at York the 15th May. I am without any Letter from
you by him or any other of the last arrivals at Bristol or here and was it
not for intelligence I have from others should be as ignorant of what is
going on in Virga. as I am of what passes on in Lapland for I have recd.
but one Letter from you since the 12th of Decr. wch. is now upwards of 6
Months. (Surely this is too much) I know not what Yr. Sales amo. too,
what Qty. of Tobacco you are like to remit, nor whether you shall want any
Fall Goods, or of what sort, & to have them in good time they should be
ship'd now, as you say yours was too late last year.

Mr. Lyde told me the other day there was 13 or L1400 of Yr Bills
come to hand wch they was advised of, but you never mentioned buying more
than 100 hhds Tobo. on their acct. wch. they well know cannot amo. to this
Sum. I have undertaken that you shall Ship Tobo. equal to the Amo. of Yr.
Dfts. - but they are angry you did not add a line to the 2 or 3 you wrote
them adviceing these dfts. to let them know how much more Tobo. you was
like to Purchase on their accts. let me again beg of you for Yr. own repu-
tations sake as well as for mine who have recommended you to this Business
to be regular in Yr. advices else all I can say or do for you will availl
nothing should you otherwys do yr Business ever so well.

Roots vs Gist (continued)
Letters of Samuel Gist to John Smith, continued:

        I have wrote you so often to make all the remittance in yr. Power
that I expect you will exert yrself to the utmost to do it, and that you
might be the better inabled to do so I have all along told you to take in
Tobo. at the Market price in order to force of as many of yr. Goods as possible for ready pay to make a remittance in, for any profits the present
prices of goods give us will never answer lieing long out of the Money, &
if you'l turn back to my first instructns you'l find that was the Plan I
set out on, to sell cheap for ready pay, that a remittce. might come round
soon, if you are not furnishd with Cash from Mr. Brook's & others suffs. to
carry on yr. Business give the Preference of what Bills you are obliged to
draw to the Gentn. I have all along recommended to you. What Tobacco you
have left after Hubbard is full ship me on the best terms you can. I before
mentioned selling it but the risque of bad Bills & the chance of the Markets
not falling has induced me to alter my Opinion & to have home all you can
get for your Debts, Goods on Consignmt. &c for the latter besides the Planters, apply to Colo. Tabb, Mr. Coutts, Mr. W. Peter Bowdoin Eyre & Smith,
Thorowgood Smith & Co., to all whom I have ship'd Good & who may have a
large Quany. to Ship wch will lower the Frt. and do not forget Col. Brooke
among the rest. I have recommend. a Tobo. remittce. to all those Gentn. as
I not only believe it will ansr. their end but will be a means of bringing
a remittance round sooner, avoid bad Bills, & save me in the advance, wch I
assure you is very considerable on their accts. as well as my own for your
Store & wch will present_ put it out of my Power to advance the Money you
may want to purchase Anderson Stiths Land with. You may be sure if I could
advance the Money I would do it for you sooner than for any Man living.
P.smentn. (? postponement?) the Sale of it to me as a thing he believes will
happen a year or two hence, then perhaps I may have it in my Power to oblige
you but so soon as you mention I cannot do it -

        My Hanover Land I know is rather too light for S Scend. Tobo. I
therefore consent they shall tend broad Green or any sort that suits it
best & they can make the most of, let the Leaf be prised as heavy as it will
bear not to hurt it. I have made good crops there, & as there is near 2400
acres of it, the greatest part of wch is level near 140 head of Cattle & the
hands reduced to 24 Workers, I think with good managemt. they might dung
Ground enough in 2 or 3 Years for their Crops of Tobo. & allways have plenty_
of Corn Field to shift on the level land. I shall not therefore part with
it yet. I should be glad to have the House rented on some terms or other,
in hopes of hearing from you soon, I remain

                D Sir   Your most obed. Sr

June -

        Since the foregoing I have your favor by Capt. Foot & observe
the Contents. You must have got your Goods soon after the Date of your
Letter & hope they will at least in part be sold for ready pay & that Yr
remittce will exceed your expectn. I long to receive a particular acct.
of your Trade that I may be able _ form some Judgmt. of it.
Mr. Lyde tells me you have pd. the diffce. of yr. acct. & Dfts. to Mr.
Atkinson

Roots vs Gist (Continued)
Letters of Samuel Gist to John Smith, continued

had too short Notice of Fearons going ...

     You are a bold Adventurer to risque so much Indian Corn as you
have done to a Market where never half that Qty. was sold before. I fear
it will not answer your Purpose let me caution you not to embark in such
schemes again without better advice than the Man who is concerned with you
is capable of giving, for it is more than an equal chance it must be re-
shipt again to Lisbon or Cadiz by wch means you'll have two Frts. & two
Insurances to pay, besides the risque of its being damaged & there is no
average pd. on Corn. I wish I may be mistaken as you are Interested in it.

                                   S. Gist

     Capt. Foot says Yr. Tobo. was sent round in a Sloop all most
without Sails. Part of Yr. Tobo. was on Deck & no covering. Heat n (?)
bad weather. The Vessel was obliged to lower her Sails ... (torn) Cover
the Tobacco ... so that she was -- Getting round wh detained the Ship
Be careful who --- employ in future --- it is essential things be attended
to -- (torn).

     Messrs. L. will take no notice to you of your overdrawing but let
me caution you never to do it again. R. A. has done so too -- his Bills that
are overdrawn will be noted wch I mention to you in confidence therefore
this must go no further. Yours might very justly have been noted too, and
perhaps would, if you had not had a friend on the spot to step forth in
your behalf. I know not in what light you may view the advice & caution I
have from time to time given you. I have no view in it but to serve you
& if after all you run into the same errors again I will Int. myself no
further abt. it - having fully discharged my duty.

                                   S. G.

         - - -

                           London July 2d 1768

Mr. John Smith

     I have allready wrote you fully by this oppy. to wch. be pleased
to be referred. as I have finished the Sale of my Tobacco & shall have but
little to do the latter part of the year I am willing to speculate a little
in Tobo. to find me employmt. in the Winter, for as Mr. Hunt will have so
large a Quantity in my Ship the sale of my part cannot hold me long. I have
recommd. a Tobo. remittance to all the Gentn. wh I have shipd Goods to,
wch it is probable some of them will come into & that there will be a good
deal left of yours after Hubb is full, should the Quantity be worth while
you may after you have got in all you can for Goods purchase 50 to 100 Hhds
if you can fill a ship at a moderate Frt. or should that Quantity not be sufft.
go as far as 150 Hhds. provided the upland York & Ja. River does not exceed
25/ the Lowland 20/ to 22/6 P Cs, giving the preference to Upland Tobo. if
the difference is no more than 2/6 P Cs & preferring York to Ja River if
the Prices are equal the heaviest Leaf & driest Stand is best the scarcity I
imagine will enable you to get the Frt. low, wch. is as great an inducement

Roots vs Gist (Continued)
Letters of Samuel Gist to John Smith, continued:

it would not do so singly, but do not let the Frt. induce you to ship in a
bad Vessell - to whatever may be left you may add a 100 or 150 hhds. by
Purchase to the above --- (torn), whether there is sufficient to fill the
ship or not if you can get Frt. for it draw yr Bills at the highest Exa.
& longest Date giving Preference to the Gentn. I before mentd.

          I suppose by this time you have Messrs. Lydes other Ship I take
Pains to serve you here although I have been offered half the Comr. by
others to Procure theirs or any other Business for them - do you endeavour
to establish yourself well there, it will be worth your while - they have
a Nephew who will be out of his time soon, when he and his Brother Mr. N.
Pool will be joined in the manufacty. and Grocery Business which the young
Gentn. is apprenticed too & wch Messrs. L. & S. Lyde will give up to them -
they will then again enter as large as ever into the Purchasing Tobo. wch
has been 2 to 3000 hhds. a year - this I tell you in Confidence & that you
may do nothing to disoblige them.

          Receive yr Customers Tobo as soon as the Inspn. opens on the same
terms your Neighbors do else it may slip thro your Fingers, & as I must
take Tobacco in Paymt I am determined to have some home early that things
may be turned about as quick as possible for nothing else can make the
Business answer - I am
                              D Sir
                                   Your most obed. St.
                                             Saml. Gist

                         - - -

                                        London   Aug 15, 1768
Mr John Smith
    D Sir
          You have herewith copy of what I wrote you by Mr. Yancy & Capt.
McNabb wh I confirm & desire you will comply with ...

          I have been thinking that Ships in York River might be dispatchd
as well in 10 days as in 2 or 3 months if the Owners of Stores at the heads
of the Rivers had a Warehouse at Cumberland to lodge their Tobacco in agst
the Ships arrivl Iron, Slaves &c might be ready on the wharfs & the ships
having nothing to do but load away the Tobo. might be sent down as it was
collected & the couny. craft would carry it down when they was out of employ for 1/2 price by wch a considerable saveing would be made & a much
greater in the Provisions and in a Ship & Seamens wages, these inducements
lead me to desire you to Purchase for me a Lot with a wharf where a Ship
can lie at Cumberland wth a good Landing if there is a Warehouse on it that
will hold 3 or 400 hhds Tobacco so much the better - if not such a place
with room to build a good Warehouse on, a very little money I should think
would Purchase the latter - £50 at most-perhaps a great deal less as the Town
seems rather on the decline than otherways. I remember when £25 would do it.
Should the Purchase Money be much more than I imagine let me know it by the
first Oppy. - if not buy me such a place as soon as you can - should a Warehouse be allready built on it the cost of it may be added to the Price above
mentioned. R. Adams has such a Place, but he may want to sell his houses

Roots vs Gist (Continued)
Letters of Samuel Gist to John Smith, continued

wth it, wch will not suit me nor indeed to go to a great price at all for
unless the Assembly will consent a Mans own warehouse should be put upon
the footg. of the Warehouses at the difft. Inspections the scheme could
not be carried into execution, as the risque of thieves & Fire would be too
great. Should you succeed in such a Purchase have a Petition preferred to
the Assembly the first time they meet. I think they cannot refuse it the
advantage to Trade will be so evident. Consult the Nelsons on the occasion
you may be sure they will be with you as the Town of Hanover will be in
some sort thereby established & the Lands above render'd of more value, &
the objection to the Badness of the navigation to Pages by Shoals in the
Summer & Freshes in the Winter would by this means in a great measure be
removed. Do not mention my Sentiments on this head till you have secured
yr. Purchase to anyone - it will be sufficient to say you want such a place
for your own convenience as your Business frequently leads you to Cumberland.
I have not yet heard if you have a Bridge over the River at Hanover Town,
if not, it is much wanted - push it forward as it will add greatly to the
trade from K Wm &c. Persuade Mr. Page it will add to the value & Sale of
his lots wh perhaps he may not otherways find out.

My mill in its present situation (tho it has cost me a great deal
of Money) brings me in very little profit - with such a one here I could
very easily clear L500 a Year. I have therefore been thinking if I was to
go to some further expence it might be made to answer better. I meane to
have it fix'd, wth 2 pair of Stones Boltings Cloths & every other necessary
for Grinding Flour for exportation. You might Purchase in your Store a Sufft.
Qty. of Wheat to keep it constantly employed & the Flour might be sold in
the County to Advantege, or on failure sent to the difft. Markets in Europe
or the West Indes as might best ansr on my acct   send me your opinion on
this head with an estimate of the expence.

I have a Lot in Hanover Town opposite to Mr. Jerdones at the first
entrance of the Road to Crutchfields Warehouse. I think if my Carpenter
Built Common Houses on it it might be let to good tenants. The lots where
you live has cost me a great deal of money. You should therefore have the
Houses well preserved & the land improved. I should think it would be a fine
amusement for you if you was to have it laid off in walks along the side of
wch & round the Pales if the choicest Fruit trees was planted in Rows. These
would form a pleasant shade & be a great relief to you in Summer. The Gardens run all in that stile here. When I heare you set about it I shall send
you some of the choicest fruit trees from here.

I have not yet departed from my old Plan of haveing Plum & Peach
Trees planted on all my Hill Sides next the Creek.   therefore put Whitlock
in mind of it & pray see that it is done for I fear Grimes neglected it
altho' I had so many Peach Stones sowed in nurserys for that Purpose. Whenever they are propperly Grown I will send in a Large Hill to distill them
into Brandy & I am sure it cannot fail answg with tolerable management for
want of wch I am sorry to say, many Promising appearances in your Country
fall to the Ground.

                I am very Respf   D Sir
                                Your most Obed. Sr.
                                            Saml. Gist

Roots vs Gist (continued)
Letters of Samuel Gist to John Smith, continued

P. S.   I formerly wrote Grimes abt. sendg. a Blacksmith to Hanr. Town but
he advised me to put one at the Plantn. where Pain lived wch I did not like
--- (torn) my own workmen --- of Money in the Year & I think a great Savg.
might be made in that article.

    I have also thought of setting up a Flat of my own. As I shall
pay more Craft hire myself and the Negroes employed in a Flat would earn
more a great deale than in the Crop & if the Mill & Warehouse scheme shd.
sucseed I should have full employment for them myself. Let me have your
opinion by the first Oppy. on these things & rent Dundee House if possible---

- - -

August 30 1769

Mr. John Smith
    D Sir
        I have already wrote you by this Oppy. chiefly to advise that sev-
seceral of Yr Dfs. had come to hand without advice - since wch. by Walker
I have your favor of the 12 July advsg. the same. I will acquaint Manduit &
Co. of Lillys Promise - I wish Coutss may be as good as his word if he is
not proceed against him, you don't say anything abt. Tunstall & Brooks nor
has Estin mentioned their names, indeed he only says in General that he has
abt. 200 hhds. of the Store Tobacco on Board ... That he shall sail abt.
the middle of August -

    My signing the Address had no reference to America or American
affairs, it was in opposition to a set of Men who seem dispond. to give all
the disturbance they could to Govermt. in hopes to get themselves into place
among whom was the very Man who was for forgeing chains for America & Docr.
Lee nor any other Man could suppose I could wish to Hurt America where I am
so largely concern'd the Docr. I suppose by this meant to make himself appear a Patriot in the Eyes of the People for I hear he solicits the Agency .
& his Brother Wm. a Man of much the same stamp sets up as a Merchant here.
I allways found the People made nearly the same Payments in a Moderate as in
a large Crop for what the Crop fell short in Qty. was generally made up in
the Price & wch has been the case these 3 Years ...

    I never blamed you for buying your Brother's Estate but when
George Thomas told me you had Bt. most of the Negroes in dispute I was much
concern'd at it, considering the conduct I had always observed to you -
Please let me know how much I am to charge you with on his acct.

    For Gods Sake why do you after such repeated requests & promises
delay sending Yr. accts. of sale of my Goods the thing is easy & short -
I therefore desire I may be no longer without it than it can be drawn if it
is not allready sent. Invoice Yr. Goods on hand wch. send me an acct. of
Balance Yr. Books & send a List of Yr Debts that I may know in whose hands
my effects are & what are my Profits, but I am in hopes this will be the
last time you will give me an Oppy. of mentioning such a thing to you -
        I am   D Sir   Your very hhble Sr
                                            Saml Gist

Rootes vs Gist   (Continued)

THE ANSWER OF WILLIAM BURTON
Concerning Deed to "Pickenochy"

        To the Honorable Creed Taylor Judge of the Superior Court of Chancery held in the City of Richmond -

        The separate answer of William Burton one of the defendants to the bill of complaint filed against him and others in this Court by Thomas R. Rootes, admor. de bonis non of John Smith, deceased.

        ... That the tract of Land mentioned in the Complainant's bill of 200 acres called "Pickenochy" now owned by your Respondent, he purchased of the defendant Richard Adams in July,1784, and paid him for it ₺600, - that he was a fair purchaser for a valuable consideration and without notice of any claim to the land by the Complainant or anyone else. A copy of his deed is hereto annexed and referred to as part of his Answer. It will be the duty of the defendant Adams to shew his title and he will no doubt do so and trace the title to William Anderson the first Admor. of John Smith, deceased.

        The plaintiffs is a stale claim and made upwards of thirty years after the sale of the property by William Anderson. If he (Anderson) was guilty of misconduct in selling the land as Admor. of Smith (which the defendant does not admit) that misconduct is not imputable to your Respondent. Your Respondent has been guilty of no fraud but is a fair purchaser from the defendant Adams, whom he your Respondent believes had a perfect and good title to the property at the time he sold it to your Respondent ...

        City of Richmond, to wit   Wm Burton

        Sworn to in the usual form before me a Magistrate of the said City
25 May 1808   B. Tate

                    - - -

EXECUTOR'S ACCOUNTS KEPT BY
WILLIAM ANDERSON

        ... "Pickenockeys charged to Wm Anderson in his Admors. Acct., altho sold to T. Smith & a deed passed. Thos. Smiths Rects. prove the delivery of the G. Books" ...

THE ESTATE OF JOHN SMITH IN
ACCOUNT WITH SAMUEL GIST

        ... 1765, May 2 - By cash for Pork sold at Pickenoky ₺4.14.6

        At a Court held for Hanover County, Thursday 5   , 1765,
Samuel Gist Gdn. of John Smith proved this account - which is recorded.

Rootes vs Gist (continued)

THOMAS SMITH'S RECEIPT FOR BOOKS

Hanover Town April 3rd   Then Recd of Capt William Anderson Executor of
Mr. John Smith deceased all the Books supposed to contain the Transactions
of his Business as Factor for Mr. Samuel Gist of London, which Books I
Promise to account for

April 1773   Thos. Smith
Test - Zach. Clarke

        Two Ledgers   One Journal
        One Cash Book   Sundry Blotters
        One Day Book   One Invoice Book

- - -

THE DEPOSITION OF MR. JOHN AUSTIN

The Deposition of Mr. John Austin of Hanover County taken at his
own house this 27th day of August 1807.

This Deponent who was 80 years old on the 14th day of September
last being first sworn deposeth and saith that He well recollects John Smith
the elder formerly of Hanover County Merchant that kept a store at his dwelling house as large as any in those times - That the Father of this Deponent
dealt with him - That some time before the death of the said John Smith as
this Deponent believes the Goods were removed to a Store house built on the
roadside and where the store continued till his death and where the said
Smith had such a store as was common in those days for Merchants to have
and it was said in the neighborhood the said John Smith died possessed of
an Estate both in land and negroes. This Deponent further states that he
knows Samuel Gist one of the Defendants that the said Gist lived with the
said John Smith as a Store Boy and after the death of the said Smith the
said Gist continued to keep store in the same house the said Smith had kept
Store in and this Deponent himself dealt with him, and the said Gist married
the widow of the said John Smith and continued to reside in the Dwelling
house that the said Smith had resided in, and to keep the Store in the Store
house that the said John Smith had kept Store in untill the said Samuel Gist
left this Country to reside in Great Britain where he has remained to the
present time as this Deponent has understood & believes ffurther this Deponent saith not

                                                    John Austin

Sworn to before Thomas Starke in the presence of Benjamin Toler & Thos. R.
Rootes & by their consent agreeing that it should be read in evidence in
the suit within mentioned ...

Rootes vs Gist   (Continued)

WILLIAM ANDERSON TO THOMAS READE ROOTES

London   18 Aug   1794 -

Dear Sir

      I received your favor of the 7th of June with a letter from Mr. Thomas Shore enclosed advising his having sold you all his right to the Gould Hill Estate, and expecting you wish either to purchase Mrs. Anderson's life Interest in that Estate, or to Rent it - or if neither of these should be agreeable to you, desire to have the Houses and Land between them and Hays - It is my wish to accommodate you, in some one of the ways you propose, and I will consult Mrs. Anderson upon the Subject after she has had time to consider it and write you more fully - in the meantime I should be very glad if you will inform me how much Sterling money you will give for the purchase or for the Rent, to be paid down in case of purchase, or if Rented, that to be paid Annually in London to save me the commission to an Agent for receiving and remitting which would be 10 Pcent -

      I have never made any use of the Land purchased of Lawson except fencing &ca - which saves the more valuable timber on the Goulds Hill Tract- Permit me to correct a mistake you have made about the negroes &c & Goulds Hill being subject to pay for the Land in King Wm for I paid for that Land out of Mr. John Smith's Estate long before. I left Virginia - and the suit in Chancery brought by the residuary legatees was to subject the King William land to be sold to pay that part of the purchase money which remained due at the time of Mr. Smiths death, as it was hard that the part of his Estate which they were entitled to should be subject to pay for lands purchased after the date of the Will -

      Mrs. Anderson joins in respectful Compliments to you and your Lady - I am

Dear Sir

Your mo. obt. Servt.

W. Anderson

-0-

Gist & Uxr) Appeal - April 1760
   vs   ) (Included in suit of
Pinchback) Rootes vs Gist)

      Be it Remembered that heretofore, to wit at a Court held for New Kent Co., the 9 day of February 1758 John Pinchback, admor. &C of Ann Pinchback decd. came into Court by John Wayles his Councel & brought his Bill against Samuel Gist and Sarah his wife & John Darracott Exors. &c of John Massie decd. which follows:

      Your Orator John Pinchback brother and Admr. of Ann Pinchback showeth that John Massie late of the County of Goochland died seized of a very considerable Estate ... and did by his last Will and Testament bequeath to his Loving niece Ann Pinchback the sum of £50 current money to be paid out of the Produce of the said Estate -when sd Ann reached 18 yrs of age...

John Pinchback's Bill of Complaint, continued:

Said Will was proved in due Form of Law in the Honble. the General
Court ...

That the said Ann Pinchback your Orator's Sister long since departed this Life an Infant under the age of 21 years & without Devising or making
any Disposition of the £50 Devised unto her as aforesaid and at this Time
would have been of the age of 20 years if Living - Whereby the Right, Title
& Interest in and to the said Legacy is become Vested in your Orator as Admr.
to said Ann.

Your Orator has frequently applied himself to the said Samuel Gist
& Sarah his wife in a friendly manner for payment of said Legacy with Interest from the Time the same became due ... but without success ...

To the end therefore that said Samuel Gist & Sarah his wife may be
compelled to pay unto your Orator said Legacy ...

ANSWER OF SAMUEL AND SARAH GIST
Barttlot Anderson, Counsel

Samuel and Sarah Gist deny that they have received sufficient
Profits of the Estate to pay all the said John Massies Debts & the Legacies
contained in the Will. That said Ann Departed this Life before she did arrive to such an age mentioned in said Will to be intitled to receive said
Legacy and are informed that said Legacy is Lapsed.

Sworn to 5 October 1758 before John Boswell.

DECREE

At a Court held on 13 March, 1760 came the Parties aforesaid by
their Counsel and Defendants still failing to return an account of said
John Massies Estate It is Decreed and Ordered that the Defendants do pay
unto the Complainant the Sum of £50 being the Legacy in the Bill mentioned
& his Costs by him in this Behalf expended ... from which Decree the Defendant Prayed an appeal to the 9th day of the next General Court which appeal
is allowed.   Barttlot Anderson, Surety for Defendant.

A Copy Test   Will. Clayton   Cl Cur

Rootes vs Gist (Continued)

Thomas R. Rootes, admr. de bonis non of   ) Box 116 - 1825
  Joseph Smith, decd. & John Smith, decd.) U. S. Cirst. Ct.
          agst.   ) 5th Virginia District
Martin Pearkes & Thomas Gregg, exors. of   )
  Samuel Gist & others   ) Dec. 4, 1818 - In Chancery

       Thomas R. Rootes respectfully shews that in a certain suit depending in your honorable court in which he as administrator of John Smith was pltf. & Samuel Gist & others defts., a decree was rendered many years ago directing a commissioner of the court to take and report certain accounts between the parties. That Samuel Greenhow then a Commissioner of the court undertook the execution of the order and made a report for which the fee charged was $40.50. That said report was by a subsequent order recommitted... and a certain William Temple undertook to perform the duty of commissioner. Said Temple made report & although much labor had been saved him by the previous report ... he has made the unsconscionable --- (illegible) of $565.00 for this service & he is now seeking the sanction of this court for this charge which upon inspection of the work done will obviously appear to be not more than 1/5 of the sum charged ...

       Your orator further states that William Temple ... has no property within the state or elsewhere known to this complainant out of which his creditors can obtain satisfaction of their debts. That said Temple was indebted to the estate of John Prosser in the sum of $870.00 with interest from 1810 to 1/3 of which debt your complainant is entitled as per certificate of the executor of Prosser hereunto annexed, the executor having assented to that claim of your orator and being willing to credit the said Temple for your orator's proportion of said debt ...

EDWARD W. ROOTES'S CERTIFICATE

       In a Schedule annexed to the last Will and Testament of the late Jno. Prosser there were sundry Persons charged by him as being indebted to "open account", among others William Temple ...

       During this time Thos. R. Rootes married the widow of Mr. Prosser & hearing that Mr. Temple had a claim against him, I suggested that there might be an arrangement made, by which one claim might be offset against the other & that whatever Mr. Rootes obtained of Mr. Temple I would charge him with on account of his wife's dower ... Sgd. E. W. Rootes - 30 Nov., 1818

     Memo - "John Prosser died on 25 October, 1810. -

                    Sgd. E. W. Rootes
                    Exor. of Prosser."

Roots vs Gist (continued)

THE ANSWER OF WILLIAM TEMPLE

William Temple answereth and saith that as a Commissioner of said Court he took an account & made a report in a suit on the equity side thereof in which Rootes as admr., etc. of John Smith was complainant & Samuel Gist and others defendants, in the year 1813 ... That the business involved the settlement of several estates & transactions of long standing, most of them having taken place before the War of our Revolution, including agreements, long accounts, and long written correspondences which required time & attention. He was engaged the greater part of his time for six or eight months, & kept an account of the time he was engaged in the business, and although he cannot state the precise time he knows that it was more than he charged to make up the account of his charge at 75¢ per hour which was the sum allowed by the Court ...

Complainant was frequently with him before it was finished & saw it when finished & also defendants charge & made no objection, but on the contrary alledged that defendant should have more for his services than the Court allowed.

Defendant left Richmond the latter part of January or the beginning of February 1814 after having given up all the property he possessed for the payment of his debts & was absent from the State a considerable part of that Year. He resided in the upper part of New Kent County on a Plantation of William H. Macon, Esq., distant about 25 mi. from Richmond all the year of 1815 and until the latter part of October 1816 when he removed to the State of Tennessee where he has since resided.

Defendant transferred his claim for taking said account to Mr. Miles Macon of Hanover County, Virginia, and in the Spring of 1818 drew on him for $500. in consideration thereof which he paid & defendant believed he had long since received the Money, never having heard to the Contrary until he received copy of said Bill.

Defendant was intimate and frequently in Company with John Prosser for many Years, while they both resided in Richmond, Virga., and frequently there spent many hours with him and others amusing themselves at a Game on Cards called Loo, and sometimes lost Money with said Prosser and sometimes won from him and others at said Game within the last 8 or 10 years of said Prossers life. He understood that Prosser kept a book in which he charged money won in this way - defendant also kept such a Book in which he charged money also won in this way, which Book is either lost or left in Virginia - He cannot therefore state how their accounts stood for Gaming transactions -

Some time after the death of said John Prosser Edwd. W. Rootes, Esqr. Exor. of said John Prosser's last Will informed him there was an account on said Prossers Books against him, when deft. informed said Executor how it originated to wit for Money won at Gaming at said Game called Loo and that he had large claims due him in this way - that when he collected them he would settle with him. Defendant never did receive the sums due him for such Debts and therefore never did settle with said Executor. Defendant knows not whether Complainant is entitled to one-third of said claim or not or whether said Executor has assented to his claiming one-third of such claim, but this Defendant is advised that if said Executor had any claim against him that could be enforced in a Court of Law, which he does not ad-

Rootes vs Gist (Continued)
The answer of William Temple, continued:

        Defendant had extensive dealings and accounts with said Prosser
and Moncure as Commission Merchants, which were all settled and closed in
the life time of said Prosser and did not owe said Prosser & Moncure or said
Prosser anything at his death except something due to him as above stated
for Money won from him at said Game of Cards called Loo in Richmond, aforesaid, contrary to Laws of Virginia on that subject, and defendant respect-
fully submits to this Honourable Court whether money won as above stated can
be made the subject of a sett off.
                                                        Will Temple

State of Tennessee   )
Davidson Circt. Ct.)   Nov. Term, 1821

        Sworn to in Court - Jac. McGavock

State of Tennessee - I Thomas Stuart one of the Judges of the Circuit Court
for the State of Tennessee and the Judge now presiding in the Circt. Ct. of
Davidson Co., do certify that Jacob McGavock is clerk of the Circuit Ct. of
Davidson Co. ... 6 Nov., 1821.   Thos. Stuart

        On motion of William Temple by his counsel It is ordered that
Robert Thruston to whom the Estate of Thomas R. Rootes has been committed
for administration do appear here on the second day of December next and
shew cause why the Rule made in this cause upon 2 June 1815 on William Temple should not be discharged and the order made on 24 November 14 set aside -

                            DECREE

        ... Robert Thruston having failed to appear ... the Court approv-
ing the report of Nathaniel Sheppard and John Robinson of the 26 May 1820
doth further adjudge and order that said Thruston do out of the effects of
Thomas Reade Rootes in his hands to be administered pay to William Temple
for the benefit of Miles Macon to whom it appears his claim has been assigned for a valuable consideration, the sum of $351. reported by said Shep-
pard & Robinson, with interest thereon from 25 Nov. 1812 till paid deducting
therefrom $20 paid by said Rootes to said Temple on the 15 January 1814 and
also $20 the cost of the proceedings in this case incurred by said Rootes,
same being allowed said Thruston as representing said Rootes in consequence
of the latter being partially relieved from the sum claimed by said Temple
of him.

                            DECREE

                        Rootes vs Gist

        On motion of the plaintiff this suit is discontinued. Dec. 9, 1822.
                            U. S. Circuit Court O. B. 11, p. 294.

SYME

Warre, Ex.	) 1797 (8)	Jones, Surv. Partn.	) 1790-2 (1)
vs	) U. S. Cir. Ct.	vs	) U. S. Cir. Ct.
Syme	) Distr. of Va.	Syme	) Distr. of Va.
	June 1794		

John Tyndall Warre a subject of the King of Great Britain and executor of the last will and Testament of William Jones late of the City of
Bristol in the Kingdom of Great Britain but now deceased, who was surviving
partner of Joseph Farrel & William Jones late of the same City & Kingdom,
Merchants and partners trading under the firm of Farrel & Jones, complains
of John Syme a citizen of Virginia in custody of the Marshall, of a plea for
this to wit, FOR THAT WHEREAS the said John Syme the defendant on the firs
day of January in the year of our Lord 1775 at the City of Bristol in the
Kingdom of Great Britain, that is to say in the County of Hanover in the district of Virginia in the middle circuit and with the jurisdiction of this
honorable Court, was indebted to the said Joseph Farrel and William Jones ...
in the sum of ₤25,000 Sterling money of the said Kingdom of Great Britain...

A Ronald pq

June, 1794 - May, 1796 - Judgt. for plaintiff ... and continued

PLEA OF JOHN SYME

And the said John Syme by William DuVal his attorney saith that the
said Plaintiff, John Tyndall Ware ought not to have or maintain his said
action therefor against him because he said that he did not undertake at any
time within Five Years next before the day of sueing forth the original
writ ... And the said Defendant by William DuVal his attorney, saith that
the said Plaintiff ought not to have or maintain his action aforesaid
against him because he saith that on the fourth day of July in the year
1776, the said Defendant became a Citizen of the State of Virginia and hath
ever since remained a Citizen thereof and resident therein; and that the
said Messrs. Farell & Jones merchants, and Partners on the said fourth day
of July in the year 1776, were and from the time of their nativity had ever
been and always since have been to the times of their Death British Subjects,
owing, yielding and paying alliegiance to the King of Great Britain which
said King of Great Britain and all his subjects, as well the plaintiff as
others, were on the fourth day of July, 1776, and continued until the Third
day of September 1783 Enemies of and at open War with the State of Virginia
and the United States of America, and that being so Enemies and at open War
as aforesaid the Legislature of the State of Virginia did at their Session
begun and held in the City of Williamsburg on Monday the Seventeenth Day of
October, in the year 1777, pass an Act entitled "An Act for sequestering
British property, enabling those indebted to British Subjects to pay off
such debts, and directing the proceedings in suits where such subjects are
parties, "That it shall and may be lawful for any Citizen of this Common
Wealth owing money to a Subject of Great Britain to pay the same or any part
thereof, from time to time, as he shall think fit, into the said Loan Office,
taking thereout a certificate for the same in the name of the Creditor, with

Warre vs Syme

an indorsement under the hand of the Commissioner of the said Office ex-
pressing the name of the Payor, and shall deliver such certificate to the
Governor and Council, whose Receipt shall discharge him from so much of
the Debt: "And the defendant says and avers that he did on the Twenty
Seventh day of November in the year 1778 on the County of --- and within
the State of Virginia while the said recited Act continued in full force,
pay into the Loan Office of this Commonwealth on Account of this demand
Debt in the Declaration mentioned the Sum of Ten Thousand Three Hundred
Pounds Curr. Money of Virginia, and on the Fifth day of April in the year
1779 in the County of --- the further Sum of Two Thousand Seven hundred and
Thirty Three Pounds Ten Shillings Current Money of Virginia ...

Receipt dated Williamsburg November 27, 1778, Signed by P. Henry

LETTERS OF COL. JOHN SYME

Virginia Hanover 9th June 1753

Gent:

By the True Patriot you have fifty hhds. of my Tobo which I intended
to have sold in Virginia, but being strongly Recommended to you, by Colo.
Peter Randolph, I have accordingly shipt. it to your House, and Do now
Confirm, the Contract with you, ... As yours is the first house I ever
ship'd any Tobo. to I hope I shall meet with proper encouragement, and
you may assure yourselves, my Endeavours to Promote your Interest, shall
not be wanting.

I have been obliged to draw largely on you this year, which was occas-
ioned by my beginning housekeeping however I have a Probability of making
an hundred hhds this year, which shall be sent your house on good Usage.
What I write you is not with an intention to Deceive you as is too often
the Case, but Desire you will enquire of Colo. Randolph, into the truth of
the Case.

You have also an Invoice of Sundry goods, which hope you'll send by the
first opportunity -

I am, Gent,

Your very hble Servant

John Syme

Warre vs Syme (continued)

INVOICE OF GOODS FOR BRISTOL
Col. Syme begins housekeeping
9th June 1753

300 yds. Cotton, 300 Ells Ozns. 15 lb. Brown thread, 3 Pieces Dutch
Blankitts, 9 Doz. Plaid Stockings, 5 M 20d nails, 20 M 10d nails, 20M 8d
nails, 5 M 6d nails, 5 M 4d nails, 5 M hob nails, 6 Pots Different Sizes, 1
Small Copper Kettle, 2 Sauce Pans - 5 Doz. Best Broad Hoes, 5 Dozn. Do. nar-
row, 3 Best broad Axes, 2 Steel Plate Handsaws, 6 Inch and Half Augurs, 6 Do.
Different Sizes, 6 Chisels Different Sizes, 13 yds. Green Cloath for Liveries
with Trimgs., 11 yds. Green Plush, 40 yds. Green Plains, 1 Dozn. Pair Green
Stockings, 2 Pieces best Irish Linnen, 1 Do. @ 2/, 2 Pieces Irish Sheeting,
1/2 Do. Brown, 1 Piece Dowlas, 20 yds. Diaper 3/4 wide, 2 hair Brooms, 2 Mops,
2 Counterpins, 3 Rugs, 1 Coal Still, 1 Dozn. Tin Pans, 1 Warming Pan, 2 lb.
Powderd Blew, 6 Shallow Pewter Dishes Difft. sizes, 6 Deep Do., 2 Dozn. Best
Shallow Plates, 1 Dozn. Do. Deep, 2 Brass Chafing Dishes, a set Casters, a
Grid Iron, 2 lb. Green Tea, 2 lb. Do. Bohea, 6 Loaves Double Refind. Shugar,
8 Do. Single, 1 Dozn. Ivory Handled Knives and Forks, 1 Oild Cloath 11 feet
wide & 15 long, 1/2 Dozn. best Brass Candle Sticks, 2 Pair Snuffers, 1 Box
Iron, 2 Flat Irons, 1 Coil Trace Rope, 4 Dozn. Butchers knives, 6 mill Pads,
2 Casks Beer, 2 Cheeses, 4 Pair Sifters, 2 small coarce saddles -

1 Silver soup spoon, 1 Dozn. Silver Table spoons, 1 Silver Punch
Ladle & Strainer, 1/2 Dozn. Tea Spoons, 1/2 Dozn. Shallow China Plates, 1
Dozn. Do. Deep, 1/2 Dozn. China Dishes Difft. Sizes, a set of white China, 3
China Cans, and one Cup with 2 Handles, 2 Glass Table Stands, 4 Silver Salts,
1/2 Dozn. Candle molds.

- - -

Virginia Hanover 27th May 1754

Gent.-

By the time this comes to hand, hope you'll have my Tobo. safe by
the Duke, and the Ramainder of my crop shall be sent you by the first of
your ships that arrives here -

I have again been obliged to draw heavily on this crop, but you may
assure yourselves, my Bills will be very triffling another year, and as I
have encreased my number of Negro's considerably and got the genuine sweet
scented Tobo. my crop will be much greater in Quantity, and much better in
Quality, so must desire my Bills may meet with Due Honour -

I have solicited many People to try you with some Tobo., but the
ill Opinion, some Gent. have taken Pains to possess the Planters with, of
your House, has made them shy at Present, however, as these things generally
wear off (especially when they are given the Lye to, by Mens Actions) make
no Doubt but you will have a considerable Interest on York River shortly -

You have an Invoice of Goods inclosed, which should be glad you
would send, with my former, by some ship that comes into York River, as it
is very inconvenient for me, to transport them from James River. I also

Warre vs Syme

should be glad you'll send them by the Fall, otherwise it will be a great Disappointment

. This comes by Mr. George Webb a young Gentleman of my Acquaintance and any Civilitys shown him shall be taken as a favour, should also be Glad you'll honour his Bill, as soon as Conveniency will Permit as he proposes to stay but a short time in Bristol. I am, With Esteem, Gent.

Your Mo. hble servt.

To
Messrs. Lidderdale Harmer Ferrell   John Syme -
     Merchts Bristol

- - -

Virginia, Hanover County 24th April 1755
Gent.-

By the time this comes to hand, hope you'll have Recd. my Tobo., both by the Planter & Packet; you have also 25 hhds. by the Camarkin Castle, towards whose Dispatch I contributed all in my Power, but could not Possibly get all my Mountain Tobo. Ready, the Remainder shall be sent you by the Patriot. A spell of snowy Weather happeninning to set in, just after the Brigs arrival, and some very odd Behaviour of Colo. Macons, I am sure Delay'd her 10 Days at Least. Colo. Macon Deliver'd us Notes and Orders, for twenty odd hhds. as soon as the Vessel came in, but upon his seeing her, gave Orders to the Inspectors, not to deliver any More, than the Capt. had already on board his Flat, and said, He was sure the Brigg would never get safe to Bristol. However, am in hopes she will answer your Expectations, in being the first Ship at Home, as there will be none to sail after her, in less than a fortnight at Least. I had Engag'd some Planters, to ship their Crops to your house, but the most Extraordinary Price given here, in our Country Prevented them, as they would be convinc'd, it was better to take 18/ Pr. Ct. I am desir'd by Isaac Winston, Junr. to acquaint you of a Mistake Concerning a hhd. of Tobo. ship't on Board the Duke of Cumberland, he is an Honest Man, and if he could be made sensible, in what Manner it was Dispos'd off, I am sure would be a Good Shipper to your House; and as I have been apply'd to by People, who make about 10 hhds. a Year, to know whether you would advance their Goods, besides the Cash on their Tobo. I should be Glad of your Instructions, how far I may go, where I know the Person to be Punctual, & to be depended on. You mention putting a good small vessell in our River, which I greatly approve off, as the People will be under no Apprehensions, of sending to James River for their Goods. Inclos'd is an Invoice, which I want again this fall; and as to my Acct., I find no Error in it, Except that the Bill, which you Mention of P. Randolph's, It is large, but shall Endeavour to lessen it Yearly, having Eight hundred & fifty Pounds to Receive this Summer of Wm. Nelson, Esq., & four hundred of Colo. Johnson, both which sums Intend to Purchase Negro's with, to seat my Mountain Lands. However it is a satisfaction to me, that I am in debt to but one House, and therefore shall be Intirely at Liberty, to Devote my Crops & Interest Accordingly -

We are now in Spirits, concerning the Ohio Expedition, as all our European Forces arriv'd in Good Order, and intend to March Next Week, to

Warre vs Syme (continued)

Attack the French Fort at Monongahella. We have the Forces from Great Brittain, Virginia and Maryland, 24 hundred Stout Men, which General Braddock seems to think sufficient, he having Discharged several, that he thought unfit for the Buisiness. We have no Certain Accts. of the number of the French, but are Sure their Forces will be inferior to Ours in Number when the Joint supplys, of all the Brittish Colonys in North America Unite, and we are assur'd they are Badly Supply'd with Provisions already; But as for our Quondam Friends the Indians I am sure will do nothing for us, till we appear on the Ohio too able to want their Assistance. I hope you'll Excuse my Troubling you, with so long a Letter, but as I imagine, the Matter in Dispute upon the Ohio, of Consequence to the Nation in General I shall as Opportunity offers, give you an Acct. of such Matters, as I may think worth your hearing, having my advices from a Person who is on the Spot.

          I am Gent,
                      Your Mo: hble Servt
                                          John Syme

N B - The set of Shoemakers Tools
was left out of my Goods, and should
be Glad you'll send them, with the
Inclos'd Invoice, & should be Glad of
the Magazines in Regular Order -

To Messrs. Lidderdale Harmer & Farrell

                        - - -

                                Virginia 12th May 1756

Gent -

          This serves to advise you, of my Draught to Doctor Shore, for Forty Pounds, which should be much oblig'd for your accepting.

          I make no Doubt, my Bills will appear large, on this Short Crop, but hope you'll Honour them, as it Came very unexpectedly; and hope by the Goodness of the Present Crop, to make some Amends, and you may Depend, on my Drawing for very little, this next Year.

          I am, Gent

                    Your Mo: hble. Servt.
                                          John Syme

To Messrs. Lidderdale Harmer & Farrel,
          Merchts   Bristol

Warre vs Syme   (Continued)

Virginia 9th Feby 1757

Gent -

My last was by the Spotswood, so Desire you to make Insurance on the
True Patriot, by whom you'll have Eighty hhds. of my Tobacco.

It gives me much concern, to have my Bills protested; the Shortness of
the Crop, was what I could not foresee, and as I have always Ship'd you my
whole Crop, and done Everything in my Power for you, I hop'd You would have
been so good, as have Honor'd them, notwithstanding my falling so far Short,
of my usual Quantity; But I have now compleated what I am about, and I shall
only Renew the Bills Protested last year, and a small Bill to Mr. Jameson,
and Capt. Richd. Heux, which will not be in the whole to the amount, of the
Present Crop.

I am truly sensible, Gentlemen, the Debt I owe you is large, but then I
pay you Interest for it, and with any Tolerable Success, I shall be now able,
to send you Yearly, considerably above an Hundred hhds, and you may Depend,
I shall not by any means Exceed ₤300 a year, both in Bills & Goods till I
have pay'd the Old Score.

I hope my Tobo. will this Year prove satisfactory, in General, as it is
Esteem'd very good here, and as I had not any Possibility, of getting one
hhd. on Board the Packet, make no Doubt, you'll not let me suffer by it,
but still Render me agreeable Sales. -

I am desired by Isaac Winston, Junr. to Require you to make Insurance
on the Planter, for two hhds. for him, and on propper incouragement he will
send more next Year; I hope you will for the future, send a Ship into our
River, as it is a great Disadvantage to you Interest, for the Shippers to
send Round their Tobo. to James River, and to bring Round their Goods, and a
forward Ship here, next Year, will meet with Great Dispatch - I mentioned
some time ago, my being Charg'd with a set of shoe Tools, which never came to
hand, should be Glad You'll send them, as they were left out before. - You
will observe two hhds. No. 17 in my Crop, the lightest is Extraordinary Sweet
Scented, and I imagine will sell very well; You will find Most of the Crop
very good, as there is but 3 or 4 Indifferent hhds. in the whole, which was
occasion'd by not being able to save seed Enough of one Sort, in the Dry
Year.   Inclos'd You have my Invoice, which should be Glad You'll send, at
the usual Time, (and if Possible) in our River, as I do assure You I have not
to this Day, got all my Goods that you sent me in the Packet.

I am   Gent
Your mo: hhble. servt.

N B   J. Syme
The Remainder of my Crop, which
will be abt. 23 hhds. shall be
sent you by Capt. Aselby

(No addressee)

Warre vs Syme (continued)

Virginia 8th May 1757

Gent -

This comes by Capt. Aselby, who I hope will in some Measure make up (by a quick Passage) for the time he has been delay'd here, by the imbargo; It was a great Mortification to me, to have my Tob: left for the last Ship, when I made use of every method, to get it Round to James River, and, indeed, put my own People in the Craft, that the Sloop might meet with the greatest Dispatch, and had Prevail'd on the Skipper to go 7 hhds. short, but to my great astonishment, he was Directed to the Contrary. - I make no Doubt Gent., when you put the Matter to yourselves, you will still render me such accounts, as a man may live by, as I am sure, my Tobo. is Reputed very good sweet scented and as such would command 21/6 P. Ct. here, tho' the common Price but 20/. You will Receive my Bill of L50 to Mr. Jameson, and another of L60 to Capt. Meux, which is all I shall Draw. And will not amount to the 80 hhds. sent, and the Remainder You shall have by the Packet. - I have not yet heard, of the Bill of L100, to Geo: Webb Junr., but if it Returns, shall Discharge it with Grain, and shall not by any means, (as I have finished everything I was about) exceed L300 a Year, in Goods and Cash, till I have pay'd the old Score.

I am Gent.

N. B.   Your Mo: Obedt. hhble. servt.

Please send me, with my   J. Syme
former Invoice, a Sain 42
fathom long, 16 feet in the
middle, & 6 feet at each end,
a pair of Strong Buck Breechs.,
for a small man, and 15 ll.
Lucern seed.

To Messrs. Lidderdale Harmer & Farrel, Merchts.
                                         Bristol
By Capt. Aselby

- - -

Virginia 19th May 1758

Sir

I have received yours of the 28th Jan'y & 10th Feb'y with regard to the Virginia Packet, and in conformity to your Request, have had a conversation with Capt. Darracott, on that Ships loading in Our River, and we think she has no kind of chance, on account of the Short Crop, and your Interest here is not yet good enough, to load two Vessels in Our River, for People can't so suddenly break off their Ingagemts.; but ours you may be Sure of, and every Person that I have Mention'd the Dissolution of your Partnership to, is much Pleas'd, and Promises to send you Tobo. next Year, but at Present we have but a Poor prospect of a Crop, there being scarce any Plants, and the few Planters, that have not Dispos'd of their Crops, have been offer'd 25/Pr. Ct. for their Tobo., and I believe will keep it till another Year, if they cant get 30/ Pr. ct., therefore as there will be so great a Scarcity, make no Doubt, my Tobo. in the Judith, will answer Extremely well.

Warre vs Syme (Continued)

Capt. Darracott goes to James River next week, to do the best he can for the Packet; as the Crop last Year is Universally short, I don't imagine she can be Loaded there, however, of this shall write you. I advis'd you sometime ago, of my Bills to F. Jerdone, Renewal to Doctor Shore, Geo: Thomas L45, J. Carter L30, and to Dickinson & Sompy. L80 which, when they come to hand, should be Glad you'll Honor; If you can by any Means get us the Gardner, it will be a Very Great favor, and if he comes, Please let him bring some Seeds, flower Roote & Gra.

I am   with Great Esteem   Sir
                      Your Mo: hhble Servt.
Mr. Farell   J. Syme

- - -

Virginia   2d June   1760

Gent.

My last was by Capt. Aselby, wth the Invoice for our Store, wch hope You'll receive, 'ere this comes to hand -

I am now to answer yours Covering Sales for my 25 hhds Tobo. wch falls greatly Short of my Expectations, & when I come to Consider the insurance, Shrinkage, interest of lying out of the Money till sold, all wch is to be deducted out of the Nt Proceeds, it reduces them much, near one half they would have sold for here; This wth a Mistake is not giving me Credit for the last 5 hhds. by Aselby, & some other things I shall mention, have swell'd my Acct. Currt. to a Prodigious Sum of late, for my Part I am heartily for Your living, & that You would let me live also; My situation in a Public Place, Obliges me to live in a Way, somewhat Expensive, whereby I am better able to serve your interest, & for wch in return, You allow Others many advantages, of Guinea Ships, Cash Comiscions & cra., that dont contribute more, or Perhaps so much to your Advantage, as myself, & in the meantime, Charge me a heavy interest on my Goods, in 6 months from the time they are Ship'd, whereas some other Merchts. do not put it to Acct. of interest, in less than 12 months, & Indeed, I think You ought to let me have the Money, for the net interest You Pay for it in England, in Consideration of my Services here, wch are Certainly Equal to your Trouble in negociating it (if you have any) but make no Doubt it is your Own, & as to any risk You may Run, I am Ready to make you any Security. I have been, & still am, very unfortunate in my Slaves dying, having lost as many of my Men, within these ten years, as Would amt. to 1000 pds., and You'll Perceive, my Crops have increased of late, wch. will readily Acct. for my heavy Drafts. This incourages me, to think of another Scheme to Cultivate my Lands, wch. is, if You'll advance me a Sum of Money, at $3\frac{1}{2}$ or 4 Pr. Ct. to be laid out in Negroes, their Crops shall be Mark'd wth a distinguishing Mark from the rest, & the Produce annually remain Untouch'd, & go to discharge the Money so advanc'd. By wch means You'll get Comissions on the Tobo. made, & I in all Probability, make something of my Lands, wch. are at present Burden'd with Taxes to support the War, & a dead weight that Yields no present Advantage. - Another Reason for Purchasing Negroes is we expect them cheap soon. Our late Assembly having taken of_ 10 Pr. Ct. of the Duty.

Warre vs Syme (continued)

You'll receive some Tobo. from Colo. Henry & he tells me, he Purposes to be a constant Shipper but Can't Promise for him.

I am with Much Esteem
N. B.   Gent Your hhble. Servt.
In the Botts. for Mr. Page, & Colo.   )   J. Syme
Baylor, a Gross is left out in each   )
Quanty. Please send the Cloaths mentd.)
before, of the finest Ratteen, and also)
6 Scythes, fix'd best manner, wth. Cra-)
dles, 6 Do. without, 12 Gr. Good Corks ）   No addressee

- - -

                                        Virginia 18th June 1761
Gent. -
        I have just had the Pleasure, of yours of the 10th March, & I am
much oblig'd, for the Trouble you have had in Procuring Juniper, and shall
be more anxious abt. him, than you can Possibly be, till he arrives. I don't
in the least doubt your care, should be Glad, you'd let the Groom be an honest Industrious Man, & bring wth him some Spancels & Crs. made use of in
Covering, and also some Bridles & Saddles, for Breaking young Colts; 2 best
Bridles, Wire Bits, a very light Saddle, 2 Broad belts, and Sircingles; It
will then be a good time, to send me some seed wheat & oats, the former coming so late, that I am afraid it will not come up; likewise 400 lb. of spant
Brown in Gd. in Oyl, 400 lb. dry, and should be Glad You'd send me, a Suit
of Best Cloath, of a Fashble Color wth two pair Breeches, made very long Over
the knees, & a Velvet Waistcoat to Suit it. Kagley has my Measure, & Please
give him a Charge to let it be the best of its kind.

        I have at last Prevailed on Capt. Meux to send you 4 hhds. Tobo. in
Walker, Colo. Lewis 6 hhds., & as many myself, wch. desire may be insur'd,
& there will be some few more. Tobo. has fell here, being from 20/ to 22/6
Pr. hundred at Present, but think it will Rise. Every ship that Comes here,
meets wth Great difficulty in Loading, Meriwether is not full, & the Lord
knows, when Walker, Thomas, or Spencer will sail.

        I wish you all manner of happiness. I am
                        Gent Your Mo: obedt.
N. B.   J. Syme
I inclose you two Memo for Goods

Messrs. Farell & Jones   P America

Memdm. - For a pair of best Peak Mill Stones the size to be about four feet
across The thickness ten inches on the brim I desire that they may be very
full of Pebble, and that it may be all over both stones as regular as possible, and to observe that the pebble is set in good hard grit, that by packing it may not fly out. If there shoul'd be occation, would be willing to
allow what you think reasonable, to a man thats a Judge in Mill Stones to
Chuse such a pair as I have Described.

Warre vs Syme   (Continued)

Virginia 10th May 1763

Gent. -
      This comes by the Friendship wth 75 hds. of my Tobo. some being left out
The Vessell not carrying near so much as we expected. I have ingaged a good
deal more Tobo. for You, wch shall put on Bd. some other Vessell, to your Port
on the best Terms I can. Excha. is now at 60 Pr. ct. You'll therefore easily Perceive, the Disadvantages I should be under, in taking up my Bills under
Protest, in Currt. Money. Besides Nelson insists on Sterlg. Money. I have
therefore, added a small matter to them, & renewed them, wch is all the Bills
I shall draw on You, except, any more of them returns, wch will not be the
case as they are very few and small. I am determined to make no more Purchases
but apply my Tobo. every year towards Paying you off, indeed those Renew'd
will not near amount to the Tobo. I shall send you this Year, so it will not
interfere wth. your Resolution agst. advancg. I owe you a good deal of Money,
& would have you inquire of Aselby abt. my affairs. I got him to take a Ride
wth. me to that Purpose. He can also inform You, whether I am of any service
to you here. I wrote you by the Planter I had advanc'd some cash for Purchasing Tobo. for Gent. here, wch. occasion'd my Bills to be so large, however,
shall not do the like again, wch. I own, to be by no means the thing. I also
told you before, the case, wth. Regard to R. and B. the latter of wch is a
Great Lyar, he writes me not to Depend on Your sending me a Horse, for you
told him you would not, but shall take no notice of the Scoundrel.

I Believe I mentioned the sums formerly sent, were to be charg'd to the Gent.
for whom they came, & the Stone Trough last sent, to Colo. P. Randolph, when
you send the ship, you tell me of Purchasing, should be glad you'd Put Cawsey
in her, for several Reasons.

Pray send me a Transcript, of Bills Paid to Old Mr. Webb, in his life time.

As we are now blest with Peace, suppose there are Plenty of Tradesmen & cra.
to be had; I am much in want of a good Plowman & Seedman. I mean a nice
hand to Put me in the Way of doing things of that sort, in a Farmer like way,
besides such a one would Do, to take care of the Horse on his Passage, wch.
hope will be Provided this Summer, as you write me. I have sent you another
Pott Axe, wch. beg you'll urge the Workman, to Pay Particular Regard to; also
a Bundle of Old Silk, wch I want Dy'd, & made up for the Girls mentd. in the
Invc., but chiefly for the eldest; It is Rap'd in the Morng. Gown sent, wch
is to be Return'd. I have sent You some finely distill'd Peach Brandy, and
with Great Regard, I am,

Gent. Your mo: obedt.

J. Syme

Since writing the above, have rec'd yours by Cawsey, & you'll have 10 hhds.
Tobo. now from Colo. Lewis, and there is more ready, wch. I will take care
off for you. I perceive you say nothing about the Horn, but must request
of you, to send me only one, & Pay those Bills, now under Protest, wch is
all I Request of you at Present, & you may Depend, I am as unalterably Determined, against inlarging my Acct. as you are agst. advancing any more cash.

I am as Before

Messrs. Farell & Jones   J. Syme

Memo. on back of letter: "the Buff to be dyed yellow A Brocade made into
Stay & Coats for the eldest Yellow into Stay & Coat for the eldest."

Warre vs Syme (continued)

Virginia Williamsburg 21st May 1765

Gent.

In mine by Anselby, I advis'd you of my intentions, of taking up my Bills to Mr. Nelson; This serves to accompany them, and to inform you, he insists on Sterlg. Money, therefore cannot imagine You'll suffer them to return, as besides that, Exchs. is at 60 Pr. Ct.

All the Bills I shall draw on you, will only be to Renew those under Protest, & a Small one to Mr. Prentis, for Quitrents & taxes; Indeed as the others were small, suppose you'll pay them. - I told you before I was fully bent, to clear off the old Score; wch you may depend on, being fully satisfied, it will be for our Mutual Advantage. But must once more desire You My Friends, not to hurt my Credit so much, as to suffer the Bills to Come Back, & I am wth Esteem,

Your Mo: Obedt. Servt.

N. B.   J. Syme
The Guns formerly sent, are to be)
charg'd to me or to the Gent. &)
the Trough to Colo. P. Randolph) Messrs. Farell & Jones Merchts. Bristol

- - -

Virginia 15th Novr. 1763

Gent.

I have mentd. the several matters contd. in your last, to Your Friends here, at wch. they seem well Pleas'd. I think one Ship of abt. 400 hhds. every Fall would be sufficient at this time & I can always get room, for the stragling hhgds. that remain in some Vessel or other. I have talk'd with Mr. Dandridge abt. it & he says little, being deeply ingag'd in the Sportg. Way at prest., however, you shall hear More fully from me by Cawsey. You are so kind as to say, you'll send me a Horse, and as I am very Particularly circumstanc'd in that Respect, Must make you acquainted wth. it. A Gent. in London hearing in what Demd. Horses were here, sent me a common Hunter on his acct. & a Blooded nag on my Own; I sold the Hunter for ₤165, & mine (wch. everything included cost me 130 Guineas) for ₤500, wch offer I refus'd till after the receipt of your Ltre. & now I am quite wth out a Stud Horse. I must therefore intreat you, to hurry one of the following List, that is by next Season, & let him be a Blood Bay (exactly Juniper's Color) & very handsome, to move well, lofty & Proud, 15 hands high at Least. I have said so much on this head formerly that I shall take up no more of your time, than to assure you, it is the Last Trouble of the kind I shall give you, therefore, can wth the more Freedom request you, to send me a good one, & to be here by next April or May. Your Expedition on this occasion, shall always be greatly remembered by Gent,

Your Mo: Obedt.

J. Syme

N. B. her follows the List above)
mentd. Vizt. Appollo, Bosphorus,)
Belford, Borcas, Pangloss, Hanby,)
Fearnought, Tarpaulin, Bosphorus,)
Sportsman, Mickleham, Americus   )

Warre vs Syme (Continued)

Virginia 2d Feby 1764

Gent.

You have herewith Copy of mine of the 15th Novr last, to wh please be referr'd. I think the Prices of my Tobo. mentd. in your last, extremely low. I am in some doubt it is owing to its being of the Frederick kind, for I am taking all the care I can to make it good; You may Depend, I shall not draw on You, to exceed one half of the nt. Proceeds of my Tobo. after Dischargg. the Interest, for I look on it, to be to our mutual advantage so to do, & if my Tobo. is faulty in any Particular, Please to mention it. I am still of the same Opinion with Regard to the Ships to be sent here, but can be a more Competant Judge when Cawsey Sails, whom I have long expected. Doctor Walker, by this Conveyance applys to you, to Purchase some Goods for him at 9 mo: Creditt, for reasons wch he gives you; I hope you'll oblige him in sendg. them, & Buying them on the Best terms. He has it much in his Power to serve you, is Punctual even to a Proverb, & has a great Deal of money Due to him, indeed it surpriz'd me, he should want to be trusted by any man till I heard his Scheme. I inclose you an Order of Joseph Rogers & his Wife, wch desire you'll secure in Your hands, we having no other way to get the money. I don't remember you ever Told me, that you had rectify'd the Mistake wth regard to the Sums, wch are to be charg'd to the Gent. who sent for them. Since the above, Capt. Aselby informs me, You have now a small Vessel, near Finish'd, to send here early next Fall; as our Tobo. does not come in so soon, as in some other Places, it would be Propper, to give instructions about Purchasing, should that be the case, for it will answer no end, to let the Ship Lye, and think you may Depend on 500 hhds.

Wth. Great Esteem, I am, Gent.

Your o: Obedt. Servt.

N. B. Please insure 70 hhds. for)
me, on bd. Cawsey, & in case my)   J. Syme
Invo. does not come in time, a)
large Stock of Negros goods, by)
the early ship)

- - -

Virginia Wmsburg 15th Novr. 1764

Gent.

I am now to inform you, the Brothrs. has been arrived about 3 weeks, & have some hopes of getting her away by Jany. tho' really must say, Your Friends here are very Slack; in Yours by Anselby, you desire to know the Reasons, it is Partly as you Suggest, owing to the Price for the Tobo. going in the Country, & the difficulty's of complying wth. their Protested Bills, wch. were drawn Contrary to my advice; Their Minds are as Unsettled, as the Markets on our River, for the Tobo., & forgettg. you have advanc'd Money for them, they only think of the Present time. This now is the case of Mr. Dandridge, Mr. Antho. Winston & Mr. L. Pope, from all whome, have only got the Promise of 45 hhds. & not one Ready yet. It will be Xmas or thereabouts, before Aselby sails, so can't tell what may be expected from James River. I shall contrive for the best, & should there be a small deficiency, shall make it up. And by no means, Purchase more than what you mention, but Tobo. will not be so high this year, as it was last wth us, & hope it will be better wth. you. I am much oblig'd, for your enquiring's after a Nag for me, but as I mentd. before, You may take no more Trouble on

Hanover County - Mar. 17th 1758/9

This figure is ye shape of 27½ acres laid off for a Town on Pamunkee River by Mr Jnº Henery. Survt. for Colº Wm Merewether

This copy taken from the original plats in possession of Colº Merewether & ye oyr 9rt. Jnº Thomson Copyd June 1744

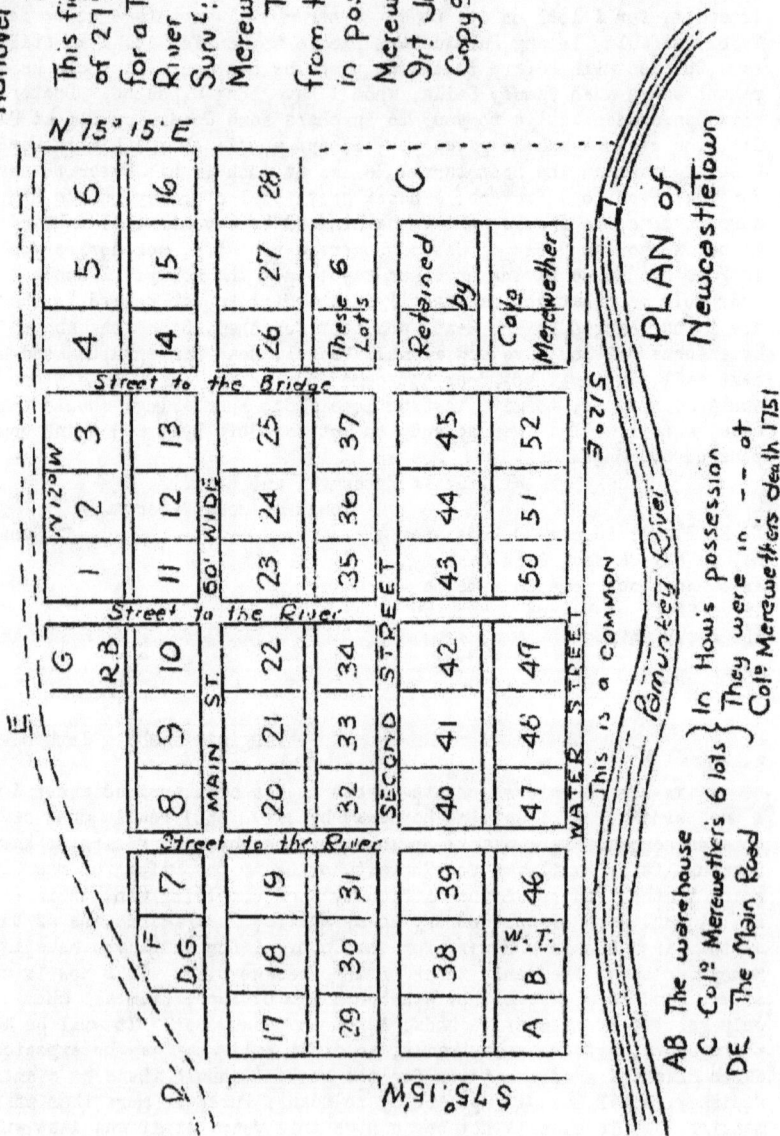

N 75° 15' E

6	5	4	
16	15	14	
28	27	26	These 6 Lots
C	Retained by		
	Colº Merewether		

Street to the Bridge

N 12° W

3	2	1
13	12	11
25	24	23
37	36	35
45	44	43
52	51	50

60' WIDE

Street to the River

G R.B	10	9	8
22	21	20	MAIN ST.
34	33	32	SECOND STREET
42	41	40	
49	46	47	

S 12° E

Street to the River

F D.G.	7
19	18
31	30
39	38
46	W.T.

17	
29	
	A	B

E

D

S 75° 15' W

WATER STREET

This is a Common

Pamunkey River

AB   The warehouse
C   Colº Merewether's 6 lots   } In How's possession
                                They were in -- ot
                                Colº Merewether's death 1751
DE   The Main Road

PLAN of Newcastletown

PLAN OF NEWCASTLE TOWN
PAMUNKE RIVER, HANOVER

Lot No.	Owner - Occupant	Lot No.	Owner - Occupant
1. Wm. Morris	- Black: Hugh's	27. --- Walters	- himself
2. Jno. Ballard	- The Heirs of Ballard	28. Mr. Chapman	- his heirs
		29. Wm. Taylor	- Mat. Anderson
3. Farg. Matthison	- Dr. Shore's	30. Wm. Belamy	- Do.
4. Wm. Taylor	- Himself	31. Do.	- Do.
5. Ditto	- Do.	32. Do.	- Dun. Graham
6. Wm. Neilson	- Himself	33. David Holt	- Do.
7. Jno. Poindexter	- Himself	34. Wm. Macon	- himself
8. Jno. Ballard	- His Heirs	35. Wm. Massie	- his heirs
9. Jno. Henery	- Col. Jno. Cheswell	36. Edd. Littlepage	- Jno. Thomson
		37 Leighton Wood	- Robt. Jennings
10. Jno. Poindexter	- Do.	38. David Holt	- David Holt, Jr.
11. Jno. Holt	- Himself	39. Peter Marks	- himself
12 James Littlepage	- Hyndman & Donald	40. David Holt	- Wm Holt
		41. Fra: Jordan	- Dun. Graham
13. Wm. Parks	- His Heirs	42. Jno. Dixon	- himself
14. Jno. Dandridge	- Himself	43. Jno. Holt	- himself
15. Wm. Neilson	- Himself	44 Richd. Littlepage	- himself
16. Samll. Hale	- Wm Coles	45. Do.	- Do
17. Jno. Thomson	- Himself	46. Peter Marks	- himself
18. Ditto	- Do.	47. Do.	- Do.
19. Wm. Parks	- his heirs	48. Neill Buchanan	- Duncan Graham
20. Jno. Thomson	- Dun. Graham	49. Jno. Dixon	- himself
21. Jos Peace	- Do	50. Richd. Johnson	- Harden Burnley
22. Wm. Johnstone	- Do. Taylor, Tennent to D. G.	51. Jno. Dandridge	- Jos. Fox
		52. Jno. Darrecott	- Dun. Graham bought of Thos. Merewether
23. Richard Johnson	- Geo. Webb		
24. Edd. Littlepage	- Donald & Hyndman		
25. Leighton Wood	- Robt. Jennings	F. Dun. Graham 1746	- Dun. Graham
26 --- Walters	- himself	G. Robt. Brown 1747	- his heirs

N. B. No. 52 was acknowledged Augt. 3d 1750
          By agreement Exempt. from Building
          Advanc'd Thos. Merewether Junr Cash for yt (it)
          before I gott the deeds acknovledgd.
          £ 16. 2. 6

On reverse side:

          Memorandy. to get my deed out of the Clerk's office for Lot No. 52
          in New Castle

The above list of lot owners and occupants was made from a negative in the
Archives Division of the Virginia State Library, lent May 28, 1940, through
Dr. Garnett Ryland - Original from papers of Henry Hill, of Mt. Gideon, Caroline Co., now in possession of his descendant, Mrs. Nannie Jackson, Richmond, Virginia. - The compilers.

Warre vs Syme (continued)

that head; Times are very hard, & Horses now, fall every Day in their Value;
I shall be uneasy till I hear of your Complying wth my Request by Pearson,
wch I think will certainly be to our mutual advantage, & as you refer me for
an ansr., till you see him, can't but hope the Proposals will be agreeable.
I must further Observe on that Particular, opings. and advantages, are greater every day. If you could send me a Smith, & Set of Tools, it would be a
good article, at this Juncture; also 60 M nails sorted, except as to 20d, of
wch have Plenty. I had almost forgot to tell you, Mr. Thos. Jones complns
of your not sending his goods, & will not give us any Tobo. for this Ship;
It is a material Article, to oblige People wth their Goods - I don't observe
you give me any Credit, for the Sums sent to Dr. Walker & Mr. Dandridge, by
Stanton. They are to be Charg'd to those Gent., as I ment'd in mine some
time since -   Wth Regard   I am   Gent

                                        Your Mo: Obedt. Servt.

                                                      J. Syme

N. B. Poor Aselby has lost his son,
drowned as suppos'd; Colo. Randolph
has between 2 and 3 hundred Negroes left
yet, on Bd. his Guinea Ship, wch Believe   Pr   Rialto
he will keep till the Spring; hope the   rec'd 12 Jany
nails & mill Work will come by Cawsey,
or Sooner   Yrs   J S

                            - - -

                               Virginia, Newcastle 4th June 1765
Gent.

        Your last was by way of London, only desir'd me, to forwd. a Pack-
et to Mr. Wayles, wch I did immediately. I have examin'd the Acct. You
Speak of & there is only Cr. Colo. Randolph for a Stone Trough, not a Word
of the Gunns, in any Acct. sent me. I return the Boltg. Cloaths bought by
Cary, except two very Coarse ones, wch. cost 15/, they are Worsted instead
of Silk, & will by no means do, besides, I ment. Silk in my directions. I
should be glad, You'd send me 50 sacks Salt by Emms, & please charge me,
wth Wm. Wades Acct.

        I perceive what you say, in yrs. of the 24th Jany. last, wth regard
to the Goods Pearson wanted, the sum of £5000, is more than I had bought of
Kirkg. in the set out, however, he tells me, You are to send us abt. £350
in the Fall. As we have hitherto made a great Sale, we shall apply to you
for some Spring Goods, wch if you'll send, it will be forwarding your Ships,
as we shall remit Tobo., & moreover, prevent your advancg. cash, to induce
People to ship that article.

        We have been very much alarm'd of late, wth an Act of Parliamt. lay-
ing Stamp Dutys, on the several Colonys in America. I herewith send you the
resolutions our Assembly came to, on that head, wch: occasions the Govern-
or, to Dissolve the House of Burgesses, & of Course, inflame the minds of
the People much. One hardship (among many others) of that Tax is, that t'is
to be paid in Silver, of wch there is scarce any in the Colony. It is certainly Bad Policy in Britain - to Tax her Colonys so heavily, as to o-
blige them, to manufacture for themselves; the consequences attending it,

Warre vs Syme   (Continued)

must be a Decrease of her Trade, & many Poor Tradesmen's wantg.bread on your
Side the Water, who are at Present supported, by her American Dominions.

A Vote has paid our House, for Borrowing the Sum of ₤240,000 Sterlg. of
the Merchts. in England, One hundred of wch was to have been apply'd towards
sinkg. the Paper Money now in Circulation, & the remaing. ₤140,000 to have
been a Currt. Coin in the Colony, but the Council rejected the Measure, as
not being Salutary at this Juncture; the Sums beforementd were to have been
repaid, by a Tax on Tobo. of 10/ Sterlg. pr hhd. in Great Brittain.

I am really much Concern'd as well as surpriz'd, at the Account you give
me, of the Purchas'd Tobo. The Inspectors still insist it was good & sure I
am the makers live upon good land, & are reputed among the best Planters here.
You may remember the Partnership Tobo., that was made mostly by the same People & Yielded a Profit. The reason of its Turng. Rotten, must be owg. to the
Packing & Prizing it in too high cases, wch I could not tell; as to being forward in the Purchase, the Orders came later than I could wish, & very unluck-
ily in a Year, when Tobo. Sold higher here, in Proportion to the Price wth
You, than for many Years Past, but this may not always be the Case, the Price
is now from 18/ to 20/ pr ct. & make no Doubt, the sale Brisker wth you, then
at that time.   I am Gent,
                    Your mo: Obedt. Servt.
N. B.   J. Syme
    Since the above have had some talks with Cawsey, abt the Scheme of send-
ing the goods, & we are both of Opinion, the advantages will be Mutual;
Please send me two Pair of Mill Stones, 3 feet Nine Inches & 4 feet, very
best sort, wth the memo. of seeds, as soon as Possible - J S

Messrs. Farel & Jones   p Betsey   rec'd 24 July

- - -

                                        Virginia, New Castle
                                        20th June 1766
Gent.
    Since mine of the 12th inst. have recd. yours by Planter You tell me
nothing of the Bills Protested, but that you'll send the Goods. I desire
they may not come, unless the Bills are Paid, wch I mentd. in mine, of the
above Date. I was oblig'd, to take them up wth Cash, or Renew them. I told
you formerly, I was oblig'd to bring Suits, for the Money Due me, & had no
other way to raise the needful, but by Sellg. the Tobo., wch I wrote you,
should come by Cawsey, & this you would not have approved of, tho' if I had
Done it, it would have been ₤5 Sterlg. in my Pocket, for every hhd. better
than your Prices You give me.

    I offer'd the Gent. Slaves, or anything I had rathr. than renew the
Bills, but that would not Do, & to be sued is grevous to me. I am trying
to sell part of my Estate; in the meantime, my Old Friends, for whom I have
Done so much, are Destined to ruin my Credit, just as I have finished my
Mills, & entered into Trade, Both greatly to my advantage, & at a time,
when they have Tobo. in hand to ansr. the Present Drafts. I shall Procure
what Tobo. is now to be had, for Cawsey. I am

                    Gent. Your Mo: Obedt
                                        J. Syme

Warre vs Syme (continued)

N. B. I am more surpris'd than you can be, that you'll still insist on cr.
being given for the guns. I have not had time to cast the Accts. over -
By next Oporty. will send you a Copy of those Accts. refer'd too

Messrs. Farell & Jones

- - -

                                          Virginia 20 July 1767
Gent.

        I am not favor'd wth anything from you, since the 10th of Feby. by
the York. since wch wrote you twice, wth regard the shortage of the Crop,
But as it was impossible to speak wth Precision at that time, I now inform
you, a third is what I expect, in General, & indeed, unless the after Part
of the Year is favorable, we shall fall short of that. As to my own Part,
I think I shall make, rather Better, than half my usual Quantity, for I have
water'd & Planted a good Deal, & seen to my People myself. Colo Peter Randolph Died the 8th inst. after being sick at times, for this several Months
Past, his last Confinement was not More than 10 or 12 Days, During wch he
was very ungovernable, & in all Probability, hastened his end. He is really
a Loss to the Publick, having distinguish'd himself as a Judge (of Late) &
a firm Attachment to the interest of His Country. I have not the Least
Doubt You'll forget your ingagements to me, as to the favors You have Con-
fer'd on Him & his Brother, & Him alone, since Colo. William's Death. You
may Depend, the Utmost Assiduity shall not be wanting on my Side. I am Sure
I can now Please You.

        I make no Doubt, You have been told of your Townsman, T. Thomas's
Marrying a Sister in law of Mine. He has made her a Settlent. in wch I am
the Trustee. She comes home now, & will take the first oporty. of waiting
on Your J F & his Lady, & your Countrywoman will (as myself) be Peculiarly
Oblig'd, for any Civilitys Shown her. Mr. Thomas has put his affrs. into my
Hands to Collect, & seems not inclin'd to have anything more to say, at Present, to the Tobacco Business, in wch he has succeeded but Poorly.

        Pray, remind Capt. Emm's, of the Smith His Carpenter was to Pro-
cure me; It will be a great Disappointment. in case He Does not Come, Also
the Tools he shall Chuse. I wait with impatience to hear from You, in Ansr.
to my several Letters, & am wth Real regard Gent
                                    Your Mo: Obedt. Servt.
N. B. The weather still   )   J. Syme
continues favorable for the)
Crops -   ) P the Chambden   rec'd 14th Septr 1767

                    - - -

                              Virginia, New Castle 25 May 1768
Gent
        Yours of the 10th Octo. & 12th Feby. & my Acct. Currt. - Also one
beginning wth the Year 60, in wch You Do dr. & cr. the Sums so often mentd.,
wch leaves the matter as it was; The point is, whether they are included,
in the Article of Merchandize for the Years 61 & 62. Certain I am you have
not given me Cr. for them, wch you tell me repeatedly, you have, & that I
shew'd Capt. Emm's, an Acct. for the Year 64, to clear up this Affair;

Warre vs Syme (Continued)

Strange indeed, Perhaps I may read as well as Yourselves, tho' I may not be such an Adept in Figures; Whether they are Charg'd as above, I will not pretend to say, but sure I am, they are not creditted, & have shewd the same to Cawsey. He brings You some stockings, You'll see the Order, they came to me in. Please let me know what was done wth the Bolting Cloaths Return'd; They were not the kind I sent for, consequently no use to me, & too much for me to Loose. To be sure I must pay Colo. Henry's Balla. and You'll oblige me, if You'll write him Pressingly on that head, wth his Acct. Inclos'd, wch may be a means of my getting it the sooner of him. I am sorry, the Tenders of my Services in Philada. prov'd so disagreeable as likewise the Favor, of Purchasing me a Horse, when the name, owner, & Place of Abode, was to be wrote down (as in Juniper's Case) The Latter, I will not Trouble You wth. again, & I can assure you as to the Former, the Correspondents I Mentd. you to had no more Idea of your advancg. money for them (to use your own Expression wth regard to the Horse) than they had, of your finding out the Longitude; However, enough of this, and now to more Serious matters.

I perceive you say nothing, in answer to that Part of my Letter, concerning what Guineamen, you may send here, for the Future, & the Collection of Debts, on your River, now Colo. Randolphs are gone, for wch Reason, Desire, You'll be Pleas'd to refer, to yours of the 14th Augst 54 - 18th Augst 60 - 18th Jany 62 - 5th Augst 66 & 4th Augst 67 - Also to Sundry of my own, Particularly those of the 15th Feby. 66 & 12th June following, Relative thereto. I can't Pass over one Observation, on Your saying, your Pride was Piqued, by my telling you your Vessels here, Were Loaded by my Assistance & that Capt. Farell had a good interest; Granted, that worthy man had, But Times were alter'd, for many Reasons, too Tedious to mention; You must remember, the Dislike to Mr. Lidderdale; People had Chang'd their Connections, & the Prices in Virginia, were always as good, & generally Better without Lying out of their Money. Do recollect, Your Own Brother, & Brother in Law,* hardly ever ship'd you any Tobacco, lately Mr. Winston has, if they did not, what could you expect from Strangers, Nay when I have been Soliciting for You, that has been thrown in the Way of others. Now, my good Sirs, you have advanc'd me Money, at a Very sufficient interest, an interest, comencing in 6 months, upon all my Necesserys Ship'd me, & wch some Merchts of your Port, have refus'd to swear, was the Precise time of Payment. I don't deny, it being the Custom generally, to do so /but not always/ And that Custom, will in the end, Ruin my Virginia Estate, Considering the Long time, his Tobo. is Selling, low Price when Sold &Cra. &Cra. unless the owner lives, on bread & Water. I believe You can't give an Instance of any Gent. doing anything to the Purpose, that was not assisted, what You have so often Promis'd me, wch I depended upon, & wch I do say, I have a Right to. I am now advancing in Life, I want to settle my Affrs. if ever I am to do anything, for myself, now is the time As for your Debt, I wrote you before it was Safe, & I am always willing to give you Landed Security, or anything to Banish your Doubts, if any you have. It will be surprising indeed, to deny me a Benefit, because you are in Adva. for me, when the Cause (Party) of that Advance, was, to Serve You & wth a Dependance, on that benefit, to Reimburse myself, & Lessen the Balla. due you. I always knew Colo. Randolph's were a Short Liv'd Family, & I was Contented wait for a Vacancy; Lay your hands on Your Breast, & say if you did not give me Reason to expect it. Clear I am, as well as many others, that 'tis my Due & I have depended on it, & can transact that Business, or any other, in the Merchantile way, as well as any man here. It did bear very hard on me, to

--- *James Winston, of Woodgrove, who m. Anne Farrell, sister of Richard Farrell. James Winston was the son of William and Barbara (Overton) Winston. LMB

Warre vs Syme (continued)

Protest my Bills, for abt ₤400, wch was all I wanted to Compleat my Schemes, greatly Beneficial, much more so, than Tobo. makg. these bad Years; You have a good deal Tobo. from the Store, & will be little or nothg. in adva. when this now sent is Sold; We are now in Debt, on that Acct. about ₤2000 Sterg. (chiefly in Glasgow) where we get goods on 15 Months Cr. & are not oblig'd to ship Tobo. Our Debts are in good Hands, amt. to ₤5460. My half of this, wth. what I before Wrote You, was Due to me here, & the Fortune already recd. wth my Wife (wch is in Bonds) gives a Debt to me, of near ₤8000 in this Colony, wch I am trying to Collect, as soon as may be. I am Promis'd a Proportion of Mr. Hoop's Estate at his Death, he is now Suppos'd, Worth ₤90,000, Pennsylva. Money. You take notice of my being away, & the delay it was to Cawsey; It may be so; but my interest of Late, is not what it was, You have Lessened it; Perhaps it may revive, when my Bills meet wth. Honor & People know, We are on good Terms. At Present, you think, I ought to do everything, can do everything, without the Means, & when all advantages are, & have been ingross'd, by the James River Gent. in Short, that I owe you, ₤6000. I am
Gent. Your Mo: Obedt. & hhble. Servt.
Messrs. Farell & Jones   J. Syme

INVOICE FOR 1768
Included the Following Items

4 Pair Shoes & Stockings, for a Girl 14 yrs old
"   "   Do. &   Do.   " " Boy 13 "   " and large
"   "   Do. &   Do. for a well grown Boy -. 9 yrs. old
"   "   Do. &   Do. " " Girl 7 yrs. old
2 Lace Hats for the Boys above mentd.
A very Genteel Sourtout Coat
6 pr. Best Sheep Skin Breeches Difft. Siz's.
4 Pr. Best Mens Shoes   4 Pr. Best Mens White Silk Stockgs.
3 Pr. half Boots for Middle size Men @ 18/.

- - -

Virginia, New Castle. 29th March - 1769

Gent.

In consequence of what I wrote you, I have been twice to Mr. Wayles (who has been long laid up) to give him the Security, he Desir'd, for your Debt, (wch was Personal) One of the Gent. I offer'd, He was Pleas'd to say, was Sufficient, but nothg. would do, but my Bond on Demand, for the whole; I Propos'd, as Did they, ₤1000 Sterlg. Pr. Year, and that you might be quite easy, You should have both the Genn. wth. Myself, in the Bonds.

I moreover offer'd, to Put into his Hands, good Bonds, for ₤6,000, ₤4000 of wch. carries the Interest of Pennsylvania, 6 Pr. Ct. All would not Do; Nothg. would Do, but Shippg. my Tobo., puttg. up wth. the Damages on my Bills thrice retd. & wch. the holders would not accept again, & loose, accordg. to Custom, considerably by the Sales of my Tobo. Why, this is to Travel on in that same Road, that has brought me to this Dilemma, & wch I should have been infatuated to have Pursued so long, had it not been for the Advantages Promis'd me wch You now refuse Because I am in your Debt;& became so, by losses in

Warre vs Syme (Continued)

Shippg.my Tobo. mentd. to you Before. I do not mean to offend or affront You,
Gent. but Justice to my rising & numerous Famy. calls aloud on me,to say what
Truth Dictates, on this Occasion.

    I can't help observg. on two things You say Vizt. What would I have
besides advancg. me L6,000, & if I was to Die, dreadful might be the Consequences. As to the first, 'tis owg. to the Disadvantages in Shippg. as above,
& quick Interest Charg'd, that has swell'd my acct. (to use Your Own expression) to that immediate Sum, & not Cash advanc'd, wch can easily be Demonstrated.

    And the Terrible Consequences (in Case of Death) must be, I am not Worth
so much Money, Alarming & Terrible indeed. Be it known to you Gent. in the
first Place, I can give two Securitys one of wch. was said, as before mentd.
to be sufficient for this Money, & to Pay it, as soon as any man, should think
Equitable, between us; I have Lands, Clear of intail, more than sufficient;
negroes without encumbrance adequate to it; and Bonds (wth. Mr. Hoop's, or
my name on them, good beyond a Doubt) indeed, that is the case, wth these Bonds
without our names; Tho' the money, can't be had directly upon all, it may be
on Part of them. Mostly Bonds have been taken, I am instructed to say, by Mr.
Wayles, on like occasions, not so good as these; I am likewise instructed to
say, time has been given others, from your House, to People that never did
so much for You, as your Old Correspondent has; and this Time will Demonstrate. I never Disappointed you in my Tobo., if I did not make it, 'twas my
Misfortune, But then I Procur'd it from others, many Gent. here know it, &
can avow it, indeed, Your Ltres. agree it. I can truly say, nothing has ever
given me so much Pain as this affair, & Your usage to me lately.

    If you have no more Generosity, than to Desire me to sell my Estate, I
am ready to sell Part of it; Can any Man in my Place, that has such large
Sums Due him, Act in a fairer Manner; is it to be suppos'd, that such a sum,
can be rais'd immediately, in this time of scarcity of Cash; This is not
what I did Propose in my Letter to You; vizt. to make you Safe; I have kept
my word Strictly, & ever will. It is really that you are endeavoring to Ruin
me, at a Time, when Friends ought to be Assisting, to a Person who has serv'd
them, & whose Schemes are ripening to much advantage; I shall ship you some
Flower &cra by Emms, & Remain   Truly
                      Your Mo: Obedt. hhble. Servt.
P Virga   J. Syme
        (Recd. 23 May)

                        - - -

                        Philadelphia 28th May 1769

Gent.
    I wrote you before I left Virga. by Asselby wch hope you will receive;
I am now to Observe, by the Proceedings after that time, of your Attorneys,
it did appear, You intended to Ruin me, or at least attempt it. Now, quite
Divested of every Sentiment, but what is actuated by Justice & Equi y, was it
Generous, was it right, to treat Your Old Friend in that Manner. - Surely
Gent. You were not offended, at my urging, what I look'd on to be my Right,
wch I have Desir'd. You would not take offence at, & wch was not intended to
give any. I can say wth great Truth, I never intended to give you Umbrage,
or Injure you in my life.

Warre vs Syme (continued)

You have said as well as Myself, I have been of Service to You, & now, that there has been a misunderstanding between us, as to the Business so often mentd., & wch. God knows, was the Reason, of my continng. the Correspondence so long, to my Loss; when I offer'd good Bonds, instead, of your open acct. or my own (accordg. to Promise) wth the best Security, in the Colony, wth reasonable Paymts I say, all these things Consider'd, was it not Hard, crust Hard, to sue an old and serviceable Correspondt. for not makg. immediate Paymt. of so large a Debt, Accumulated, by so many Years beneficial, greatly beneficial intercourse, to your House, & such manifest Loss to me. You Gent. had time to Pay Mr. Lidderdale. If any Person upon earth, has a Right to expect it, I have.

I came here with an intention of Raising Money & making You a Considerable remittance, for settling Estates, or any other Method will not do it, at the Present in Virginia, & by the Court, could keep you out of it, many years, & you are without Security. As to wch Please be refer'd to my last. Since that, one of the Gent. Waited on Mr. Wayles in Person, to that Purpose; but all in vain, & by everything, He could collect, of your Orders, they were, to ruin me, was his Expression; This must Ruin any man, & to take away those triffling Commission's, for Purchasing Tobo. under the name, of its being for Cawsey, was very Mortifying, & exposing me to ridicule, knowing my connections wth Your House and what Trouble, &Cra I had had, in Your Business, & well Pleas'd I am, that you have Prosper'd so well. My own affairs, as unsettled as they are, I must be Contented to struggle wth. But can it really be any Pleasure to You, or Gratifycation, to any Anger, you may have taken up, against me, upon misinformation, thus to hurt my Rising & numerous Famy., in your present Affluence, & as much Money, as you enjoy.

My Father in Law Mr. Hoops, writes Mr. Wayles on this occasion, as he is unacquainted wth. You; As soon as He can Collect Cash, from the Large Sums Due him, he will Assist me; I should in the meantime be glad to know, what time of Payments, You will Give me, in wch when You consider everything & are quite Dispassionate, You will not endeavour to Destroy me, when you can Be made Safe, & have Your Money as soon. Most certainly it will be no great Glory to Your House, to Blast the Credit of a Man who has serv'd you so long, Thinks, there is a Great Mistake, between You & him, Breaks the Correspondence wch has Prov'd greatly to his Disadvantage, & does not Propose shippg. his Tobo. to anyone; Under those Circumstances, & the Large Sum of Money, you have made by me, I think it but a request, any Gent. would grant, to stay a Little, for the large Sum I owe You. I am

Your mo: obedt. Servt.

J. Syme

N. B. I shall also, be getting my Cash on the Bonds
in Virginia

Via Londo.

Messrs. Farell & Jones

(recd. July 16)

Warre vs Syme (Continued)

New Castle 14 March 1774

Sir

      Amid the Deep Distress, & real Heartfelt Affliction of my Fam'y. Yrs
of the 12th came to Hand. I dare say, Sir, You will readily conclude, it
is but little time, I can at present devote to Business; Yet, mindful of
the Day You Promis'd me, Have sent to Augusta, & Colo. Bassett offering Himself a Mediator, as to Colo. Harrison, & Promising to make the matter agreeable to You, wait his ansr; my Hopes are really Sanguine on that Head. I
doubt not, from your known Humanity, it would give You Pleasure to adjust
these mattrs, agreeable to the Interest of Messrs. Farell & Jones, at the
same time, paying some regard to the people Concern'd. I can't say anything
agst Your proposal to me, except as to the April paymt. wch from everything,
that pas'd between us, I did certainly expect, wd not be call'd for so early
in the Year; I have on my Honour, (wch. I beg to Demonstrate to you when You
come here) wth a Dependance on that's being the case order'd my Drafts &Cr
&Cr will give You Directly & Satisfy You I am sure, at all points, being
with real regard & Esteem

                         Your Mo: obedt. Servt.

                                            J. Syme

N. B. We think the sickness
          wth us, on the Decline.

To Thos. Evans Esq
          at
       Hanover Town

By Richd Syme

                              - - -

May 1796 - Judgt for Plt. on Demn. to repln. to plea of Payment into Treas.
& Cont.

We of the Jury find for the Plaintiff Fifty Three Thousand, nine Hundred and
fifty four Dollars and Seven Cents Damages

                                        David Lambert

Warre vs Syme (Continued)

Byrd vs Watson   ) 1817 (59)
Byrd vs Watson & Love) U. S. Circt. Ct. Va. 1800

WILL OF ADAM HOOPS
of
Pennsylvania

D. 7 June, 1771
P. 6 July, 1771

In the Name of God Amen, I Adam Hoops, of the Falls in the County
of Bucks and Province of Pennsylvania being of Sound and perfect Mind and
Memory blessed be God for the same, do this Seventh day of June in the year
of our Lord one thousand Seven hundred & seventy one make and publish this
my Last Will and Testament in manner and form following (that is to say)
Imprimis I commend my Soul to God that gave it me, and my Body to the Earth,
to be decently buried at the discretion of my Executors hereinafter named,
in hopes of a Joyful resurrection through the merits of my Savious Jesus
Christ; And as for that Worldly Estate wherewith it hath pleased God to
bless me with, I dispose thereof as follows, first I will that all my Just
debts and funeral Expenses be fully paid and discharged by my Executors
hereinafter named; I give devise and Bequest unto my dearly beloved Wife
Elizabeth Hoops my Southernmost Messuage Tenement and Lot of Ground which I
purchased of William Henderson now in the tenure of William Clifton and Sisters Situate on the East Side of Third Street in the City of Philadelphia
to hold the same during her natural life Also I give & Bequeath unto my
said beloved Wife the sum of two hundred and fifty pounds Current Money of
the province aforesaid to be paid her yearly and every year during her natural life Also I give such of my Household Goods furniture and Servants as
She shall chose, to the amount of five hundred pounds at a reasonable appraisment; also I give my beloved Wife my Chariot, furniture, and two Horses
belonging thereto.

Item I give devise and Bequeath unto my Son Robert Hoops my plantation in West Jersey called Paquess together with the Grist Mill and two Saw
Mills; with the appurtenances, and the Horses, Cows, Household furniture,
Store and Store Goods, which he has now in his possession, to hold to him,
his Heirs and Assigns forever, which was delivered to him by Jos: Watson
about two years ago which I Estimated at four thousand pounds.

Item I give devise and bequeath unto my Sone David Hoops after
the decease of his Mother all that Messuage Tenement and Lot of Ground with
the Appurtenances (which she is to have during her natural life) to hold to
him his Heirs and Assigns forever. Also I give and bequeath unto my said son
David the sum of two thousand pounds current money aforesaid.

I give devise and Bequeath unto my Son Adam Hoops my Northernmost
House and Lot in third Street aforesaid, adjoining that given to his Mother,
which I also purchased of William Henderson, to be by him possessed when he
arrives to the Age of twentyone years, to hold to my said Son Adam and his
Heirs and Assigns forever; Also I give and Bequeath unto my said Son Adam
the Sum of two thousand pounds money aforesaid, to be put to use for him as
soon after my decease as may be conveniently, and the principal and Interest
thereof paid to him when he arrives to the age of twenty one years.

(Warre vs Syme) Will of Adam Hoops

Item I give unto my daughter Jane Clarke, wife of Daniel Clarke, one
thousand pounds (which I paid to her said Husband more than a Year ago)
Also I give devise and Bequeath unto my said daughter Jane Clarke all that
my Plantation and Tract of Land Situate in lower Makefield in the County of
Bucks aforesaid, to hold to them during their Natural lives, or the life of
the longest liver; or if they chuse it should be sold with my other Lands
In such case I give and Bequeath unto the said Daniel & Jane Clarke the annuity or Sum of Eighty Pounds Money aforesaid to be paid to them yearly and
every year during the life of the Longest liver of them.

Item I give devise and bequeath unto my daughter Isabel Mays, wife of
John Mays all that my House and Lot in front Street in the City of Philadelphia, which I purchased of the Executors of David Callwell deceased to hold
to them their Heirs and assigns forever, which with the Cash he hath had I
Estimate Two thousand and two hundred and twenty Pounds.

Item I give devise and Bequeath unto my daughter Sarah Sims wife of
Coln. John Sims the sum of four thousand pounds money of Pennsylvania which
I have paid to her said Husband by a Bond on Colnl. Harrison for about two
thousand pounds Sterling which with the Interest makes the said four thous-
and pounds Currency.

Item I give devise and Bequeath unto my daughter Mary Barclay my House
and two Lots of Ground Situated on the East side of Water Street in the said
City of Philadelphia which I purchased of John Malcolm, and John Knowls to
hold to her, her Heirs and Assigns forever, The lots House and Money her Husband Thomas Barclay has had of me I Estimate at two thousand Eight hundred
twenty one pounds.

Item I give and Bequeath unto my daughter Margaret Hoops the Sum of
two thousand pounds money aforesaid.

Item I give and Bequeath unto my Grand daughter Elizabeth Sims five
hundred and fifty three pounds Seventeen Shillings and one penny which is
now in the hands of her father which he received of Colonel Birrd & Tho:
Willing bonds: and two drafts he drew on me; the dates of which will appear
by my Books; which I desire may be paid to her when She arrives to the age
of Eighteen years. Also I give my said Granddaughter a Bond due to me from
Colnl. Adam Stevens with the Interest due and to become due thereon.

Item I give and Bequeath unto my Sister Margaret Cummings the Sum of
fifty pounds P Annum to be paid to her yearly and every year during her
natural life.

Item I give and Bequeath unto my Nephew Robert Cummings the sum of
three hundred pounds money aforesd.

Item I give and Bequeath unto the Children of my Sister Ann Evans,
deceased, the Sum of three hundred pounds money aforesaid to be equally
divided amongst them share and share alike.

Item I give and Bequeath to Mary Emerson Wife of James Emerson the
sum of one hundred pounds money afsd.

(Warre vs Syme) Will of Adam Hoops

I give unto my Wife's Niece Jane Taylor the Sum of --- (mutilated) hundred pounds and also I give unto the said Jane Taylor one half of a certain Tract of Land which I purchased of Robert McCrea situate in Cumberland County. The other half of the said Tract being given to her by her Uncle Alexander Finney.

Item I give and Bequeath unto Frances Batchelder wife of Edward Batchelder the sum of one hundred pounds money aforesaid.

All the rest Residue and remainder of my Estate both real and Personal after my Just debts and funeral Expences and Legacies hereinbefore mentioned are paid and discharged I give & bequeath unto my dear Children, to wit, Jane, Isabol, Robert, Sarah, David, Mary, Margaret and Adam to be divided in Such Manner that my Son Robert Shall have fifteen hundred pounds more than any of the rest of my said Children accounting for and reckoning the sum he has already received according to the Estimate I have herein mentioned, and my daughter Isabel Mays to have fifteen hundred pounds less than the rest of my Children accounting for reckoning what she has already at the Estimate hereinbefore Expressed and my other Children to be made Equal in their dividends accounting for and reckoning the Several Sums they respectively --- (mutilated) Daniel Clarke had of me before he failed shall not be accounted to him, I having received my dividend of the proceeds of his Effects, and I do hereby nominate Constitute and appoint my beloved Wife Elizabeth Executrix and my Sons Robert Hoops and David Hoops, Executors of this my last Will and Testament, giving them and the Survivors or Survivor of them, full power and authority to sell and dispose of all my Estate both real and personal --- (mutilated) before Bequeathed, of what kind soever and wherever to be found and to Convey and Confirm the same to such purchaser or purchasers by good and Lawfull Deed or Deeds as fully as I myself could have done if personally present; and I do Nominate and Appoint my Sons in Law Daniel Clarke and Thomas Barclay Merchants to be Trustees of this my Last Will and Testament, requesting the favour of them to give their advice and Assistance in the Execution of it according to my Intent and Meaning herein before Expressed, and for their Extraordinary trouble and service it is my Will that my Executors pay unto Each of them the sum of one hundred pounds Exclusive of their dividend of my Estate above mentioned.

And lastly I do hereby revoke disannul and make void all other and former Wills by me made, and ratifie this to be taken for my Last Will and Testament Containing two Sheets. In Witness whereof I the said Adam Hoops have to the first Sheet set my Hand and to the second thereof set my Hand and Seal the day and Year first above written.

Signed Sealed Published and Delivered   Adm. Hoops   (Seal)
by the said Adam Hoops as and for his
Last Will and Testament in the presence
of us and in whose presence we subscribe
our Names as Witnesses
James Emerson   Timothy Taylor   Mahlon Kirkbridge

The foregoing is a true Copy of a Writing lodged in my office as the Testament and Last Will of Adam Hoops Esqu deceased, and as such propos'd to be prov'd as soon as the Witnesses thereto can come to Town for that Purpose. Witness my Hand at Philadr. the 6th Day of July Anno Dom. 1771.

Benjamin Chew Regr. Gl.

Hoops vs Syme - Continued:

SYME to WALKER

Feb. 27, 1762. John Symme of the County of Hanover, Gent., to Thomas Walker
of the County of Louisa, Gent. Consideration, L400 currt. money. 1650 acres
of Land formerly in the County of Hanover, now Albemarle, whereon the said
Thomas Walker now lives, beginning at several marked trees on the west side
of Turkey Run Mountain, which Land formerly belonged to Nicholas Meriwether,
the Elder, by him conveyed to Nicholas Meriwether the younger his Grandson &
heir by Deed dated 5 December, 1734, recorded in Hanover County Court, and on
the Death of Nicholas Meriwether the Younger Intestate descended and came to
Mildred his only Daughter and heir with whom the said John Symme intermarried
and with her consent agreed to sell the same to the said Thomas Walker for the
consideration aforesaid but before any conveyance was executed for the said
Land, the said Mildred died leaving issue John Symme her son & heir an Infant
to whom the reversion & inheritance of the said Land descended, expectant on
the death of the said John Syme who is intitled to the same for life as tenant by the courtesy of England ...

                                                     J. Syme   (LS)

Wit.: Robert Cobbs   Jo Moore
Henry Tyler   Andr. Johnston
John Hawkins   John Walker

Recorded in Albemarle County D. B. 3, p. 169, xiii May, 1762 - J.Nicholas,Cl.

SYME to CRENSHAW

4 November, 1782. John Symo the Younger of the County of Louisa, to William
Crenshaw, of the County of Albemarle. Whereas Mildred formerly the wife of
John Syme the Elder of the Town of New Castle in the County of Hanover and
mother of the said John Syme the Younger at the time of her intermarriage
with the said John Syme the Elder was seized in fee Simple of Sundry Lands
and Tenements, among which was a Tract of Land in Louisa containing about 300
acres of which the said John Syme the Elder became possessed in Virtue of the
intermarriage aforesaid, and finding it to the interest and advantage of his
family to dispose of the same, did covenant to sell it in fee simple to the
above named William Crenshaw, and did Receive Consideration Money agreed on
for the same, but before legal conveyance was made said Mildred departed this
life leaving said John Syme the Younger her Eldest Son and Heir at Law, whereby the Legal Estate of the said 300 acres aforesaid will be vested in said
John Syme the Younger after the death of the said John Syme the Elder, who
during his life would have been Tenant by the Courtesy of the same in Equity
and good Conscience, the said William Crenshaw ought to hold the same in fee
Simple agreeable to the terms of the Sale aforementioned. And the said John
Syme the Younger, having arrived at the age of Twenty-one years, doth assent
to the sale of the said Land and is willing and doth hereby Ratify and Confirm the same ...

                                                  John Syme   Junr   (LS)

Wit.: W. Howes, Jas. Harvie
John Hawkins junr   B. Bruce
T. Woolfolk   John Key
Jo.: Morton   Walter Carr

Recorded in Albemarle County D. B. 8, p. 78, July Court, 1783.H.Martin,Dy.Cl.

Syme - Continued

WILL OF NICHOLAS MERIWETHER, GENT.
of Hanover County
D. 12 Dec., 1743; P. 26 Nov., 1744
(Not a part of this suit but included because of its obvious interest.)

To Granddaughter, Judeth Littlepage, 459 acres in King William County, over against my Son William Meriwether's Plantation; also Eleven Negro Slaves now on said Land. If she should die without heirs or her heirs should die without heirs, I give and bequeath unto my Son William Meriwether the aforesaid 459 acres of Land; also I do give unto my two Sons William Meriwether and David Meriwether the aforesaid Negro Slaves and their increase, equally to be divided between them.

To my Grand Daughter, Judeth Littlepage two malatto boys by name Charles and Jamey to be delivered to her at her marriage or when she shall come of age of twentyone years, and her heirs, and (in case of failure of heirs) to my Grand Son John Meriwether and his heirs forever.

To my Daughter, Ann Johnson, Land and Plantation whereon she formerly lived on the East side of the branch that parts it and the Land I bought of Edward Hix, being about 630 acres, during her natural life, at her decease to my Grand son William Johnson, son to the above Daughter Ann, and to his heirs, and (in case of failure of such heirs) to my son William Meriwether.

To my Daughter, Ann Johnson, my Plantation commonly called and known by the name of Roundabout together with Thur hundred acres of Land, etc.

To my Grand Son Nicholas Lewis the son of Mr. Robert Lewis my Planta-tion and land whereon I now live, Containing by Patent 1020 acres, together with 119 acres, part of a greater Tract bought of Thomas Graves to be laid off in the most Convenient manner and joyning to the Thousand and Twenty aforementioned, etc.

To my abovesaid Grand Son Nicholas Lewis one Negro boy about six years of age to be Delivered at the Division of my Slaves hereafter mentioned, also 20 head of neat Cattle and 20 head of Hoggs after my Wife's Death. That is to say, 10 head of cattle and 10 head of Hoggs from the Plantation whereon I now live, and 10 head of Cattle and 10 head of Hoggs from off the Plantation whereon Robert Dalton formerly lived, etc.

To my Grand Son Richard Meriwether Son of my Son William Meriwether, 700 acres of Land in Goochland, part of 819 acres bought of Thomas Graves.

To Son David Meriwether my ffork Plantation he now lives on together with 400 acres of Land.

To Mildred Meriwether, Daughter of Nicholas Meriwether, deceased, one Negro Girl of about her own age, to be delivered to her at the Division of my Slaves.

To my Loving Wife Elizabeth Meriwether One hundred Pounds Sterling money of Great Britain together with what new Goods and plate I shall have in my house at my Death.

Syme - Continued: Will of Nicholas Meriwether, cont.:

To my Son-in-Law Mr. Robert Lewis 1500 acres of Land whereon he now lives, as will appear by a Deed in Hanover Court.

I Lend to my Loving Wife Elizabeth Meriwether twelve working Negroes and two Negro Girls, she having her choice, as also all my household goods and 90 head of neat Cattle and 90 head of Hoggs, Young and Old, and all my working horses, with four Choyce breeding mairs during her natural life and at her Deth I do give and bequeath the above mentioned 14 Negroes and their Increase to be equally Devided between my Seven Grandsons and three Granddaughters, Viz.: John Meriwether, Thomas Meriwether, and Richard Meriwether Jane Meriwether, Sarah Meriwether, and Mary Meriwether, Sons and Daughters of William Meriwether, and to Nicholas Meriwether, ffrances Meriwether, James Meriwether, William Meriwether, Sons of David Meriwether, and their heirs forever, etc. Stock of Hoggs, Cattle, horses and Mairs and what shall be left of my household goods after the death of my Wife, to be equally Divided between them and their heirs forever.

To Mary Lewis, Daughter of Mr. Robert Lewis, a Negro Girl of near her own age, &c.

Unto Mildred Lewis, Daughter of Mr. Robert Lewis (similar bequest).

Unto Robert Lewis, Son of Mr. Robert Lewis, Negro Boy of near his own age.

Unto Isabella Lewis, Daughter of Mr. Robert Lewis, Negro Girl ...

Unto Nicholas Meriwether, Son of my Grandson Thomas Meriwether, a Negro boy about his age.

Item [This paragraph is crossed out]: I do give and bequeath unto my Gr.-Daughter, Elizabeth Bray, two Negro boys, by name, Ton son of old Tom that I bought of James Blackwell, and Tom son to Tom and Doll his Wife, to be delivered to her at her marriage or when she shall come to full age, and if she should die before marriage or before she shall come to Twenty-one years of age then said two Negro boys to my Grand Son Nicholas Lewis ...

October, 1743 - I have delivered these two to Mr. Philip Johnson, her husband.

Item - Unto John Meriwether, Son to my Son William Meriwether, 2000 acres of Land that is Laid of next his Brother Nicholas Meriwether deceased, Including where his Quarter is built.

Item - Unto my Grandson Nicholas Meriwether, Son to my Son David Meriwether, 2000 acres of Land joyning to John Meriwether's line and to include the Plantation whereon he now lives -

Item - Unto my Grandson ffrances Meriwether, Son to my Son David Meriwether, all that Land that lies between Mr. Robert Lewis's line and Nicholas Meriwether deceas'd line, being about 1600 acres more or less.

Item - Unto my Grandson James Meriwether, Son to my Son David Meriwether, 1150 acres on Beaverdams, where old Toby lives ...

Syme - Continued; Will of Nicholas Meriwether

To my Grandson William Meriwether, Son to my Son David Meriwether,
1270 acres that lies between Mr. Robert Lewis's line and Capt. Tho. Meriwether's line, being the place where old Jack lived, etc.

Item - To my Grandson, Thomas Meriwether, Son to my Son William Meriwether, after my Wife's Death, all the Land that I have below Nicholas
Meriwether's line of my first Mountain survey to Mr. Robert Lewis's line
that he bought of Capt. Christopher Clark, to him and his heirs forever.

Item - To my Grandson, William Meriwether, son to my Son David Meriwether, 450 acres that his ffather had a Quarter on.

Item - To my Grandson Richard Meriwether, Son to my Son William Meriwether, my quarter and Land where Negro Jemy lives, that I bought of Edward
Hix, with some more Land added to it in all about 300 acres -

Item - To Catharine Holladay, Daughter of Capt. William Holladay,
who now lives with Mr. Bick----- (mutilated), of King William County, 26
shillings Current money, to be delivered to her when she arrives at the age
of twenty-one years or marries.

Item - To Jane Lewis, Daughter of Mr. Robert Lewis, Twenty-five Pounds
Sterling Money of Great Britain.

Item - Unto my Seven Grand Sons and three Grand Daughters, Viz.: John
Meriwether, Thomas Meriwether, Richard Meriwether, Jane Meriwether, Sarah
Meriwether and Mary Meriwether, Sons and Daughters of my Son William Meriwether, and ffrances Meriwether; James Meriwether and William Meriwether,
Sons of my Son David Meriwether, all of my Negro Slaves that I have not yet
disposed of Equally to be divided between them and their heirs forever. Also
I give and bequeath unto my Ten Grand Children (above named) all my Stocks
of Hoggs & Cattle, Horses and Mairs, not yet disposed of, to be Equally divided between them ... Slaves to be laid off into two equal Lotts to be divided among the said Ten Grandchildren when the first comes to lawfull age,
&c. At the Death of my Wife my aforesaid two Sons and my Son-in-law, Mr.
Robert Lewis, to divide Negroes, Stock, and household goods left at her
Death, the said ten Grandchildren to draw equal Lotts as aforesaid &c.
Slaves already delivered to certain Grandsons to be reckoned in the final
division.

To Grand Son, John Meriwether, son of my Son William Meriwether, two
other Negroes now in his possession, these also to be reckoned in the final
settlement.

Item - To Son-in-Law Mr. Robert Lewis, ffifty Pounds Sterling Money of
Great Britain.

Item - Estate not to be brought to an appraisement. Wife Elizabeth
Meriwether, and Son-in-Law Mr. Robert Lewis, Exx. and Exor.

Dated 12th Day, December, 1743.   Nicholas Meriwether   (Seal)
Wit.: Pet. Jefferson, Samuel Dalton
George Taylor, Chas. Lynch

Recorded at a court held for Goochland Co. Nov. 26, 1744   Hon. Wood Clk.

SYME

Hoops	)	1820 - Box 91
vs	)	U. S. Circt. Ct.
Syme	)	5th Cirt. Va. Dist. (1804)
	)	June 1830 - abates by defts. death

To the Honourable the Judges of the Court of the U. S. for - Circt., District of Virginia

Humbly complaining sheweth ...

Your Orator David Hoops a Citizen of the State of New Jersey, that John Syme, Gent., the Defendant hereto who is a citizen of the Commonwealth of Virginia, previous to your Orator's marriage with Mildred, a Daughter of the said John Syme, did expressly promise your Orator that in case he married his said Daughter Mildred that he the said John Syme would give his sd Daughter for her Marriage portion One Thousand Pounds Sterling and a Negro Girl.

Your Orator sheweth that having an affection for the said Mildred & Relying on the said Marriage promise that your Orator did marry the said Mildred who afterwards died about the year 1778, having issue two Sons both of whom are since Dead.

Your Orator also sheweth that he had sundry dealings with the sd. John Syme, Gentleman; that he never paid the Marriage Portion; that he now owes your Orator the whole thereof; that there is a balance due from the sd Defendant of about Twenty Seven hundred pounds Current Money of Virginia.

Your Orator refers to Account No. 1, Letters of John Syme, Gent., etc., which your Orator prays may be taken as a part of this Bill of Complaint. ...

ACCOUNT OF COLO. JOHN SYME WITH DAVID HOOPS

Dr. Novr. 2d. 1772. To One thousand pounds sterling which you contracted to give as the Marriage Portion of your Daughter Mildred

To which is ad_ 33-1/3 Excha.   £ 1333.6.8

(Various other items are included, - horses, prints, furniture, etc., through October 26, 1782.)

Cr. May 10, 1773. By Store account to this date   £   31.12.9

(This represents transactions at New Castle Mill in 1776 and Rocky Mill Store in 1780, through March 14, 1781. No totals are given.)

SYME

Hoops) 1807 - Box 36
vs   ) U. S. Cir. Ct.
Syme &c) 5th Cir. Va. Dist. (1803)
         5 Dec., 1807 - "Dismissed, of course."

To the Honourable the Judges, etc.

Your Orator David Hoops a citizen of New Jersey; married one of the
Daughters of Col. John Syme; soon after her death, to-wit, in May, 1779, John
Syme, jr., the Son of Colo. Syme married and being improvided with a House
and home of his own entreated your Orator who was about to move to New Jersey
to sell him the valuable Tract of Land and the improvements whereon your
Orator Lived, lying near Albemarle in Louisa County, and containing 1300 acres
by Estimation, which Land your Orator bought of Doctor George Gilmour, and
had paid the purchase Money, but the legal Title thereto, the said Doctr. Gilmour had neglected to obtain from his Brother John Gilmour of the State of
Georgia, from whom the said George Gilmour had purchased the said Land. Your
Orator sold the said Land on the 11th day of May, 1779 to the said John Syme,
jr. at his request for £2500 specie, and it was understood that your Orator
would be indulgent to him and not be vigorous in demanding payment as Colo.
Syme, his Father, had sold his said sons real Estate when a Minor and under
age. That a great intimacy subsisted between your Orator and the said John
Syme, jr. Your Orator gave the said John Syme jr an Order on Doctr. George
Gilmour to make him a Title for the said Land which was obtained, but your Orator neglected to take any Bond or note in writing from the said John Syme, jr
respecting the sale of the said Land. Your Orator when he moved to the Jerseys
left all his Slaves, Plate, Household and Kitchen Furniture, and his cattle in
the care and safe keeping of the said John Syme jr, the amount of the Household and Kitchen Furniture, Cattle and Plate will appear by Account No. 1.

That the said John Syme jr departed this Life about the year ---.(1)
Previous to his Death to protect his Land and Slaves for his Children he
conveyed the same to John Warden. That the Land and about forty Slaves are
worth about Four Thousand Pounds.

That Nicholas Syme Esqr. is indebted to the Estate of his Brother
for the Purchase of the New Castle Land in a considerable Sum, which your
Orator is advised is secured by a Mortgage on the said New Castle Land. The
said John Syme jr died intestate, leaving a Son, John Syme, jr.for whom your
Orator is informed that the said Nicholas Syme was appointed Guardian, and
a Daughter named --- (2), who intermarried with Doctor William Cochrane; all
of whom are residents and citizens of the State of Virginia, and your Orator
prays may be made parties Defendants hereto ...

In tender consideration whereof, etc.

----

(1) John Syme, jr. died before 21 December, 1796, when the Court ordered administration to be made upon the same. See p. 73, this volume.
(2) Dr. William Cochran was the son of David Cochran, merchant of New
Castle, Hanover County, and his wife, Lucy, the daughter of William Winston,
of St. Paul's Parish, Hanover. For his will see Volume I of this series,
Dr. Cochran's wife Mildred Syme daughter of John Syme junr.

Hoops vs Syme, continued:

ACCOUNT NO. 1

Dr. The Estate of John Syme Junr deceased in A/C with David Hoops Cr.

1779 - To one Tract of Land containing by estimation)
May 11 1300 acres, situate in Louisa and Albemarle   )   ₤ 2500.0.0

To furniture consisting of

five feather beds with Bolsters & pillows comp.
10 pr. Sheets, 10 pr. Blankets
10 Coverlids
12 Green Windsor Chairs
2 Arm Do.
12 Walnut Ditto with leather bottoms
2 Mahogony Card Tables
1 Large Silver Tankard, 1/2 Gallon
1 set Silver Castors, with silver boxes for)
Sugar, Mustard, & pepper; & cut flint   )
glass cruits with Silver Tops   )
16 Table Spoons - 11 Tea Spoons
1 Soup Spoon

2 Yoke of Oxen and
17 Head of Cows and Young Cattle

. . .

In Hanover County Court
January 17th 1799

It appearing to the Court that the order made the twenty first of
December 1796 directing Elisha White late sheriff of this County to take the
estate of John Syme junr deceased into his hands and administer the same according to Law, not being acted upon, It is ordered that Thomas Tinsley gentleman present sheriff of this County do take the estate of the said deceased into his hands and make sale of so much thereof by public auction as
the payment of debts shall make necessary or as shall be perishable, and
otherwise dispose thereof as the law directs.

A copy Teste   Tho. Pollard D C H C

It does not appear from the Records of the County Court of Hanover
that any proceedings have been had concerning the estate of John Syme junr
since the 17th day of January, 1799 -

Tho. Pollard D C H C
Mar. 19th 1805 -

Hoops vs Syme, continued:

THE DEPOSITION OF NICHOLAS SYME, ESQR.

The deposition of Nicholas Syme, Esqr. taken this 17th day of May 1806 at William Hazelgrove's Tavern in the neighborhood of New Castle, in the suit depending in the Federal Court of the United States for the fifth Circuit in the Virginia District, wherein

David Hoops is pltf and John Warden, Nicholas Syme, John Syme, jr by Nicholas Syme his gdn., William Cochran and --- his wife, Defendants.

"This deponent being first sworn on the Holy Evangelist of Almighty God, deposeth and saith, that in the Fall of the year 1778 or Spring of 1779 as nearly as this deponent now recollects, his Brother John Syme then called John Syme, jr, father to the defts., John Syme and Mildred Cochran, wife to William Cochran, purchased of David Hoops a plantation in Louisa & some Household Furniture & stock as this affiant understood.

That as nearly as he recollects, though he cannot be positive, his Brother gave ₤2500 & took possession of the premises. That in part pay, according to the impressions on the mind of this defendant, his Brother let David Hoops have a Saddle Horse, which Horse at this day would be worth ₤60 and Horses at that day were higher than they now are. That about the year 1786 David Hoops came from the Northward, & carried his Slaves from Virginia with him; that at that time John Syme the Brother to this affiant & this affiant himself lived on the New Castle Estate, doing Business together, & that this affiant did not at that time hear either of the parties say anythin about the demand for the Land &c, and from that period (ie) 1786 this affiant continued to do Business for his Brother till his death, which happened about the Spring of 1793 that during that period altho this affiant was in the Habit of paying money for his Brother and acting generally as his Agent, he Never heard from either of the parties anything of their debts due to either.

That his Brother frequently spoke anxiously about his debts & at length made preparations by the sale of the New Castle Estate for their payment & mentioned to this affiant what debts he did owe, & he did not mention any debt due from him to Mr. Hoops, nor does this affiant recollect but two other debts of any magnitude which he did not mention which appeared afterwards.

That about the yr 1781 Mr. Hoops went to the Northward & from that time to the death of John Syme, the said Hoops only came twice to Virginia as this affiant recollects, and remained but a few days each visit -

Signed   Nicholas Syme

Hanover County   towit

This day Nicholas Syme made oath before us as magistrates for the county aforesd (Mr. Hoops & Councel for the defts. being present) to the truth of the foregoing deposition

17 May 1806   Signed   P. Street - John Kilb

Hoops vs Syme, continued:

HOOPS TO HOOPS
Power of Attorney

I David Hoops of the Township of New Town County of Sussex and State of New Jersey have ... constituted Robert Hoops of the County of Hanover and State of Virginia my true and lawful attorney to recover &c certain sums of money ...

29 May 1795   Signed   David Hoops

State of New Jersey, County of Sussex: Acknowledged before Jonathan Willis, Esq., one of the Judges of the Court of Common Pleas in and for the County of Sussex.   29 September 1795

DEPOSITIONS
To be Taken

To Nicholas Syme, John Syme Junr. Wm. Cochran and Mildred his wife

Be pleased to take notice that I shall on the 8th day of April next at the Tavern belonging to Mr. Jos: Smith, Blue Run, in Orange County, take depositions in my suit ...

22 March 1805   Signed   David Hoops

NOTICE OF SERVICE

Hanover Co. to-wit - This day Adam Cockburn came before me a Justice of the Peace for the aforesaid county, and made Oath that he did deliver to Doctr. William Cochran of New Castle, and to Mrs. Nancy Syme, the wife of John Syme, on the 22nd day of March 1805 a notice of which the within is a true copy -

25 March 1805   Signed   John Kilby

SUBPOENA

To Summon Nicholas Syme, John Syme, Minor, and William Cockrane and Milly his wife, the said John and Mildred being the children heirs and representatives of John Syme Junr, deceased, and John Warden and Humphrey Brooke trustees of said John Syme Junr deced - 16 January 1804.

DEPOSITION OF JOHN T. HAMILTON

The Deposition of John T. Hamilton, of lawful age, taken at Mr. Smith's Tavern on blue run in Orange County on 9 April, 1805:

Question put by Plaintiff: "Did you live on intimate terms with Capt. John Syme while he lived in your neighborhood, at the place now Mr. Waddles?"   Ans.:   "Never two Brothers more so."

Hoops vs Syme, continued: <u>Dep. of John Hamilton, cont.</u>:

"Have you heard Capt. Syme say or do you know that Capt. Syme purchased the plantation whereon the Revd. Mr. James Waddle now lives from David Hoops and on what terms?" Ans.: "I recollect hearing Capt. Syme say that he purchased that place from David Hoops at a certain price in Specie but at how much I do not recollect ..."

Sgd.   John T(aylor) Hamilton

Notice to defendants that depositions would be taken on 18 May, 1805 at the house of Mr. John Davidson, merct., near Mrs. Walker's Mill in Albemarle, at ten in the morning, and between 3 and 6 o'clock in the afternoon of the same day at the Tavern belonging to Mr. Smith, Blue run, Orange County.

On reverse side of above notice:

"Hanover Co. To wit: This day Frederick Hawes made oath that he delivered notice to John Syme on the 7th of the present month (May) and to Mrs. William Cochran on same day in the Houses and places of Residence of said John Syme and Wm. Cochran. Dated 9 May, 1805. Sgd. John Kilby."

Deposition of Doctor Thomas Crystie, of New Castle, taken in open Court: "Saith that David Hoops had been husband of a sister of said John Syme Junr."

John Cunninghame,* New Castle, 13 Feb. 1787, to Mr. David Hoops, bill for Horse bought Jan. 12, 1786, and other things, from Capt. Syme.

ANSWER OF JOHN WARDEN

The joint answer of John Warden one of the Trustees of John Syme decd. (who in his lifetime was distinguished by the Appelation of John Syme Junr) and Sally his wife, and of John Syme Junr, and William Cochran and Mildred his wife, which John and Mildred are children of said <u>John Syme and Sally</u> <u>his wife and have now each attained the full Age of 21 years, Defendants</u> ...

John Warden saith that on the 21 day of February 1792 the said John Syme Junr and Sally his wife now <u>both deceased</u> executed an Indenture under their Hands and Seals whereby they conveyed to John Winston now deceased, this Defendant and Humphrey Brooks a Tract of Land therein said to contain 300 acres or thereabouts, 34 slaves, and also assigned to them a writing obligatory of the Defendant Nicholas Syme of even date with said Indenture and conditioned for the payment of £2000, and also a Mortgage from said Nicholas Syme and Elizabeth his wife, of one thousand acres of land be the same more or less, intended for the greater security of the monies due on that writing obligatory, and one other of equal Date with a collateral condition agreeably to the condition thereunto annexed IN TRUST for the Purpose in said Indenture mentioned, and those several writings are now either by originals or authenticated copies in the hands of this Defendant ready to be produced at the hearing of this cause if required ...

*   See Va. Migrations, Hanover Co., Vol. I, pp. 32-33-34, for ancestry of John Cunninghame, son of Sir William Cunninghame, Bart.

Syme (Continued)

WILL OF MARTHA H. SYME *
D. 12 June, 1820
P. 18 Oct., 1824

    In the name of God, Amen! I, Martha H. Syme, of the County of Hanover, and Commonwealth of Virginia, being in perfect health both of mind and body, but calling to mind the uncertainty of life and wishing to dispose of my earthly estate by last will and testament, do devise and bequeath as follows:

    In the first place, having under the advice of council, instituted a suit in the Chancery Court of the City of Richmond against John T. Swann and wife and Lemuel Riddick for the purpose of recovering that portion of the estate of my deceased Father to which I have been advised that I am entitled under certain deeds of marriage settlement between my deceased parents, and having been informed that it has been suggested by the first named of my opponents that he is in possession of a paper which will prove the said deeds fraudulent, but which on application he has refused to produce, I deem it an act of just respect and reverence to the memory of my deceased parents that the said suit aforesaid may and shall be continued in or my said opponent may be constrained to use the aforesaid paper in his defense, as I have understood he has threatened to do, or to confess the allegation to be a calumny on the memory of my honored parents; as I believe it to be; I do, therefore, enjoin it on my executor hereinafter named and particularly on my nephew, John S. Fleming, to cause the said suit aforesaid to be prosecuted to a close; and that no compromise be ever made which shall not remove the said reproach from the memory of my parents.

    Item. In case the said suit shall be decided in my favor, I give, devise, and bequeath to my said nephew, John S. Fleming, one-half of all the estate, real, personal, and mixed of which I may be seized and possessed, to him and his heirs forever. In case the said suit shall be decided against me, I devise to the said John S. Fleming one hundred and five acres, part of the Rocky Mills tract, of which I am now seized, to him and his heirs forever.

    I enjoin it on my executor to see to the execution of certain bequests, which, for particular reasons, cannot now be reduced to writing, but which I propose to reduce to writing and to cause to be annexed to this will.

    Item. In case the case aforesaid against the said Swann and wife and Riddick should be decided in my favor and the servant Harvey who now attends me should in the division of the slaves fall to my lot, it is my wish that he, together with his wife, Mary, whom I purchased on his account, should be free at my death; should the suit not be decided in my favor, and should he not fall to my lot, it is my will, and I do accordingly direct that my executors should purchase him from the personal funds of my estate and cause him to be emancipated; his wife, Mary, being now my property, I direct in any event to be free at my death; and I request that if at that time an Act of the Legislature of Virginia should be necessary, or any order of Court should be required to enable them to a residence in Virginia, my executor and particularly the said John S. Fleming may cause the necessary steps to be taken for that purpose.

    Finally, I do hereby constitute and appoint my nephew John S. Fleming and my friend Dr. Thomas Curd executors of this my last will and testament.

Will of Martha H. Syme, continued:

In witness whereof I have hereunto set my hand and seal this twelfth day of June in the year of our Lord one thousand eight hundred and twenty.

                                    (Signed)   Martha H. (X) Syme (Seal)

Signed, Sealed and
acknowledged in the
presence of
    The words "the memory
    of" on the first page;
    the word "particularly"
    on the second page;
    "should be decided in my
    favor", "my" and "parti-
    cularly" on the third
    page and "my friend" on
    the fourth, entered be-
    fore signing.

Wm. Wirt
Robt. Copeland
William Copeland

CODICIL

Agreeable to the conclusion of the paragraph under the first item, I now proceed to make the bequests mentioned to be annexed to my will, to which I hereby again enjoin the attention of my Executors.

'Tis my will and desire that my executors sell all the estate of which I may die seized, which is not heretofore disposed of, and of the money arising from such sale, I make the following disposition, viz.:

Item. I give to my young friend Agnes C. Wirt, daughter of William Wirt, Attorney General of the United States, one thousand dollars together with all my books in consideration of my friendship for her and her Father.

Item. I give to my niece, Jane T. Fleming, Five hundred dollars in consideration of my affectionate regard for her.

Item. I give to my friend Margaret M. Crew three hundred dollars in consideration of my friendship for her.

Item. I give to my friend Martha H. Burruss, two hundred dollars in consideration of my friendship for her.

Item. To my friends, Jane and Catherine Dabney, I give the sum of one hundred dollars each, in consideration of my friendship for them.

Item. The residue of my estate after paying the foregoing bequests I give and bequeath to my nephew, John F. Fleming, leaving it to him to make such provision as he may think proper for my two servants, Harvey and

Will of Martha H. Syme, continued:

wife to whom I have willed freedom at my death. And farther I bequeath to
my said nephew John S. Fleming the miniture of my dear departed Mother together with a silver can and water bearing the cipher of both my parents;
also the miniture of my uncle, Patrick Henry, should it be recovered from
the publishers of his life; and I hereby reserve the articles in the last
bequest to John S. Fleming from the sale directed in the first clause of
this codicil, and also the miniture of my Aunt Clarke and my late friend
Helen Campbell now deceased, the latter of which I bequeath to my cousin
Maria T. Coulter and the former to my niece Eliza Maria Swann.

          A few other articles of jewelry which will remain, I also wish
reserved from the sale before mentioned, which together with clothes I wish
said nephew John S. Fleming to dispose of amongst his sisters as he may think
proper.

                                        --- ---

          At a Monthly Session Court held for Goochland County at the Court
House on Monday the 18th day of October 1824

          This writing with the Codicil was presented in Court and proved by
the affirmation of Walter Crew to be the last will and testament of Martha
H. Syme dec'd, and ordered to be recorded.

          Then on the motion of John S. Fleming who made oath according to
law and with William Miller, his surety, entered into and acknowledged a
bond in the penalty of eight thousand dollars, probat thereof was granted
him in due form.

                    Teste   W. Miller C G C

          At a Monthly Session Court held for Goochland County at the Court
House on Monday the 20th day of December 1824 this writing was again presented in Court and except the Codicil was proved by the Oath of William
Copeland to be the last will and testament of Martha H. Syme dec'd and
ordered to be recorded.

                    Teste   W. Miller C G C

_____
          *The above will is from the collection of Judge Leon M. Bazile,
Judge of the Fifteenth Judicial Circuit of Virginia, through whose courtesy it is here included. - E. G.

Thompson   )   Louisa County, Virginia
vs   )   L. F. 1819
Thompson   )   (August T-Z) Judgments

WILL OF JOHN THOMSON *
D. 21 July, 1758-P. 7 June, 1759

In the name of God, Amen, I john Thomson of the Parish of St. Paul in the County of Hanover, being of perfect sense and memory, praised be God for it, do make this present writing to be my last will and testament in manner following, that is to say

Imprimis: I give, devise and bequeath unto my son Joseph Thomson and to the children of his body lawfully to be begotten forever (which children of his body lawfully to be begotten are to have the same equally amongst them, be they son or Daughter, or sons and Daughters, after the decease of the said Joseph, all of my houses and land with the appurtenances whatsoever that are situate, being and lying in the said County of Hanover and also the following eight Negroe slaves and their future increase to be annexed to the said lands and to be intailed therewith in manner aforesaid, which said eight slaves are called and named as followeth, to-wit: Sukey, Aggy, Venus, Lucy, Suk, daughter of Bess, Hannah, Cupid, Moore and Tom, which said Houses, Lands and appurtenances and the said Negroe slaves thereto annexed, I devise and give to him my said son Joseph and to his children, lawfully to be begotten, in manner aforesaid (save only the reservation thereof hereinafter mentioned) and I also devise, give and bequeath unto him my said son Joseph and to the children of his body lawfully to be begotten, to be divided in manner aforesaid my land and plantation that has a mill thereon with the appurtenances situate lying and being in the County of Louisa to him and them forever.

Item: I lend unto my wife Kerchuhappt (1) my manor house and plantation whereon I now live with about eight hundred acres of land adjacent thereto and the appurtenances thereunto belonging during the term of her natural life, it being part of the lands given to my said son above mentioned.

Item: I lend unto James Brown and his wife Mary, (my daughter), the use of the plantation whereon they now live and two hundred acres of land thereto adjoining including the place called Bryant's and that I bought of Gabriel Hill (it being a part of the above mentioned lands given to my said son aforesaid) which said plantation and two hundred acres of land is to be laid off for them which I purpose to do that they may know the bounds thereof which said two hundred acres of land the said James and Mary, his wife, are to occupy and possess during the natural life time of the said Mary and no longer.

Item: I give, devise and bequeath unto my daughter Elizabeth Thomson my tract of eleven hundred and ninety-five acres of land in Albemarle County called Meadow Creek with six negroe slaves annexed to the same, by name, Rose, Lucy, Mary, Peter, Doll and Bartlet and the future increase of the said slaves, which said land with the appurtenances and alsves annexed thereto I devise, give and bequeath to the said Elizabeth and the children of her body to be lawfully begotten forever (which children of her body lawfully begotten are to share the same equally amongst them be they

----

* From the collection of Judge Leon M. Bazile and here included through his counteau -- Eugenia Glazebrook

Will of John Thomson, of Hanover, continued:

son or Daughter or sons and Daughters after the decease of the said Elizabeth) saving only that the Plantation on the said land with one hundred acres
adjacent thereto shall be preserved to the use of my above said wife during
her natural lifetime.

Item: I give, devise and bequeath unto my daughter, Elizabeth,
tract of two hundred and sixty-six acres of land and appurtenances lying in
Albemarle County, the same that I purchased of Thomas Wenton, which said
land and appurtenances I give to her my said Daughter Elizabeth and her heirs
forever;and I also devise and bequeath unto my said Daughter Elizabeth and to
her heirs forever another tract of four hundred acres of land and appurtenances lying in the said County of Albemarle and taken up by me in partnership
with one Charles Lynch, the patent for which remains at present in the Secretary's Office to be taken out.

Item: My will and desire is and I order it so that my said wife
shall have the use and benefit of all the lands and slaves hereinbefore given
unto my said son Joseph and Daughter Elizabeth for and in their behalf until
they the said Joseph and Elizabeth come of age or marry, the use and profits
of which are to be applied for and toward the bringing up, education and maintenance of them the said Joseph and Elizabeth in their minority, and that my
said son Joseph be kept at school until he is eighteen years old.

Item: I give, devise and bequeath unto the children of my daughter Mary, the wife of James Brown, now of her body that are born and likewise
the children of her body that shall hereinafter be born to be equally divided
amongst them and the heirs of their bodies lawfully begotten forever, one
tract or parcel of land and appurtenances containing eleven hundred and sixteen acres lying in the County of Albemarle on Beaver Creek part of the tract
of land taken up by me in partnership with the aforesaid Charles Lynch the
patent for the same remains in the Secretary's Office, now to be taken out,
and also I give and bequeath to the said children born and to be born of the
body of the same in the same manner six negroe slaves and their future increase to be annexed to the said eleven hundred and sixteen acres which said
slaves are called and named as followeth, to-wit: Lucy, a woman, her two
children Tom and Peter, Sall, Judy and Frank to go and be with the said land
unto the said children now born and to be born of the body of the said Mary
to be equally divided between them and the heirs of their bodies lawfully
begotten forever, save only that the six negroes in this bequest named and
the profits thereof shall be to the use of my said Daughter Mary for her support during her natural life, and after her death immediately then to go to
her said children without the control or hindrance of him the said James
Brown but that my Executors shall take charge and care of the same for the
said children.

Item: My will is and I order it so that my goods left in my store
and what other personal estate I have that my said wife hath not occasion to
use shall be sold and the money arising by said sale together with outstanding
debts due to me when got be put out on interest and be applied (after my debts
and charges are paid) and go to the use and benefit of the legatees in the
manner following: I order and will that the same money so raised shall be
be divided into four equal parts and one part thereof I give to my said son
Joseph; another part thereof I give to my said daughter Elizabeth; another
part I give to be equally divided amongst the children now born and to be
born of the body of my daughter Margaret, the wife of the Revd. Mr. Todd (2);

Will of John Thomson, continued:

and the other part thereof I give to be equally divided amongst the children now born and to be born of the body of my said daughter Mary, the wife of James Brown; and that my Executors take charge and care of the part that is for the said Mary's children so that the same may not come into the hands of the said James Brown.

Item: I lend unto my said wife during her natural life time all the rest of my estate (not hereinbefore mentioned under the restriction, to-wit, if in case she should marry, then and in that case she is to have only such a part thereof as hereinafter is mentioned in case she should marry and after the decease of my said wife I give the same remainder and rest of my estate in this bequest mentioned to be equally divided into four parts and my said son Joseph to have one part thereof; my Daughter Elizabeth to have another part thereof; the children now born and to be born of the body of my daughter Margaret to have another part thereof, equally amongst them; and the children now born and to be born of the body of my Daughter Mary to have another part thereof equally amongst them and that my Executors take charge and care of what goes to the children of the said Mary in the manner as aforesaid, and in case my said wife should marry then she shall have only twelve of my negroes (not hereinbefore named such of them as she shall choose and one third part of my personal estate that hereinbefore is ordered to be sold and outstanding debts during the time of her natural life and the rest and remainder to be taken care of for the legatees in the same manner as if my wife had deceased.

My will is that if the profits of my said son Joseph's part be not sufficient to maintain and educate him then the deficiency shall be made out of my personal estate.

Item: My will and I order it so that after my wife has deceased what negro slaves not herein particularly named that shall be allotted and divided amongst the said Legatees shall be annexed to the land hereinbefore given them and go and remain with the said lands in the same manner as herein before mentioned to every legatee respectively.

Item: It is my will and I desire that the Legatees herein mentioned that are under age may receive their portions as they come of age or marry respectively as near as can then be estimated what their parts may be.

My will is that my said son Joseph shall be put to such employment as his genius most leads him to.

Lastly I constitute, appoint and ordain my said wife Executrix, Mechzielek Brown and William Holt Executors of this my last will and testament, hereby revoking and making void all other wills and testaments heretofore by me made and confirming this and none other to be my last will and testament.

In testimony whereof I have hereunto set and affixed my hand and seal this thirty-first day of July in the year of our Lord Christ one thousand seven hundred and fifty-eight.

Wit.: Bartelot Anderson   John Thomson (Seal)
Roger McClelland, Robert Glass

Will of John Thomson, of Hanover, continued:

          At a Court held for Hanover County on Thursday the 7th day of June
1759

          This last will and testament of John Thomson dec'd was offered
to proof by Kerenhappuch Thomson Executrix therein named and was proved by
the oath of Bartelot Anderson and Roger McClelland two of the witnesses
thereto and also by said Executrix who took the oath of an Executor thereto
and admitted to record.

                Teste   William Pollard D. C. H. C.

    March 1807

     A Copy   Teste   Tho: Pollard D. C. H. C.

―――――

(1) Keren-happuch - Job's third daughter - Job, 42:14 - L. B.

WATSON

Mercer & Wife) 1840 - Box 145   Note - The following Hanover deed was
        vs   ) U. S. Cir. Ct.   found in this suit which had no other
Selden   ) (1819)   connection with that county.- E. G.

At a Superior Court of Chancery held in the town of Fredericksburg, on the 16th day of October, Before the Honble. William Brown,
Judge of the said Court

Be it remembered that heretofore, to wit, on the 6th day
of December, 1819, came Edward Swann, John Swann, and others by Counsel, and
sued out of the Clerk's office of the Superior Court of Chancery for the District of Winchester, returnable to the first Monday in January thereafter, a
spa: to answer in the usual form against William Carey Selden and others ...

DEED - WATSON TO LOGWOOD

This Indenture made this 16th day of October in the year of
Christ 1773, between John Watson and Annie his wife of the county of Hanover,
of the one part, and Edmund Logwood of the county of Cumberland of the other
part - WHEREAS John Watson late of the Parish (sic) and county of Hanover,
decd father of the first mentioned John Watson was in his lifetime, and at th
time of his death, seized in fee simple of sundry tracts of land in the count
of Hanover and Goochland, being so seized, by his last will and testament
bearing date the 21 day of January, 1762, and recorded in the county Court of
Hanover, after devising to his son Joseph Watson all the land that he bought
of William Johnson, 630 acres, whereon he then lived, lying and being in Hanover County on little Allen's Creek, and also 118 acres of land lying in the
said County, which he bought of William Baker, joining Richard Loving's land,
he did devise to his said son, the first above mentioned John Watson, the remainder of the land that he held, provided he dies with a lawful heir of his
body, them he gave to them forever; but if he should die without such heir
he gave the said land to his two sons Jos: Watson and William Watson to them
and their heirs and assigns forever, which last devise included a tract or
parcel of land lying and being in the said counties of Hanover and Goochland,
on the waters of Tuckahoe, & adjoining the lands of Robert Haston, Wm. Barret
Robert Anderson, John Anderson, Joseph Watson, William Price, James Clarke,
John Oron, George Hamock, & John Rowe, and contains 1046 acres - by virtue of
which devise the said John Watson first above mentioned entered into the said
last mentioned premises with the appurtenances and became seized thereof as
tenant in fee tail special, and the said John Watson the son and Annie his
wife being minded to sell the land and have the entail, have lately sued out
a writ in the nature of an ad quod demnum, bearing date the 25th day of May,
1773, to the Sheriff of the said County of Hanover directed, whereby he was
commanded that by the Oath of good and lawful men in his County, by whom the
truth of the matter might be better known, he should diligently enquire if it
might be to the damage or prejudice of our Sovereign Lord the King or others,
or not if the said John Watson the son should sell the said 1046 acres of
land with the appurtenances and if it be to the damage of our said Lord the
King or others, then to what damage or prejudice to others, and of what value the said land is, of good and lawful money of Great Britain, and whether

Mercer & Wife vs Selden   (Watson), continued:

the same be a separate parcel, and not parcel and contiguous to other entailed lands, in the possession and seizin of the said John Watson; to which
writ Edmund Taylor sub:sheriff of the county of Hanover answered, that by
the Oath of twelve good and lawful men of the said County, who being sworn
and charged, upon their Oath, did say that it will not be to the damage or
prejudice of our Lord the King, if the said John Watson should sell the said
land with the appurtenances, but that it will be to the damage of the issue
of the said John Watson and those claiming in Remainder & reversion:

And further the Jurors aforesaid upon their oath aforesaid did say
that the said land and appurtenances in the said writ mentioned were of the
value of £167:7:2:1, Sterling money of Great Britain, and no more, and is a
separate parcel, and not parcel of, or contiguous to other entailed lands in
the possession of Seizin of the said John Watson by the said recited writ and
return remaining of record in the Secretarie's office more fully and at large
doth and may appear:

Now this Indenture witnesseth that the said John Watson and Anne
his wife for and in consideration of £627:2 current Money of Virginia to the
said John in hand paid by the said Edmund Logwood, - the receipt whereof is
hereby acknowledged and confessed: have granted, etc. unto Edmund Logwood,
his heirs, etc., the aforesaid tract of land lying in the County of Hanover
containing by estimation 1040 acres be the same more or less, and bounded as
followeth:

Beginning at a post oak in a branch at William Burnett's line,
thence N 12 E 76 poles to a corner, thence N 33 E 232 poles to a white oak,
thence N 64 E 89 poles to pointers, thence N 57 E 126 poles to a corner white
oak, thence S 10 E 33 poles, thence S 34 E 20 poles, thence S 15 E 101 poles
to a corner white oak, thence N 66 E 53 poles, thence N 76 E 8 poles, thence
N 60 E 88 poles to pointers by a patch, thence N 79 E 40 poles to a corner
post oak, thence S 15 W 162 poles to a white oak, thence S 5 W 265 poles to
a corner dogwood, thence N 71 W 66 poles to a corner, thence S 31 W 111 poles to
two white oaks, thence N 63 W 603 poles to a poplar, thence S 46 W 194 poles
to a white oak, thence S 16 W 123 poles to a corner white oak, thence N 24
W 64 poles to a corner, thence S 80 E 6 poles to a corner, thence N 20 E 191
poles to a poplar on the aforesaid branch thence up the said branch as it
meanders to the beginning.

And all houses, buildings, gardens, orchards, etc. ...

In witness whereof the said John Watson and Anne his wife have hereunto set their hands and affixed their seals the day and year first above
written.

Witnesses: John Watson   (LS)
                                                  Anne Watson   (LS)
Nicholas Davis, Thomas Stuart
Royal Richd. Allen, Julius Allen
Julius Allen, Jr., John Hughes
Hastin Bartlett, Richd. Johnson

Mercer & Wife vs Selden (Watson), continued:

Whereas by the within deed of conveyance from the said John Watson to the said Edmund Logwood, the said land are conveyed and being in the full possession and free occupation of the said John Watson, but in fact Eliner Black is intitled to 82 acres thereof for her life, and in case Sarah, wife of John Black, survives her husband she will be intitled to 60 acres or thereabouts for her dower, of which said Edmund Logwood had notice in due time,

Now it is agreed that Eliners right as well as the said Sarah's contingent right be excepted out of the warrantee within mentioned: that the said John Watson and his heirs are not to be answerable for the same.

Witness my hand and seal this 16th day of October, 1773.

(Witnesses same as to deed)   Edmund Logwood   (Seal)

Virginia, Sct:

George the 3rd by the grace of God of Great Britain and Ireland ...

To Joseph Woodson and John Woodson, Gentlemen, Greeting:

Whereas John Watson and Anne his wife by their certain Indenture of bargain and sale dated 16 October, 1773, have conveyed to Edmund Logwood of the county of Cumberland the fee simple Estate of 1046 acres in the county of Hanover and Goochland: and whereas said Anne cannot conveniently travel to our General Court of this Dominion to make acknowledgment of the said Conveyance

Therefore we do give you or any two or more of you power to receive the acknowledgment which the said Anne shall be willing to make before you of the conveyance aforesaid ... which is hereto annexed: And we do therefore command you that you do personally go to the said Anne and receive her acknowledgment of the same, and examine her privily and apart from the said John her husband ... and that you certify us thereof in our General Court under your seal sending therewith the said Indenture to this writ:

Witness   John Earle of Dunmore our Lieutenant Governor General at Williamsburg, 21 day October, in the 13th year of our Reign

                                                   Ben: Waller

Virginia Sct: At a General Court held at the Capitol the 14th day of November, 1773 This Indenture and the memo: indorsed were proved by the oaths of Nicholas Davis, Julius Allen, Jr., and Richard Johnson, witnesses thereto ... and ordered to be recorded

                              Teste   Ben: Waller C. G. C.
                  A Copy   "   Peyton Drew C. G. C.

Apparently John Watson and Anne, his wife, were living in Goochland County in 1773, as Joseph and John Woodson were residents of that county.

WINSTON

Bayne	) 1841 - Box 147
vs	) U. S. Cir. Ct.
Street, admr. of Winston & als	) 5th Cir. Va. Dist. Filed 1827

To the Honorable the Judges ... Your Orator George Bayne a citizen of Kentucky sheweth that on the 18th of November 1801 an agreement under the seal was entered into between your orator and a certain William Overton Winston for the sale of a tract of land in the County of Botetourt, Virginia, for the sum of $600 ... Said Winston executed a bond as security for the title to the said land, with William Lewis, John Haden and A. Haden his securities. William Lewis resided in the said county of Botetourt near the said land and was agent and attorney in fact for said Winston.

That your orator, having completed his payments for the said land and the said William Lewis having a letter of attorney for that purpose from the said Winston, he the said William Lewis on the 22nd of May, 1804 executed a deed to your orator which was duly acknowledged by said Lewis and recorded in the County Court of Botetourt. Soon after these transactions your orator sold the land and has ever since resided in the State of Kentucky.

In the year 1823 your orator learnt that long before his purchase towit in the year 1797 a certain John Meux had filed a bill in the Superior Court of Chancery for the district of Richmond against the said William O. Winston and others alledging that he was the owner of the said land, that he had executed a letter of attorney to a certain Richard Littlepage and that the said Littlepage had conveyed the said land to the said Winston ... and that after sundry proceedings had been had in the said suit the representatives of said Winston having been made parties to the suit on his death, a decree was entered on the 27th of January, 1823, setting aside the sale and directing that the said land should be delivered to the complainant, and it was further ordered that an account be made. That on the 21st of January, 1826 Meux waiving the account of profits and having recovered possession of the land an order was made putting an end to the said cause.

Your orator having sold the land with warranty was apprized by the purchasers and those holding under them of the said suit and decree and notified that he would be held liable for the value of the said land and all damages ... Your orator did not appear as a purchaser but furnished the funds or repaid the amount of the purchase money and thus quitted the title ...

The said William O. Winston having departed this life about ---his estate was committed to Parke Street Sheriff of the county of Hanover. The said William O. Winston left several children: Henry B. Winston, Philip B. Winston and William O. Winston, sons; Catharine, the wife of Henry Shore, Martha, the wife of Laney Jones, Molly T., the wife of Benjamin Pollard, and Alice B. Winston, a daughter. He also had a daughter, Barbara O., the wife of Paul Thilman. The said Barbara O. died in the year --- and the said Paul Thilman is also dead, and they left two children, William Thilman and Paul Thilman. That William O. Winston after his said sale to your orator made sundry voluntary conveyances to his said sons' of land and other property in the county of Hanover and elsewhere in Virginia. In tender consideration ...

Note: 1827, June - abates as to Molly T. Pollard and Paul Thilman, by their death.

HANOVER MARRIAGES

"A List of Marriage Licences Granted in Hanover
County between the 1st day of April and the first
Day of October, 1777". Virginia State Library.

June 11th - Benjamin Anderson and Frances Wily

July 3d - George Phillips and Ann Pettus

"Between 1st October, 1777 and 1st April, 1778".

1777
Octr. 6th - Michael Anderson and Sally Thomson

      8th - To His Excellency Patrick Henry, Esq., and
            Miss Dorothea Dandridge

Novr. 12th - Nicholas Walters and Sarah Price

      19th - William Nelson and Milley Day

Decr. 6th - John Gardner and Anna Richardson

      7th - Thomas Chiles and Mary James

1778
Jany. 1st - Constantine Riddick and Mary Bizer

     28th - John Slaughter and Martha Kent

     30th - Henry Timberlake and Ann Austin

Feby 3rd - Henry Smith and Mary Luck

     5th - Aaron Marsh and Mary Booz

     7th - Benjamin Carter Waller, Gent. and Miss Catherine Page

    12th - William Frazier and Eliza. Mitchell

    13th - Lewis Turner and Agness Turner

Mar. 4th - William Sydnor and Sarah Garland

"Between 25th October, 1780 and
25th April next following"

Oct. 25th - Gideon Grantland and Sarah Bradford

Dec. 14th - Wm. Radford and Rebecca Winston

        - Wm. Johnson and Dorothea Thomas

HANOVER MARRIAGES - 1777 - 1787, cont.:

1780
Dr.   19th - Francis Mills and Agnes Mills

      20th - Wm. Harris and Diana Goodwin

1781
Jany. 4th - Henry Fear and Sarah Lipscombe

      29th - George Hollings and Nancy Lewis

       5th - Robt. Clopton and Fanny Anderson

      31st - Jno. Worsley and Susanna Thomson

Feby. 1st - Jno. Wingfield and Rebecca Nelson

      17th - Jno. Lysaught and Sarah Tyler

Mar.   1st - Thos. Austin and Eliza. Anderson

       8th - Davd. Robinnet and Patsey Anthony

      13th - Thos. Smith and Lucy Snead

                    August 27th, 1781, Sworn to before J. C. Randolph
                                        William Pollard Junr   Clk

                              . . .

          A List of Marriage Licenses Granted in Hanover
          County between 29 October, 1831, and 8 March, 1847.
          (Photostat copies of bonds contained in "Hanover
          Miscellany - 1727-1858" - Virginia State Library

29 Oct., 1831 - Robert Crew, widower, and Sarah Adams, spinster

10 Nov., 1832 - John Via, bachelor, and Miss Martha Parsley

15 May, 1833 - Bowling Batkins, bachelor, and Miss Emily Whitlock

 7 May, 1833 - Thomas French, bachelor, and Miss Lucretia Wade

12 Nov., 1833 - Francis Tait and Miss Elizabeth Kerby

26 Dec., 1833 - James Waters, widower, and Miss Judy Toombs

15 Jan., 1834 - George W. Livesay, bachelor, and Miss Oriana F. McGhee

 7 Feb. 1834 - Josiah Martin, bachelor, and Miss Mary Hollins

13 June, 1834 - Charles Hughes, bachelor, and Miss Charity Woodward

Hanover Marriages, continued:

30 Sept., 1834 - Benjamin M. Falkener, bachelor and Miss Catherine H. Tyree

 9 Dec.,   "   - John P. Parsley, bachelor, and Miss Eleanor J. White

13 Dec.,   "   - Henry Tucker, bachelor, and Miss Sarah Barker

29 Dec.,   "   - Isaac Burnett, bachelor, and Miss Sarah Hughes

23 Jan., 1835 - John Willeroy, widower, and Miss Mary Jane Faulkner

24 Mar.,   "   - Collin Jarvis, widower, and Miss Mary White

21 Apr.,   "   - Francis Childress, widower, and Miss Eveline R. Meredith

20 May,   "   - Nathaniel Childress, widower, and Mrs. Gilley Vines

 1 June,   "   - Claiborne Grubbs, bachelor, and Miss Catherine Clarke

 6 June,   "   - John Puryear, bachelor, and Miss Ann S. Chesterman

24 Nov.,   "   - Francis C. Messinger, bachelor, and Miss Mildred Frazer

30 Nov.,   "   - Thomas Davidson, widower, and Miss Coley White

16 Jan., 1838 - Henley D. Clopton, bachelor, and Miss Mary Parsons

26 June,   "   - Edward T. Melton, bachelor, and Miss Martha Ann Tucker

22 Jan., 1839 - Francis W. Johnson, bachelor, and Miss Eliza Ann Mantlo

13 May,   "   - Charles S. Tucker, bachelor, and Miss Eliza B. White

23 July,   "   - Samuel White, bachelor, and Mrs. Ann W. Jones

29 July,   "   - George S. Earnest, Jr., widower, and Miss Agnes Hughes

14 Oct.,   "   - Thomas G. Turner, bachelor, and Miss Margaret A. Via

26 Dec.,   "   - John Gibson, widower, and Miss Emily G. Mileston

 7 Feb., 1840 - William Traylor, bachelor, and Miss Elizabeth Allison

11 Mar.,   "   - Hanswood Talley, bachelor, and Miss Mary Talley

 8 Apr.,   "   - Richard Chadick, widower, and Miss Catherine McGhee

16 May,   "   - Fayette Wright, bachelor, and Miss Mary Johnson

25 July,   "   - Francis Adams, bachelor, and Miss Sarah Boaze

 1 Aug.,   "   - Henry Timberlake, bachelor, and Miss Mary E. Tyler

HANOVER MARRIAGES, continued:

12 Aug., 1840 - Reynolds Parsons, bachelor, and Miss Coley Kerby

 9 Sept., 1840 - Robert Kent, bachelor, and Miss Lucretia Martin

22 Sept., 1840 - Harman Hughes, bachelor, and Miss Mary Ellen Davis

29 Sept., 1840 - Isaac Perrin, Jr., bachelor, and Mrs. Jane Kersey

 2 Nov., 1840 - Henry C. Richardson, bachelor, and Miss Elizabeth Melton

24 Nov., 1840 - Charles Martin, bachelor, and Miss Elizabeth Martin

30 Nov., 1840 - David Wood, bachelor, and Miss Martha E. Burnett

26 Jan., 1841 - James Talley, bachelor, and Miss Elizabeth McDougle

13 Feb., 1841 - Edmund W. Allen, bachelor, and Miss Eliza D. Talley

 4 Jan., 1842 - Billy W. Talley, bachelor, and Mrs. Mary E. Jones

 8 Feb., 1842 - Benj. A. Timberlake, jr., bachelor, and Miss Elizabeth J.
                                                              Archer

 7 Sept., 1842 - John W. Tinsley, bachelor, and Miss Eliza Martin

11 Nov., 1842 - Thomas Batkins, bachelor, and Mrs. Mary E. Cluvieres (sic)

30 Nov., 1842 - William B. Clarke, bachelor, and Miss Caroline E. Thomas

 6 Dec., 1842 - David S. Slaughter, bachelor, and Miss Lucinda F. Gentry

14 Dec., 1842 - Benjamin H. Shelton, bachelor, and Mrs. Eliza Burnett

19 Dec., 1842 - Bowling Talley, bachelor, and Miss Elizabeth Barker

20 Dec., 1842 - Nelson Hundley, bachelor, and Miss Sarah Wright

21 Jan., 1843 - William Gibson, bachelor, and Miss Henrietta J. Jones

20 June, 1843 - Henry Kerby, bachelor, and Miss Edy Martin

 9 Dec., 1843 - William E. Gauldin, and Miss Emeline Tucker

10 Jan., 1844 - James Bosher, bachelor, and Miss Jane Nance

30 Jan., 1844 - Arthur Q. Wooddy, bachelor, and Miss Martha Ellen Thomas

30 Jan., 1844 - Augustine D. Wooddy, bachelor, and Miss Mary E. Bootwright

18 May,   1844 - Thomas Harwood, bachelor, and Miss Lucretia White

18 May,   1844 - William T. Martin, bachelor, and Miss Sarah Adams

 1 Aug., 1844 - William Martin, bachelor, and Miss Susan Kerby

Hanover Marriages, continued:

6 Sept., 1844 - Allen W. McGregor, bachelor, and Miss Sarah Martin

22 Sept.,   "   - Robert Anderson, widower, and Miss Mary F. Jordan

16 Nov.,   "   - Absalom H. Jenkins, bachelor, and Miss Martha Tucker

25 Dec.,   "   - Thomas W. Richardson, bachelor, and Miss Polley Salley

30 Jan., 1845 - Daniel Wood, bachelor, and Miss Margaret Burnett

6 May,   "   - Joseph Tucker, bachelor, and Miss Ann Wright

9 May,   "   - Richard Heath, widower, and Miss Sarah Ann Tuck

26 June, 1845 - William B. Jinkins, bachelor, and Miss Caroline Franklin

29 July,   "   - George W. Chappell, bachelor, and Mrs. Maria Wade

8 Sept.,   "   - Ithama Harman, widower, and Miss Ann Mantlo

19 Dec.,   "   - Bartholomew Martin, bachelor, and Miss Sarah Wright

24 Dec.,   "   - Winfrey Tucker, bachelor, and Miss Elizabeth Barker

27 Dec.,   "   - Benjamin Garthright and Margaret Ann Gaulding

30 Dec.,   "   - Edward Kerby, bachelor, and Miss Mary Martin

6 Nov.,   "   - George Barker, widower, and Miss Mary Wade

14 Jan., 1846 - William Bosher, jr., bachelor, and Miss Judith Talley

27 Jan.,   "   - Billy W. Talley, widower, and Miss Mary Elizabeth Pate

16 Mar.,   "   - James B. Barrick, bachelor, and Miss Martha Mileston

9 Nov.,   "   - Nathan B. Clarke, bachelor, and Miss Martha B. Allen

20 Jan., 1847 - Henry Talley, bachelor, and Miss Agnes Stewart

8 March,   "   - Albert D. Wicker, bachelor, and Miss Mary Peace

also

12 Sept., 1816 - Thornton S. Kendrick, bachelor, and Miss Martha Elmore

and

"1817 February, 14th Is the day I married Bailey S. Johnson and Sarah L.
White, Boath of Hanover County and the Licence wass obtained of Cleark of
said county." (Not signed - fragment.)

MARRIAGES FROM VIRGINIA NEWSPAPERS
Intermittant Records

VIRGINIA GAZETTE

Jan. 28, 1775. Mr. Thomas Anderson, Junr., of Hanover, to Miss Sally Howard, late of Buckingham.

Jan. 16, 1772. The Rev. James Stevenson, Rector of Berkeley Parish, Spotsylvania County, to Miss Fanny Littlepage, of Hanover.

Oct. 14, 1773. Robert Page, Esq., of Hanover, to Miss Molly Braxton, eldest Daughter of Colonel Carter Braxton, of King William.

Dec. 30, 1773. Peter Lyons, Esq., of Hanover, to Miss Judith Bassett, of this City, a lady of great merit.

RICHMOND ENQUIRER

Jan. 31, 1807. (Saturday) In North Carolina on Monday Evening last, Mr. David Timberlake to the amiable and much accomplished Miss Sarah Hill, only daughter of James Hill, Esq., of Hanover County.

Mar. 17, 1807. (Tuesday) On Thursday, 12th inst., William Lightfoot, Esq., of Sandy Point, Charles City, to Miss Ann C. Ellison, of Hanover County.

Mar. 29, 1808. (Tuesday) On Wednesday, 9th inst., Lewis Berkeley, Esq., to the amiable and much admired Miss Elizabeth Darracott, both of Hanover.

Oct. 18, 1808. Tuesday) On Thursday evening last, by the Rev. John D. Blair, at Ratcliffs in Hanover county, Mr. John F. Price, of this city, to Miss Maria O. Winston.

Sept. 16, 1808. (Friday) On the evening of Saturday, the 10th inst., Charles L. Wingfield, Esq., of Hanover Co., to Miss Eliza Wilson, eldest daughter of Thomas Wilson, of this city.

April 4, 1809. (Tuesday) On Thursday Evening, 23rd inst., by the Revd. John D. Blair, Mr. Anthony Street, to Miss Susan Goodall, both of Hanover.

May 29, 1812. (Friday) On Thursday evening, the 14th inst., by the Revd. Reuben Ford, Mr. Granville Timberlake to the amiable and much accomplished Miss Mary Richardson, all of Hanover County.

July 30, 1813. (Tuesday) In Gloucester, Sunday, the 17th ult., Doctor Henry Curtis, of Hanover, to Miss Christiana B. Tyler, youngest daughter of the late Judge Tyler, of Charles City.

March 9, 1815. (Saturday) On Wednesday the 6th inst., by the Rev. John D. Blair, Mr. George Perkins of Cumberland, to Miss Eliza S. Richardson, daughter of Captain John A. Richardson, of Hanover.

August 12, 1817. (Tuesday) On Thursday the 7th inst., by the Rev. John D. Blair, Mr. Peter Demouville, of Charles City, to the amiable and accomplished Miss Mary Anne Winston, daughter of Mr. John P. Winston, decd., of Hanover.

Marriages from Virginia Newspapers, continued - Richmond Enquirer:

Dec. 30, 1817. (Tuesday) On the 18th inst., Major John Wyatt, of Fayette county, Kentucky, to Miss Patsey Harris, of Hanover county, Virginia.

Feb. 29, 1820. (Tuesday) On Thursday évening, the 17th of this month, by the Rev. Mr. Ford, Mr. V. M. Hambleton, of Hanover, to Miss Mary R., daughter of Mr. Nathaniel Anthony, also of Hanover.

May 9, 1820.   (Tuesday) In Hanover the 14th of April, by the Rev. Mr. Wydown, Mr. David Davenport to Miss Susan Valentine, all of Hanover County. Mr. Davenport is 67 years of age and is one of the patriots who volunteered under Patrick Henry in his celebrated gunpowder expedition, before the commencement of the Revolutionary War.

July 25, 1820. (Tuesday) On Tuesday the 18th inst., by the Rev'd Mr. Courtney, Mr. Francis Pledge, of this city, to the amiable and much accomplished Miss Kitty Hughes, of Hanover.

May 19, 1845. (Friday) At Bolling's Island, on Wednesday, the 10th inst., by the Rev. R. W. Wilmer, Richard K. Cralle, of Lynchburg, to Miss Elizabeth W., youngest daughter of the late Richard Morris, of Hanover.

July 7, 1843. (Friday) At Sexton Point, in Hanover, on the night of the 4th inst., by S. S. Sumner, Mr. Thomas T. Chandler, of Caroline, to Miss Edwina Williamson, youngest daughter of Capt. Dabney Williamson.

Aug. 29, 1843. (Tuesday) On Thursday, the 24th inst., by the Rev. Wm. V. Bowers, Mr. Wm. James Carpenter, to Miss Sarah Jane, daughter of William Fulcher, Esq., of Hanover.

Ibid. On Thursday, 24th inst., by the Rev. Alexandér Mebane, Mr. Benjamin B. Whitlock, of Hanover, to Miss Catherine R. Wynne, of this city.

June 5, 1858. (Saturday) On Wednesday evening, the 2nd inst., by the Rev. Thomas Hooper, Dr. Thomas H. Kinnéy, of Staunton, to Miss Mary T., daughter of the late Wm. T. H. Pollard, Esq., of Hanover County, Virginia.

Nov. 3, 1858. (Wednesday) On the 4th ulto. at Whitehall, Mr. John Ballard Smith, of Augusta County, Virginia, to Miss Maria Louisa, daughter of Dr. Edwin A. Rowzie, of Hanover County, Virginia.

Ibid. On the 3d. ulto., at Thornsburg, Dr. E. J. Rowzie of Hanover county, to Miss Imogen S. Jerrell, of Spotsylvania.

RICHMOND WHIG & PUBLIC ADVERTISER

Feb. 6, 1857. (Friday) On Thursday, 29th of January, at the residence of Mr. W. F. Wickham, in Hanover county, by the Rev. Mr. Peterkin, Mr. Julius T. Porcher, of South Carolina, and Miss Mary Fannie, - and Mr. George H. Byrd, of Baltimore, and Miss Lucy Carter, - daughters of the late Mrs. E.F. Wickham.

RICHMOND SEMI-WEEKLY EXAMINER

May 19, 1857. (Tuesday) On May 7th, in Darlington Dist., S. C., by the Rt. Rev. Mr. Spain, Dr. Benj. C. Norment, of Hanover, Virginia, to Miss Lou H., daughter of Gen. J. B. Nettles, of Darlington, S. C.

OBITUARIES FROM VIRGINIA NEWSPAPERS
VIRGINIA GAZETTE

Died, Mr. John Smith, a Merchant of Note, and one of the Representatives for Hanover, in the Flower of his Age. He was a Gentleman universally beloved and respected, and is as generally lamented. January 28, 1773.

Died, Mr. John Bickerton, of Hanover. February 25, 1775.

Died last Monday in Hanover, Mrs. Howard, relict of the late Mr. Benjamin Howard, of Buckingham. April 1, 1775.

RICHMOND ENQUIRER

August 29, 1804. Mrs. Anna Maria Riddick died lately at Rocky Mills, in the flower of her youth.

August 7, 1807. Mrs. Elizabeth Syme, the amiable consort of Mr. Nicholas Syme, of Hanover, died on the 14th inst.

Friday, May 19, 1809. Died the 1st of this month at Santee, the place of her residence in Hanover County, Mrs. Patsey Perkins Street, consort of Capt. Parke Street, and daughter of Col. Goodall.

Thursday, February 11, 1808. Departed this life in Hanover county on Friday morning last, Mr. Matthew Timberlake. A man much esteemed and loved by all who had the pleasure of his acquaintance.

Tuesday, March 15, 1808. Died on Monday evening, the 7th inst., Mr. Francis Timberlake of Hanover county. He left an affectionate wife and 7 children.

Thursday, May 12, 1808. Died on the 1st day of this month at Red Hill in Charlotte County, Mrs. Ann Henry, consort of La Fayette Henry, Esq., and daughter of Mr. Lion Elcan. She had not yet attained her 19th year. She is survived by her husband and an infant child.

Tuesday, May 23, 1809. Died on Monday, the 13th of March last, Nathaniel Pope, of the County of Hanover, in the 49th year of his age. - Son, brother, husband, and father. - Volunteer in the Revolutionary War.

Wednesday, June 21, 1815. Died on the 13th inst., at Scotchtown in Hanover County, of a lingering indisposition, Mrs. Landon Berkeley, widow of L. C. Berkeley, and daughter of Mr. John H. Sheppard. She is survived by Father and Mother, also younger sisters and brothers.

January 11, 1816. Died on the 8th inst., at his seat on the Brook, Captain Izard Bacon, a respectable inhabitant of this (Henrico) county, aged abt. 76.

Thursday, January 11, 1816. Died on the 6th inst., Col. Parke Goodall, of Hanover County, in the 74th year of his age. His county has sustained a great loss in this patriot. He was first seen in early life, holding a commission, and marching in the first volunteer company that ever marched in defense of the rights of man against Monarchies cal (sic) ursurpation in this State.

Obituaries from Virginia Newspapers; Richmond Enquirer, cont.:

Saturday, February 3, 1816. Died on the 26th ult. in the upper end of Hanover, Mrs. Sarah Cranshaw, relict of Mr. Charles Crenshaw, and sister of the late Capt. I. Bacon, of Henrico, aged about 77 years. Thus in the short space of 18 days hath death put a period to the temporal existence of a brother and a sister, the last that remained of the family.

Saturday, March 30, 1816. Died in this City, Saturday the 23d, after a short but painful illness, Miss Sally Turner, daughter of Mr. Nathaniel Turner, late of Hanover County.

Tuesday, March 4, 1817. Departed this life at his seat in Hanover County, on the 25th inst., Col. Cole Diggs, an old Revolutionary officer, in the 63rd year of his age, after a short but painful illness.

Friday, September 12, 1817. Died at Rocky Mills on the 2nd inst., John S. Swann, only son of Doctor Swann, in his 11th year.

Tuesday, May 2, 1820. Departed this life Wednesday, 26th ult., at his seat on Taylor's Creek, in the upper end of Hanover county, Mr. William Morris, Senr., in the 86th year of his age.

June 16, 1820. Died at Wingfield's Tavern in Hanover County, on the 9th inst., Samuel Richardson, Esq., Commonwealth's Attorney for the county, after an illness of five weeks. Of his family, but one child, a son, is now living.

Friday, September 15, 1820. Died on the 10th inst., on Richmond Hill, after a severe illness of twenty-one days, Capt. William White, lately a resident of Hanover County, in his 48th year. This gentleman had lately removed with his family to this place in search of health ... On the 11th his remains were interred at his farm in Hanover.

February 14, 1826. Died, Mrs. Mary R. Diggs, at her residence in Hanover on the 20th inst., in the 59th year of her age, after a tedious illness. She is survived by four children.

January 19, 1843. Died at the Family residence in Hanover on the morning of the 10th ult., after a short and painful illness, Hugh Thomas Nelson, eldest son of Thomas Nelson, Esq., in the 36th year of his age.

May 19, 1843. Died on Thursday morning, 2nd inst., after a very short illness, Mr. John Kimbrough, one of the oldest and most worthy citizens of the county of Hanover.

August 18, 1843. Died on the 29th of July, Mr. Joseph Thomson Brown, at the residence of his father, Mr. Miller Brown, in the lower end of Hanover county.

Obituaries from Virginia Newspapers,

RICHMOND WHIG AND PUBLIC ADVERTISER

February 13, 1857. Died at "White Oak", Hanover County, at the residence of her husband, on the 8th day of February, 1857, Mrs. Elizabeth White, wife of Col. William L. White, of pleuro-nonia, aged 60 years. Her ancestors were among the first settlers in this old county, and distinguished themselves in our Revolutionary struggle. She was a member of the Methodist Church.

February 23, 1857. Died of Asthma at his residence in Hanover county on Jan. 23d, Edward Maynard, in his 79th year. A native of Charles City county he came to Hanover when quite a young man, where he married and raised a large family of children, who are now widely separated through the country. He bore an honorable part in the late war of the United States against the Mother Country.

March 14, 1857. Died in Hanover county on the 10th inst., at the residence of his father, Mr. William C. Winston, Lewis Coleman Winston, aged 3 years.

May 22, 1857. Died at Scotch Town, Hanover County, Monday, May 18, after a long and painful illness, James L., son of John J. and Lavinia L. Taylor, in the 16th year of his age.

May 29, 1857. Died at her husband's residence in Hanover county, on the 25th inst., Catherine C. Parsley, aged 37 years, leaving seven children.

June 5, 1857. Died on the Morning of the 25th of May, in the 67th year of her age, Mrs. Ann, relict of Thomas Swift, of the county of Hanover.

THE RICHMOND DISPATCH

May 11, 1871. Died in Hanover County, Apr. 29, 1871, R. E. Hundley, aged 52.

May 20, 1871. Died Feb. 11, 1870 at his residence in Hanover, William H. Graves, formerly of Richmond, in his 71st year.

June 27, 1871. Died in Hanover County on the 13th inst., Mrs. Nancy A., wife of Jesse Harlow, in her 84th year.

July 14, 1871. Died on Saturday, July 8th, James Monroe, youngest son of Sarah F. and the late Wm. E. Harper, of Hanover Co., aged 6 yrs. and 7 days.

Sept. 12, 1871. Died at his residence in Hanover Co. on the 6th ulto., Spotswood James, in his 77th year, leaving a widow, 3 sons, and 4 daughters.

Sept. 29, 1871. Died at the residence of his father in Hanover County, Thursday, Sept. 28, O. T. Baker, aged 39 years, brother of Van Lew Baker, of this city, and son of William A. Baker. - California papers please copy.

Oct. 18, 1871. Died at his residence in Hanover County on the 14th inst., Capt. John Beal in his 61st year.

Oct. 27, 1871. Died on Wednesday, Oct. 25, at the Old Dominion Granite Wks., Chesterfield Co., the residence of her parents, Isabella Edna, only daughter of James M. and Maggie A. Wheat, aged 6 years, 10 mos., 10 days. Interment in Hanover County from the residence of her grandfather, Francis Wheat.

VIRGINIA MIGRATIONS - Hanover County, Volume II

ABSENTEE LAND OWNERS, YEAR 1814
FORMER RESIDENCE IN HANOVER IMPLIED

Land Taxes - St. Paul's Parish
John Glazebrook, Commissioner of Revenue

NAME	PRESENT RES.	ACRES	LOCATION	MILES FROM C. H.	
John Adams	Richmond, Va.	1	Beaverdam (Grist Ml.)	15	east
William Brockenbrough	" "	403	Adj. Hanover	7	"
George Blackey	" "	951	On Pamunkey adj. Spencer Roane & Parke Street	11	s. e.
Christiana Bowles	"	"216 3/8	Adj. Jas. Wooddy & on Tototomoy Creek	9	south
Jesse Cross	Goochland	73	Adj. Jno. Frazier & Wm. Hendrick	11	west
Spotswood D. Crenshaw	Louisa	40	Adj. Wm. Bowles and Martin Baker	7	"
Benj. Cogwell	Richmond, Va.	50	Adj. John Anthony, Sr. and others	13	s. w.
Samuel Davis (In poss. of Lucy Davis)	Petersburg,"	150	On Mechumps Cr. adj. Nataniel Davis and F. Ragland	5	s. w.
Hugh Davis	Richmond, Va.	100 266	Adj. Wm. Davis) " Jno. Austin &) James Davis)	5	west
George Dabney	King William	1 lot	Hanover Town, No. 13	3	east
Samuel Gist	England	2337	Adj. Laney Jones and Benj. Timberlake		
John Glazebrook,s. of Jas. (In poss. of John King, Junr.)	Ky.	126	(For life) Adj. John Starke & Peter Bilbow	10	s. w.
Wm. F. Gaines (In poss. of James McGrize?)	King William	84	Adj. Thos. White and Walter Crenshaw	15	west
John J. Grosjean, Est.	Kentucky		New Castle	3	east
Joel Hill	Caroline Co.	66	Adj. Wm. Hooper & Joel Hanes	3	west
Austin Hill		66	Adj. Obediah Hooper & Joel Hill	3	"

Absentee Land Owners, Year 1814, St. Paul's Parish, cont.:

NAME	PRESENT RES.	ACRES	LOCATION	MILES FROM C. H.
John Hendley, Gdn. for Peter Martin	Tennessee	45	Adj. Robt. Snead & Jno. Harlow	15 s. w.
John Hendley, Gdn. for Sarah Martin	"	34	Adj. Wm. E. Harris & Robert Ellett, Jr.	15 s. w.
John Harlow	Henrico	183	Adj. Wm. Liggon on Chickahominy Swamp	17 s. w.
Edward Hallam	Richmond	2	Hanover Town Nos. 7&8	3 east
John T. Kilby	Suffolk	22½	Adj. Wm. Drinkard Est.	20 s. e.
James Lyons	Richmond	90	On Pamunkey Riv. adj. A. Stevenson	4 east
John Lambert	"	12	Adj. Robt. Carter's Est. & Banj. Wingfield	2 west
John Lyon	"	1050	Adj. Wm. Gardner & J. L. Wooddy	9 s. e.
" "	"	600	Fork Quarter, adj.Col. Tho.Tinsley & McGuin	5 south
" "	"	69½	Adj. John Haw &c	6 "
" "	"	80	Adj. Benj. Pollard &c	6 "
Samuel Murry	"	87	Adj. Obediah Fawcett & Robert Lumpkin	7 "
Carter B. Page	"	1789	On Pamonkey Ri., adj.) Dr. Lyons, Tho. Pol-) lard & John Temple) (Conv. from John W. Page to Carter B. Page, 948 a. added to said C. B. Page's former tract)	2½ east
Charles C. Page	King Wm.	458	Near Hanover Town, adj. Mann Page's Est.	8 east
George Pickett	Richmond	2 lots	Hanover Town,Nos.15-26	8 "
Rebecca Ragland	Louisa Co.	274½	On Matidiquin Cr., adj. William Cocke	3 s. e.
Andrew Stevenson	Richmond	473-3/4	on Pamunkey Ri. adj. Samuel Gist	4 east
George W. Smith	"	300	Adj. Robt. Carter's Est., & Wm. Y. Dejarnett	2 west

Absentee Land Owners, Year 1814, St. Paul's Parish, cont.:

NAME	PRESENT RES.	ACRES	LOCATION	MILES FROM C. H.
John Seabrook	Richmond	388	Adj. Thomas Starke & E. G. Snyder	13 s. e.
Wm. Smith	New Kent	330	On Pamunkey Ri. adj. George Turner	13 west
Stephen Stone	Henrico	75	Adj. Peter Bilbow & Randolph Thacker	12 s. w.
Dr. James Turnan	Powhatan	214) 100)	On Chickahominy Swamp at lower end of County	20 s. e.
John Temple	King William	924	On Pamunkey Ri. adj. Tho. Pollard & B. O. Jones	$\frac{1}{2}$ n. e.
John Thomason	Henrico	100$\frac{1}{2}$	On Chickahominy Swamp adj. Wm. Liggon & George Dabney	17 s. w.
John Turner	Richmond	400	Adj. John Milestone & Anthony Street	16 s. e.
Edmund Taylor	Caroline	700	Adj. John Temple & Richard Taylor's Est.	2 n. e.
Mann Valentine (Imstead of Bartholomew)	Richmond	301	Adj. Jacob Christian & Andrew Grubbs	12 s. w.
Thomas Wade	Henrico	119	Adj. A. Nuckols & Fleming Brown	14 west
Hugh White	Richmond	61$\frac{1}{2}$	Adj. John Parker & Elisha Wicker	12 s. e.
Lucy White	Louisa	200$\frac{1}{2}$	(For life) Adj. Wm. Peace and on Elder Swamp	16 s. e.
Frances Wicker	Richmond	101	Adj. Wm. Wicker, Jr. & Thomas Boze	11 s. e.

Absentee Land Owners, Year 1814, continued:

ST. MARTIN'S PARISH
Pleasant Terrell
Commissioner of Revenue

NAME	PRESENT RES.	ACRES	LOCATION	MILES FROM C. H.
John B. Anderson	Louisa	252-3/4	Adj. Wm. Morris & Edmund C. Goodwin	25 west
John Bowles	Bedford	400	Adj. Nathl. W. Dandridge & Wm. Pulliam	28 "
John Bowles, Junr.	Louisa	105	Adj. Anderson Bowles & John Bowles, Senr.	32 "
Eliza and Mariah Bullock	Kentucky	231	Adj. Wm. Pulliam & Lying on Sou.-anna Ri.	30 "
Henry C. Coleman	Caroline	222	On North Anna Ri. adj. Wm. O. Winston	22 "
Freeborn G. Crenshaw	Richmond	5	On No. si. So. Anna Ri. Adj. Tho. Wingfield	18 "
James Cason	Tennessee	22½	Adj. John L. Phillips & Saml. Ragland (Life)	25 "
Thomas Dew	King & Queen	773	In Forks of North & Little River	7 "
Garland Dickinson	Louisa	51½	Adj. Jos. Woolfolk & David Spicer	25 "
Henry Dandridge	Goochland	135	Adj. Wm. Richardson & Archibald B. Dandridge	25 "
William S. Dandridge	Louisa	12½	Adj. Arch. B. Dandridge & Unity L. Dandridge	25 "
William W. Fountain	Henry	142½	Adj. Nathl.W. Dandridge & Mary W. Ellis	25 "
Edward Garland	Louisa	1098	On Fork of N.& S.Anna	5 "
Walter Boyd Gilliam	Pr.Geo.	560	Adj.Saml. Mosby & partly in Goochland	25 "
Edmund Grady	Henrico	113	Adj. James Doswell & William Harris	13 "
Tho. C. Howard	Richmond	546	Adj. Tho. Hatton & John Richardson's Est.	18 "

VIRGINIA MIGRATIONS - Hanover County, Volume II

Absentee Land Owners, Year 1814, continued: St. Martin's Parish

NAME	PRESENT RES.	ACRES	LOCATION	MILES FROM C. H.
Joseph Hawkins	Kentucky	444	Adj. George Philips & Edmund Thompson	28 West
John Minor	Spotsylvania	$106\frac{1}{2}$	On N. Anna Ri., adj. Reuben Goodwin's est.	16 "
James Madison	Caroline	$31\frac{1}{2}$	Adj. James Byars & on N. Anna River	14 "
Robert Morris	Philadelphia	1128	Adj. Nancy Netherland & Edmund Thompson	26 "
Thomas Mallory, jr.	Henrico	274	Adj. Nathl. Thompson & Anthony Thornton	15 "
Dr. James McClurg	Richmond	1200	Adj. Thomas Stanley & John Maddox	22 "
" " "	"	700	Adj. Francis Nelson & Wm. Fountain's est.	18 "
Henry H. Mallory	Kentucky	20	Adj. Thos. Price, Jr. & Francis Blunt	12 "
Peter Nelson (Conveyed 297 to J. Thornton)	Caroline	970	Adj. Wm. Nelson & Robt. Honeyman	17 "
Samuel Nuckols	Goochland	$80\frac{1}{2}$	Adj. Spotswood Childress & Thos. Nuckols	22 "
Thomas Nelson	Richmond	349	Adj. Francis Nelson & Obadiah Stanley	20 "
" "		360	Adj. Saml. Moody's Est. & Saml.Baker's Est.	21 "
Lucy Nelson	Williamsburg	400	(Life) Adj. Wm.Fontaine's Est.& Jno.M.Sheppard	18 "
Robert Nelson, Jr.	"	260	Adj. Lucy Nelson & Charles Crenshaw	18 "
George Phillips	Caroline	200	Adj. Snelson Smith & Little River	22 "
" "	"	72	Adj. Wm. Mason & Geo. Pickett	21 "
" "	"	24	Added by direction of the owner	

Absentee Land Owners, Year 1814, St. Martin's Parish, cont.:

NAME	PRESENT RES.	ACRES	LOCATION	MILES FROM C. H.
George Pickett	Richmond	834	Adj. Thos. Clay-brook & Jas.Doswell	21 West
Mariah O. Price	"	323	Adj. Horatio Wins-ton & Wm.O.Winston	25 "
Jordan Pleasants	Louisa	100	Adj. Martin Kenady & David Spicer	25 "
Thos. Richardson	Richmond	405¼	Adj. James Doswell & Chas. Colley	26 "
William Richardson	Spotsylvania	377	Adj. Walter Cole & Nathl.W.Dandridge's Estate	26 "
" "	"	471	Adj. John M.Sheppard & John Kinbrough; conv. by William Broadduss	16 "
Henry Robinson	Richmond	623-3/4	Adj. Thos.Duke & Edmd. Taylor	10 "
John Richardson	Lynchburg	150	Adj. Thomas Jones & Horace White; stood chgd.to E.C.Goodwin	10 "
Samuel Richardson	Louisiana	500	Adj. Walter Crew & Thos. Richardson	21 "
" "	"	116	Adj. Thos.C.Howard & Walter Crew	21 "
Agness Smith	Spotsylvania	221	Adj. Edward Rowzee & Jos. Woolfolk	26 "
" "	"	115	Adj. Austin Yearman & Wm. D. Goodwin	25 "
Meriwether Smith	Louisa	185	Adj. John Lively & Garland Dickerson	25 "
Nath'l Selden's Est.	Henrico	247	Adj.Robt. Snead & Richard Maccall	17 "
Robt. & Saml. Terrell	Caroline	50	Lying on Little Riv. known by name of Offley Mills, conv'd 50 a. by C. Moman	17 "
" " " "	"	244½	Adj. sd. Offley Mills & Edmund Berkeley, conv. by C. Moman	17 "

Absentee Land Owners, Year 1814, St. Martin's Parish, cont.:

NAME	PRESENT RES.	ACRES	LOCATION	MILES FROM C. H.
James Vaughan	Charles City	156	Adj. Chas. Crenshaw & William Gammon	18 West
Lewis G. White	Spotsylvania	100	Adj. Jos. Woolfolk & John Lively	24 "
Hezekiah L. Wight	Henrico	20	Adj. Chas. Crenshaw & Plummer Harris conv. by C. Moman	18 "
" " "	"	180	Adj. Chas. Crenshaw & Benj. Bates's Est. Conv. by C. Moman	18 "
Philip Woodson	Goochland	579	Adj. Thos. Puryear & Lying on So. Anna Ri.	22 "
" "	"	200	Adj. Walter Cole & Nathl. Dandridge's Est. on S. Anna Riv. Conv. by John Woodson	25 "
Wm. O. Winston, Jr.	New Orleans	323	Adj. Henry C. Coleman & Horatio G. Winston	25 "
Sally Waddy	Louisa	235	(Life)Adj. Saml.Moody's Est. & Thos. Nelson. Stood chgd.to R.Waddy	25 "
Horace White	Caroline	216	Adj.John B.Anderson & William Morris	25 "
Elizabeth Woodson	Powhatan	247	(life) Adj. John T. Swann & Chas. Hughes	
William Woodson	Goochland	106-3/4	Adj. Thos. Under-wood & Aug. Watson	24 "
" "	"		Adj. Jas. & Allen Den-ton & Spots. Childress	20 "
Augustin Watson	Prince Edwd.	674	Adj. Thos. Puryear & Thos. Underwood.Conv. to P. Woodson 579 a.	20 "
Tho. B. Wadkins	Goochland	180	Adj. Saml. Nuckols & Ben. Wadkins	

I, Thos. Pollard, deputy clerk of the County of Hanover, hereby do certify that I have carefully and deliberately examined the foregoing land tax, and I have compared with the land tax of the preceding year with the records in my office, where necessary, and with the law, and that I find the same to be correct. Given under my hand this 25 May, 1814.

Absentee Land Owners, Continued: (Alterations since 1814):

ST. PAUL'S PARISH
1815

NAME	RESIDENCE	ACRES	LOCATION	MILES FROM C. H
Thomas Auphin	Henrico	44½	Adj. Laney Jones & Pleasant Tyler	7 South
Matthew Anderson	"	1	Lot #55, Hanover Town	8 East
Nathaniel "	"	3	Lots 18-19-11 " "	8 "
Chappel F. Carrel	New Kent	49-3/4	Adj. Mary Wade & Co. Line	14 S. E.
Spotswood D. Crenshaw	Lynchburg	441	" Jas. Lankford & Wm. King, Senr. (187 a. from Tho. Sims, Exor. of W. Sims)	7 S.
Wm. Smith	King William	330	Adj. Geo. Turner on Pamunkey River	13 West
Richard S. Tayler*	" "	100	Adj. Elizabeth Tayler	2 North
Edmond Taylor	Caroline	700	" John Temple's Est. & Pamonkey River	2 "
George Whitlock	Lynchburg	122	Adj. William Toler & John Darricott	8 West
* Elizabeth Taylor	Hanover	386	(Life) Adj. John Temple's Est. & Pamunky Ri. From Rich. Taylor's Est.	2 North
Mary B. Taylor (Infant)	"	155	Adj. Edmund Taylor of Caroline; Elizabeth Taylor, Guardian	2 "
Ann M. Taylor (Infant)	"	82	Adj. Richard Taylor &c. Elizabeth Taylor, Gdn.	2 "
" " " "	"	92	Adj. E. Taylor & Pam. Ri.	2 "
John R. Taylor (Infant)	"	82	Adj. Ann Taylor, Elizabeth Taylor, Gdn.	2 "
" " " "	"	108	Adj. Paul Thilman's Est.	2 "
Daniel Taylor (Infant)	"	155	Adj. Edmund Taylor, of Caroline; Elizabeth Taylor, Guardian	2 "

Absentee Land Owners, Continued: (Alterations since 1814)

ST. MARTIN'S PARISH
1815

NAME	PRESENT RES.	ACRES	LOCATION	MILES FROM C. H.
Nathl. Anderson	Caroline	77	Adj. Nathaniel Anthony & Henry B. Jones's est.	25 West
John Ambler	Richmond	878½	Adj. Thomas Harris	18 "
" "	"	100	" Free.Crenshaw, B. Bates	18 "
Izzard Bacon	Henrico	395½	Adj. Jos. F. Price & Nath. Thompson	18 "
Jesse Crew	Charles City	22½	Adj. John Ambler & John Clough	19 "
Freeborn G. Crenshaw	Richmond	5	On South Anna Riv. & adj. Thos. Crenshaw	18 "
Freeborn G. Crenshaw (Conv. by Jesse Crew)	"	14	Adj. John Ambler & Thos. Harris	19 "
Mary W. Estes	Caroline	47	Adj. Thos. Price & Nathan Bumpass	14 ".
John Jones (Conv. by Edmund Goodwin)	Louisa	98	Adj. James Goodwin & Matthew Anderson	30 "
Thomas Mallory	Richmond	274	Adj. Nathl. Thomson & Anthony Thornton	15 "
George Winston	"	374	On North Anna River Adj. Nathl. Lester	11 "
Isham Woodson	Louisa	50	Adj. John Woodson & Richard Woodson	25 "

ESTATES FOR SALE (Virginia Gazette)

Jan. 20, 1767. To be Sold. 1400 acres of rich, level tobacco Land, in the
County of Hanover, on Turkey Cr... The subscriber will show property ...
N. W. Dandridge

Mar. 19, 1767. To be Sold. Tract of Land adj. the Meadow Bridge, in Hanover
Co., 1,000 acres ... There are three commodious situations on said Land; one
a well accustomed ordinary; another the plantation whereon Mr. Thomas Wild
formerly lived; they all lie very compact, with all convenient outhouses in
good order. Fine peach, apple and cherry orchards. Sgd. Daniel Truehart.

Mar. 26, 1767. Valuable Tract of Land in Hanover County, 432 acres; good
dwelling house, four rooms below, two above; all convenient outhouses built
but a few years; large peach orchard and young apple orchard of the best
fruit; large quantity of valuable creek low grounds ... Apply to Col. John
Syme, or to the subscriber on the premises. Sgd. Harry Tompkins.

Apr. 2, 1767. To be Sold, 30th inst., before Mr. Hay's door, in Williamsburg,
3,200 acres on Pamunkey river, Hanover county, being the plantation whereon
the late Col. James Littlepage lived ... Many fine houses thereon ... A very
fine Mill will be sold with or without the Land. Sgd. Peter Randolph, William Byrd, John Lewis, Geddes Winston.

Oct. 21, 1773. For Sale in Town of Newcastle, Three lots on the Main Street
whereon is a large and commodious Dwelling House, Kitchen, Dairy, and Smoke-
house, a Garden newly paled in, and every other Convenience for a Family;
the Whole in very good Order. Lately the property of William Muir of said
Town. Will be sold at next Hanover Court by Virtue of Trust from him to
Samuel Pearson, William Johnson, and Charles Tinsley.

23 Jan., 1778. To be sold in the upper end of Hanover Co., 550 acres; commodious dwelling house, 34x32', underpinned with fine brick cellar; four
rooms on lower floor and fire places in each; neat built kitchen; neat house,
barn, corn house; the whole built about 10 years, with about 1000 bearing
peach trees of the best sort, 2 apple orchards, etc. Situation high, on Lo-
cust creek and Little river. Very convenient to churches and meetings of
worship, mills, etc. In fine order for cropping and working 10 or 12 hands.
Sgd. Thomas Swift

Mar. 23, 1778. Hanover: I have just completed a Saw Mill in this county near
Bear Garden, about 10 miles from Hanover town, and about the same distance
from Richmond. Will furnish plank, etc.   Sgd. David Rowland, junr.

Apr. 1, 1778. Hanover Co. Stag Creek. For Sale, and may be entered on next
December, Valuable Tract containing 156 acres on above Creek; good dwelling
house with four rooms below and 2 above; kitchen, meat house, dairy, stable,
tobacco house, garden, peach orchard. Perhaps one of the most valuable
spots of land on the continent. Abounds in pitt coal, and is within 7 miles
of water carriage where flat bottomed boats can convey it down the Pamunkey
river; the coal lies in the side of a very high hill from whence the water
will run off as fast as the pitt is opened. Also innumerable quantity of
grind stone rock, equal in quality to any ever imported. Apply to Mr. Zachariah Rowland in Richmond, or to the subscriber on the premises.
Sgd. Geo. Rowland

Estates for Sale (Virginia Gazette) - (Continued):
(and other items of interest)

Apr. 24, 1778. To be sold at Hanover town, on 19 May, for ready money,
household and kitchen furniture, cattle, hogs, horses. Sgd. Francis Irwin.

May 8, 1778. Taken up on Little River in Hanover, a red cow ... David Cosby

May 15, 1778. To be sold to the highest bidder, on the 10th of July next,
on the premises, tract of land belonging to the estate of the late James
Shackleford, deceased, containing 143 acres, about one mile from Hanover
Courthouse. All persons who have demands against said estate are desired to
send in their accounts by the first of June. Sgd. Judith Shackleford, Exx.

May 15, 1778. Hanover, April 29, 1778. On August 6th will be rented for 5
years on the premises, and possession given in December, the Tavern and
part of the plantation at Hanover Courthouse with every necessary house for
tavern keeping ...   Sgd. Paul Thilman

July 17, 1778. For Sale. My estate (called Newington) in King and Queen,
on the Mattopony, containing 2450 acres, and the improvements thereon; very
valuable. Also a large tract in King William and one in Hanover, near Newcastle, called Dixon's lands. For terms apply to Nathaniel Littleton Savage.

Nov. 27, 1778. For Sale. Valuable Tract of Land in Hanover, containing 570
acres; good dwelling house and apple orchard, about 10 miles above Courthouse
on the south side of the South Anna river whereon William Tompkins deceased
formerly lived. Apply to me in King William County, or to Christopher Tompkins, Junior, in same county, whom I have empowered to sell.   John Cocke.

Ibid. I intend to leave this State very shortly. Hanover, Nov. 11, 1778.
                                        Sgd. William T. Bickerton.

Dec. 4, 1778. Lost on the 16th ult. between Pipingtree Ferry and West Point
in King William County, a red Leather Pocket Book in which were 120 dollars,
with several bonds of importance, also some receipts, a copy of the register
of the ages of Henry Cobbitt's children, and a certificate of the oath of
fidelity and allegiance of the subscriber to this commonwealth ... Ten Pounds
reward (to be paid) by the subscriber in Hanover, about three miles from
New Castle.   Sgd. William Richardson

April 2, 1779. For Sale. Tract of Land containing by estimation, 700 acres,
on the Pamunkey river below and joining the town of Newcastle in Hanover co.
The Land is exceedingly good, low grounds; dwelling house, offices, and a
very fine orchard. Also another Tract of 400 acres on the Matotoquin creek
in the aforesaid county, 4 miles below Newcastle. Fine situation for a Mill,
a never failing stream. Apply to the subscriber, living in the upper end
of Hanover.   Sgd. William Waddy

April 16, 1779. All persons having demands against the estate of the late
John Smith, Esq., of Hanover, are requested to apply for payment immediately,
and those indebted to the estate either on account of private dealings with
Mr. Smith or to the store kept by him in Hanover town, are also earnestly desired to pay off their respective balances as the situation of the estate
requires a speedy settlement.   Sgd. William Anderson

ORDER OF PUBLICATION

Richmond Whig & Public Advertiser
Friday, Jan. 5, 1835; page 3

At Rules holden in the Clerk's Office of the Circuit Superior Court of Law & Chancery for the County of Hanover, on 11 February, 1837:

Samuel Perrin and Susan N., his wife, formerly Susan N. Bowe, widow and relict of Nathaniel Bowe, deced., Nathaniel Davis and Martha, his wife, formerly Martha Bowe, Polly V. Cross, formerly Polly V. Bowe, in her own right, and as administratrix of Oliver T. Cross, deced., and guardian of Araminta A., Martha B., Mary A., John F., Frances, and Charles P. Cross, infant children of said Oliver T. Cross, deced., and John B. Green and Elizabeth, his wife, formerly Elizabeth Bowe, Hudson M. Wingfield and Sophia D., his wife, formerly Sophia D. Bowe, Jesse D. Yarbrough and Nancy, his wife, formerly Nancy Bowe, Benjamin Wingfield, Trustee for the benefit of the said Susan N. Perrin and her infant children, Ariadna B., and Eugenia N. Perrin, Thomas H. Goddin, who intermarried with Amanda M. Bowe, who died in the lifetime of the said Nathaniel Bowe, and the said Thomas H. Goddin as the guardian and next friend of Mortimer and Thomas H. Goddin, infant children of the said Thomas H. Goddin and his late wife, Amanda M., Archibald B. Timberlake, who intermarried with Emily R. Bowe, now deceased, and David, Algernon and John H. Timberlake, infants of tender years, by the said Archibald B. Timberlake their next friend, Nathaniel F. Bowe in his own right, and as Executor of Nathaniel Bowe, deceased, and Hector Bowe, and John J. Wingfield and Harriet, his wife, formerly Harriet Bowe, defendants,

In Chancery

The defendants, Nathaniel Davis and Martha, his wife, not having entered their appearance ... and it appearing by satisfactory evidence that they are not inhabitants of this Commonwealth ... it is ordered that the said defendants do appear here on the 1st day of the April term next and answer the bill of the complainants.

A Copy, Teste   Benj. Pollard, Jr., D. C.

The above named defendants are hereby notified that on Monday, the fifth day of February, 1838, at the Mechanicsville Tavern (kept by James B. Smith), in the county of Hanover, State of Virginia, between the hours of 8 A. M. and 6 P. M., I shall proceed to take the depositions of Thomas G. Clarke, Benj. Hazlegrove and others ...

Hanover, Dec. 1, 1837   Samuel Perrin

Perrin vs Susanna Bowe, widow, and others, continued:

According to the order of publication on the preceding page, Nathaniel Bowe and his wife, Susanna, had the following children and grandchildren:

I. Martha, who married Nathaniel Davis, and removed from the State of Virginia before 1837.

II. Polly V. Bowe, who married Oliver T. Cross. The latter died before 11 February, 1837. Issue (All under age in 1837):

      i. Araminta A. Cross
     ii. Martha B.   "
   iii. Mary A.   "
    iv. John F.   "
     v. Frances   "
    vi. Charles P.   "

III. Elizabeth, who married John B. Green.

IV. Sophia D., who married Hudson M. Wingfield.

V. Nancy Bowe, who married Jesse D. Yarbrough.

VI. Amanda M., who married Thomas H. Goddin. Amanda M. died in the lifetime of her father, Nathaniel Bowe. Issue:

    i. Mortimer Goddin - under age in 1837
   ii. Thomas H. "   "   " " "

VII. Emily R., who married Archibald B. Timberlake, and died before 11 February, 1837. Issue ("Infants of tender years"):

    i. David Timberlake
   ii. Algernon   "
  iii. John H.   "

VIII. Nathaniel F. Bowe.

IX. Hector Bowe.

X. Harriet Bowe, who married John J. Wingfield.

Susan N. Bowe, the widow of Nathaniel Bowe, married second, before 11 February, 1837, Samuel Perrin. Issue ("Infants" 11 February, 1837):

    i. Ariadna B. Perrin
   ii. Eugenia N.   "

The foregoing analysis is included for the benefit of those who might find the order of publication confusing. - E. G.

www.ingramcontent.com/pod-product-compliance
Lightning Source LLC
Chambersburg PA
CBHW021854020426
42334CB00013B/320